WITHDRAWN

WAKAN

THE SPIRIT OF HAROLD BENJAMIN

A collection of the writings
of Harold R. W. Benjamin

by

ROBERT M. BRUKER
Southern Illinois University
Edwardsville, Illinois

WITHDRAWN

Burgess Publishing Company

426 South Sixth Street • Minneapolis, Minn. 55415

The inspiration for all of Harold Benjamin's
work has been his wife, Georgia

It is to her memory that this collection is dedicated

Preface

Running Antelope was a chief in the Ogala division of the Teton-Dakota tribe of the Sioux Indians. His people were hungry, his warriors restless. Many moons had passed since their last great buffalo hunt, and they wanted Running Antelope to tell them where to find meat. By each campfire the braves talked about the great hunts of the past; with the coming of each new sun they waited anxiously for their Chief's direction.

Each evening Running Antelope went to the bluff overlooking the Mud River and prayed to *Wakan. Wakan,* the Great Spirit without whose guidance the Chief would not start a hunt or go to war. *"Wakan,* have mercy on me and my people. We thank you for the sun of the day and the stars which guide our feet at night, the plains and the hills, and all your bountiful goodness. Now lead our scouts to the herds of buffalo and give us a great hunt. *Wakan,* have mercy on me and my people."

After six days *Wakan* directed Running Antelope and his braves to the herds of buffalo and enough meat was taken to last the tribe through the winter. When the hunting party returned to their village with the kill, their first action was to give thanks to *Wakan.*

To most Ogala Sioux Indians *Wakan* was the divine power that directed their every movement. They sought his guidance before starting a great hunt, engaging another Nation in war, moving the tribe to a summer or winter camp-site, or making any other important decision. *Wakan* was the greatest single influence on their lives.

Harold Benjamin has certainly been a *wakan* — a Great Spirit — for education in this and other countries of the world over the last half century. He has had an illustrious career as a soldier, serving his country faithfully in two great world wars, as well as participating in the Mexican Border War. He entered the army as a private and today has a reserve rank of Lieutenant Colonel. He has been an elementary and high school teacher as well as a university professor; an administrator in the public schools; and a dean of two Colleges of Education. He has written many books and articles and at one time in his lifetime served as editor of a newspaper in Oregon. His work in the field of Comparative Education is legend. He assumed the leadership in this area shortly after being separated from the United States Army following World War I. At that time, when it was needed most, he gave the movement spirit and direction. He was instrumental in improving public schools and higher education in the countries of North Africa and in Japan, Korea, Afghanistan, and Denmark, as well as other European and Asian nations. One of his most recent investigations was made in Central and Latin America and has been published by McGraw-Hill under the title, HIGHER EDUCATION IN THE AMERICAN REPUBLICS. It covers some twenty countries and during the years of the study Benjamin lectured at the University of Buenos Aires, the University of Cordoba, the University of Chile, and the University of San Marcos.

Few people in any field have had the ability to convey their thoughts and ideas in a manner that is always fresh and pertinent. Professor Benjamin is one of those unique individuals who possesses this talent. He has been actively writing and speaking for more than forty years and most of his work is as apropos now as it was the day it was written. I have traced Dr. Benjamin's writings from 1924, and find the vast majority of them to be inspiring and thought-provoking. His SABER-TOOTH CURRICULUM, written in 1939 under the *nom de plume*, "J. Abner Peddiwell, Ph. D.," has become an educational classic which will never become dated. It is probably the most popular paper back edition every published by McGraw-Hill. THE CULTIVATION OF IDIOSYNCRASY, delivered as the Inglis Lecture at Harvard in 1949, is in the sixth or seventh printing. Among his well-known books are UNDER THEIR OWN COMMAND, TRUE FAITH AND ALLEGIANCE, and MAN, THE PROBLEM SOLVER. He recently completed THE SAGE OF PETALUMA, the biography of J. Abner Peddiwell.

A class with Benjamin is an experience not to be soon forgotten. Many graduate students, I fear, eventually reach a stage in their development at which they become impervious to new ideas. They conform to the "system," find a niche into which they fit, and steadily grind out their term of indenture. Not so in Benjamin's classes; he invites them out of their shell and challenges them to think, to be creative, to savor their work. In my first class session with him he made it clear that a graduate seminar paper should be professionally written, and in a manner suitable for publication.

Benjamin's graciousness, magnetic personality, and vast knowledge completely dominate a classroom, and it doesn't take one long to develop an appreciation of these factors. His graciousness reflects his belief in the human worth and dignity of each individual, his great personality commands respect and loyalty, and his knowledge is that of a scholar who has traveled far and studied long. Certain of his basic beliefs have become evident during my association with Dr. Benjamin, and they are presented here as I see them:

1. *Education is a behavior-changing process. Teachers act as behavior-changing agents functioning within behavior-changing institutions (the schools) to enhance the behavior-changing process.*

2. *The strength of a nation lies in its people. The strength of the people is determined by the education they receive. Education is the most important force in the world.*

3. *The individual differences of human beings should be cultivated and developed to their fullest.*

4. *An inherent faith in the people of the United States.*

In 1881, Burke A. Hinsdale, president of Hiram College, quoted President James A. Garfield as saying:

> *I am not willing that this discussion should close without mentioning the value of a true teacher. Give me a log hut, with only a simple bench, Mark Hopkins on one end and I on the other, and you may have all the buildings, apparatus, and libraries without him.* [1]

This pretty well sums up my feelings about Harold Benjamin. If I were a young high school graduate and found a college which had less than great wealth, old and battered buildings, an insufficient number of laboratories, and an inadequate library, but with Harold Benjamin on the faculty, I would unhesitantly enroll in that institution.

When I first approached Dr. Benjamin concerning the possibility of putting together this collection he threw up his hands and exclaimed. "That's a horrible idea! And a great waste of your time." I hope I have proven him wrong.

RMB

---

[1]Burke A. Hinsdale, *President Garfield and Education: Hiram College Memorial.* Boston: J. R. Osgood and Company, 1882. p. 43.

Acknowledgments

Expressions of gratitude and appreciation are difficult to make for fear of omitting someone who was singularly important. At the offset of this task I shall apologize to anyone who might be slighted by a careless lapse of memory on my part.

The idea for this collection was my own, others, however, have offered encouragement and constructive advice. Dr. Harry Smith and Dr. Gordon Bliss, of the faculty at the Edwardsville Campus of Southern Illinois University, have frequently taken their valuable time to offer assistance. They also acted as gadflies who prodded me to be sure I didn't fall too far behind. I appreciate sincerely their consideration. The Research Committee of the Graduate Council of our University has made available funds which have enabled me to secure typing and other clerical assistance as well as to defray the expense of legal fees involved in securing rights to certain publications. To that body I am deeply grateful.

Dr. A. L. Crabb, of George Peabody College for Teachers, graciously forwarded to me copies of many articles and speeches which originally appeared in the *Peabody Reflector* and the *Peabody Journal of Education.* Dr. E. I. F. Williams, former Editor of *The Educational Forum,* made available ". . . And With the Other Hand . . . A Weapon," the article based on the 1957 Frank Lee Wright Memorial Lecture, which Dr. Benjamin delivered at Washington University in St. Louis. Special mention must be made of Mr. C. B. Ulery, Managing Editor of *Education,* who very generously searched out a copy of "Nature of Curricular Problems," which was out of print, and had a special copy prepared for me. Needless to say how much I appreciate Mr. Ulery's kind attention. The office of Dr. Jean E. Battle, Dean of the College of Education at the University of South Florida provided me with a copy of their *Educational Review,* which included "The Curious Case of Homo the Sap and his Seven Smart Sons." Mr. Vernon Sternberg of the Southern Illinois University Carbondale Campus read the entire manuscript and his suggestions concerning its improvement were the most beneficial comments I received. To Mr. Sternberg I owe a special tanks.

Not only individuals but organizations were considerate of my requests for material. One of the most helpful was the Commission on Professional Rights and Responsibilities of the National Education Association, which granted permission for me to quote at length from TRUE FAITH AND ALLEGIANCE. When I solicited Kappa Delta Pi for permission to use portions of UNDER THEIR OWN COMMAND, I was once more greeted with graciousness and cooperation as they freely consented to my request. An immediate response from the McGraw-Hill Book Company allowed me to use chapter two of THE SABER-TOOTH CURRICULUM. Harvard University Press has provided world rights for use of the 1949 Inglis Lecture. THE CULTIVATION OF IDIOSYNCRASY.

In my own office I must give recognition to Mrs. Evelyn Oglesby and Miss Mary Lou Riggins who assisted in the typing of the manuscript. My wife, Jane, long after the children were put to bed, labored with the reading of proof and probably is better acquainted with Dr. Benjamin's work than I. To her I am especially indebted. Other individuals and other organizations whom I cannot identify positively have also been of invaluable assistance. I have several letters from people whom I have never met and probably never will, offering encouragement and expressing interest.

There are three gentlemen whom I owe an especial thanks for their help in getting this volume published. They are Dr. H. Lee Hornbake, Vice-President for Academic Affairs at the University of Maryland, Dr. H. Dene Southwood of Southern Illinois University, and Dr. Adolph Unruh of St. Louis University.

The most important individual was Harold Benjamin himself. The class sessions I spent with him during his year as Distinguished Visiting Professor on our Carbondale Campus, were the most interesting, the most challenging, and the most inspiring I have ever been privileged to attend. Whether he was lecturing on comparative education, discussing American public education, commenting on a seminar paper, delivering a discourse of J. Abner Peddiwell, or encouraging the class members to become more efficient and considerate practitioners of their profession, he was always stimulating and thought-provoking.

Though Dr. Benjamin seldom retains copies of his addresses and articles he was often able to tell me where I might obtain a copy of a particular selection which I had been unable to uncover. During the year he kept me advised of the dates and places he was to speak. In several instances I was able to obtain copies of these addresses, in others he gave me the copy from which he delivered the speech. Without his assistance and permission I would never have been able to complete this collection.

In drawing this collection together I have attempted to assemble the most important of Professor Benjamin's work. The process of sorting and deciding which selections to use and which to by-pass was the most difficult task in the entire project. I take this opportunity to apologize to any reader who might look in vain from his favorite Benjamin article or speech.

Contents

I PEDDIWELLIAN PROSE

Since the initial publication of THE SABER-TOOTH CURRICULUM, in 1939, the name of "J. Abner Peddiwell, Ph. D.," has become a familiar one to professional educators. To many he is a real flesh-and-blood person, just as Sherlock Holmes is to the more avid readers of Sir Arthur Conan Doyle's stories. Benjamin has assumed this pseudonym on various occasions and for various reasons for nearly forty years, always with freshness and imagination. Through the years Peddiwell has advanced from educational historian to Professor of Education and, finally, to Professor Emeritus. His alma mater has subsequently progressed from teachers college to four-year state college, to its present position as Petaluma State University. The exact geographic location of this institution of higher education, however, is unknown.

Peddiwell, though he has aged, has never lost sight of the important issues and problems on the American educational scene. Through extensive travel and diligent study he has managed to keep abreast of the issues and to offer authoritative suggestions for their solution. His lucid and penetrating style coupled with a keen and ready wit have enabled him to present the problem areas in their proper perspective and to focalize the various paths of action available. Educators, in turn, can select the plan of attack which best fits their particular situation.

Through Professor Peddiwell Dr. Benjamin has been able to send a special message to all educators – public school teachers, administrators, and college professors alike. He offers a challenge to them, a challenge to present and educational program that is personal and individual, one which does not merely pay lip-service to individual differences but that provides for those differences. Benjamin and Peddiwell offer an admonition to school administrators. They are cautioned that educational policy today is not what it was three decades ago, nor will it be the same thirty years hence. The function and purpose of the public schools is constantly changing and administrators, more than any other group, should be cognizant of this fact. The educational program which Harold Benjamin proposes, and which he often supports with J. Abner Peddiwell, can be realized only through the efforts of administrators who are dynamic rather than static; ones who recognize that subject-matter which is relevant at one time may

1

not be relevant at another, and subject-matter which is pertinent to one geographic area may not be pertinent to another.

The first public appearance of J. Abner Peddiwell, Ph. D., was during the late 1920's while Benjamin was an associate professor at Stanford University. Peddiwell was frequently mentioned in Benjamin's graduate classes and became quite well known to his students there. Peddiwell's nationwide reputation was earned in about 1939 when the series of lectures, THE SABER-TOOTH CURRICULUM, was published as a "stunt" for a winter meeting of the American Superintendents Association. Two thousand copies were printed as gifts for superintendents and professors of education. As word of the book began to spread, McGraw-Hill became overwhelmed with requests for copies. It was reprinted and has been a best seller in university bookstores ever since. Chapter two of THE SABER-TOOTH CURRICULUM is included in this collection because it is in this chapter, more than any other, that Peddiwell takes apart many of the cherished educational ideas and shibboleths. In a concise manner the learned professor chastises an educational system which teaches children to develop skills which are already obsolete under the guise of character building. The satirist is evident in many of Peddiwell's discourses as the reader will discover. He is probably at his best in the selection entitled, "What Should Our Children Inherit?"

In the fall of 1965 McGraw-Hill published a book dedicated "to the readers of THE-SABER TOOTH CURRICULUM . . .," entitled THE SAGE OF PETALUMA, with foreword appropriately provided by Harold R. W. Benjamin. This is the autobiography of Peddiwell and it is a wonderfully warm and moving story. Peddiwell's first encounter with formal education was at age six when his foster father presented him to Medicine Horse, a chief of the Lacotah Sioux. It was from Medicine Horse that Abner learned of *wakan,* the unique spirit in man which makes him sincere and considerate in his dealings with others.

The most memorable portion of Peddiwell's autobiography is that which deals with his military career. Of particular interest are the stories of Sergeant Cobb, who was unjustly court-martialed, and that of "Toot Sweet," who was Peddiwell's Army horse in Europe during World War I. Abner devoted eight years of his life to active Army duty and his military experiences served to reinforce his belief that in a democratic society every man is just as good as every other man and he must never be debased.

J. Abner Peddiwell is, of course, a fictional character, a means of conveying a message, a vehicle used by a great teacher to better communicate with his students. The message of Peddiwell, however, is very real as the reader will soon discover for himself.

The Saber-Tooth Curriculum

The first great educational theorist and practitioner of whom my imagination has any record (began Dr. Peddiwell in his best professorial tone) was a man of Chellean times whose full name was New-Fist-Hammer-Maker but whom, for convenience, I shall hereafter call New-Fist.

New-Fist was a doer, in spite of the fact that there was little in his environment with which to do anything very complex. You have undoubtedly heard of the pear-shaped, chipped-stone tool which archeologists call the coup-de-poing or fist hammer. New-Fist gained his name and a considerable local prestige by producing one of these artifacts in a less rough and more useful form than any previously known to his tribe. His hunting clubs were generally superior weapons, moreover, and his fire-using techniques were patterns of simplicity and precision. He knew how to do things his community needed to have done, and he had the energy and will to go ahead and do them. By virtue of these characteristics he was an educated man.

New-Fist was also a thinker. Then, as now, there were few lengths to which men would not go to avoid the labor and pain of thought. More readily than his fellows, New-Fist pushed himself beyond those lengths to the point where cerebration was inevitable. The same quality of intelligence which led him into the socially approved activity of producing a superior artifact also led him to engage in the socially disapproved practice of thinking. When other men gorged themselves on the proceeds of a successful hunt and vegetated in dull stupor for many hours thereafter, New-Fist ate a little less heartily, slept a little less stupidly, and arose a little earlier than his comrades to sit by the fire and think. He would stare moodily at the flickering flames and wonder about various parts of his environment until he finally got to the point where he became strongly dissatisfied with the accustomed ways of his tribe. He began to catch glimpses of ways in which life might be made better for himself, his family, and his group. By virtue of this development, he became a dangerous man.

This was the background that made this doer and thinker hit upon the concept of a conscious, systematic education. The immediate stimulus which put him directly into the practice of education came from watching his children at play. He saw these children at the cave entrance before the fire engaged in activity with bones and sticks and brightly colored pebbles. He noted that they seemed to have no purpose in their play beyond immediate pleasure in the activity itself. He compared their activity with that of the grown-up members of the tribe. The children played for fun; the adults worked for security and enrichment of their lives. The children dealt with bones, sticks, and pebbles; the adults dealt with food, shelter, and clothing. The children protected themselves from boredom; the adults protected themselves from danger.

"If I could only get these children to do the things that will give more and better food, shelter, clothing, and security," thought New-Fist, "I would be helping this tribe to have a better life. When the children become grown, they would have more meat to eat, more skins to keep them warm, better caves in which to sleep, and less danger from the striped death with the curving teeth that walks these trails by night."

Having set up an educational goal, New-Fist proceeded to construct a curriculum for reaching that goal. "What things must we tribesmen know how to do in order to live with full bellies, warm backs, and minds free from fear?" he asked himself.

To answer this question, he ran various activities over in his mind. "We have to catch fish with our bare hands in the pool far up the creek beyond that big bend," he said to himself. "We have to catch fish with our bare hands in the pool right at the bend. We have to catch them in the same way in the pool just this side of the bend. And so we catch them in the next pool and the next and the next. Always we catch them with our bare hands."

Thus New-Fist discovered the first subject of the first curriculum — fish-grabbing-with-the-bare-hands.

"Also we club the little woolly horses," he continued with his analysis. "We club them along the bank of the creek where they come down to drink. We club them in the thickets where they lie down to sleep. We club them in the upland meadow where they graze. Wherever we find them we club them."

So woolly-horse clubbing was seen to be the second main subject in the curriculum.

"And finally, we drive away the saber-tooth tigers with fire," New-Fist went on in his thinking. "We drive them from the mouth of our caves with fire. We drive them from our trail with burning branches. We wave firebrands to drive them from our drinking hole. Always we have to drive them away, and always we drive them with fire."

Thus was discovered the third subject — saber-tooth-tiger-scaring-with-fire.

Having developed a curriculum, New-Fist took his children with him as he went about his activities. He gave them an opportunity to practice these three subjects. The children liked to learn. It was more fun for them to engage in these purposeful activities than to play with colored stones just for the fun of it. They learned the new activities well, and so the educational system was a success.

As New-Fist's children grew older, it was plain to see that they had an advantage in good and safe living over other children who had never been educated systematically. Some of the more intelligent members of the tribe began to do as New-Fist had done, and the teaching of fish-grabbing, horse-clubbing, and tiger-scaring came more and more to be accepted as the heart of real education.

For a long time, however, there were certain more conservative members of the tribe who resisted the new, formal educational system on religious grounds. "The Great Mystery who speaks in thunder and moves in lightning," they announced impressively, "the Great Mystery who gives men life and takes it from them as he wills — if that Great Mystery had wanted children to practice fish-grabbing, horse-clubbing, and tiger-scaring before they were grown up, he would have taught them these activities himself by implanting in their natures instincts for fish-grabbing, horse-clubbing, and tiger-scaring. New-Fist is not only impious to attempt something the Great Mystery never intended to have done; he is also a damned fool for trying to change human nature."

Whereupon approximately half of these critics took up the solemn chant, "If you oppose the will of the Great Mystery, you must die," and the remainder sang derisively in unison, "You can't change human nature."

Being an educational statesman as well as an educational administrator and theorist, New-Fist replied politely to both arguments. To the more theologically minded, he said that, as a matter of fact, the Great Mystery had ordered this new work done, that he even did the work himself by causing children to want to learn, that children could not learn by themselves without divine aid, that they could not learn at all except through the power of the Great Mystery, and that nobody could really understand the will of the Great Mystery concerning fish, horses, and saber-tooth tigers unless he had been well grounded in the three fundamental subjects of the New-Fist school. To the human-nature-cannot-be-changed shouters, New-Fist pointed out the fact that palcolithic culture had attained its high level by changes in human nature, and that it seemed almost unpatriotic to deny the very process which had made the community great.

"I know you my fellow tribesmen," the pioneer educator ended his arguments gravely, "I know you as humble and devoted servants of the Great Mystery. I know that you would not for one moment consciously oppose yourselves to his will. I know you as intelligent and loyal citizens of this great cave-realm, and I know that your pure and noble patriotism will not permit you to do anything which will block the development of that most cave-realmish of all our institutions — the paleolithic educational system. Now that you understand the true nature and purpose of this institution, I am serenely confident that there are no reasonable lengths to which you will not go in its defense and its support."

By this appeal the forces of conservatism were won over to the side of the new school, and in due time everybody who was anybody in the community knew that the heart of good education lay in the three subjects of fish-grabbing, horse-clubbing, and tiger-scaring. New-Fist and his contemporaries grew old and were gathered by the Great Mystery to the Land of the Sunset far down the creek. Other men followed their educational ways more and more, until at last all the children of the tribe were practiced systematically in the three fundamentals. Thus the tribe prospered and was happy in the possession of adequate meat, skins, and security.

It is to be supposed that all would have gone well forever with this good educational system if conditions of life in that community had remained forever the same. But conditions changed, and life which had once been so safe and happy in the cave-realm valley became insecure and disturbing.

A new ice age was approaching in that part of the world. A great glacier came down from the neighboring mountain range to the north. Year after year it crept closer and closer to the headwaters of the creek which ran through the tribe's valley, until at length it reached the stream and began to melt into the water. Dirt and gravel which the glacier had collected on its long journey were dropped into the creek. The water grew muddy. What had once been a crystal-clear stream in which one could see easily to the bottom was now a milky stream into which one could not see at all.

At once the life of the community was changed in one very important respect. It was no longer possible to catch fish with the bare hands. The fish could not be seen in the muddy water. For some years, moreover, the fish in this creek had been getting more timid, agile, and intelligent. The clumsy, stupid, brave fish, of which originally there had been a great many, had been caught with the bare hands for fish generation after fish generation, until only fish of superior intelligence and agility were left. These smart fish, hiding in the muddy water under the newly deposited glacial boulders, eluded the hands of the most expertly trained fish-grabbers. Those tribesmen who had studied advanced fish-grabbing in the secondary school could do no better than their less well-educated fellows who had taken only an elementary course in the subject, and even the university graduates with majors in ichthyology were baffled by the problem. No matter how good a man's fish-grabbing education had been, he could not grab fish when he could not find fish to grab.

The melting waters of the approaching ice sheet also made the country wetter. The gound became marshy far back from the banks of the creek. The stupid woolly horses standing only five or six hands high and running on four-toed front feet and three-toed hind feet, although admirable objects for clubbing, had one dangerous characteristic. They were ambitious. They all wanted to learn to run on their middle toes. They all had visions of becoming powerful and aggresive animals instead of little and timid ones. They dreamed of a far-distant day when some of their descendants would be sixteen hands high, weight more than half-a-ton, and be able to pitch their would-be riders into the dirt. They knew they could never attain these goals in a wet, marshy country, so they went east to the dry, open plains, far from the paleolithic hunting grounds. Their places were taken by little antelopes who came down with the ice sheet and were so shy and speedy and had so keen a scent for danger that no one could approach them closely enough to club them.

The best trained horse-clubbers of the tribe went out day after day and employed the most efficient techniques taught in the schools, but day after day they returned empty-handed. A horse-clubbing education of the highest type could get no results when there were no horses to club.

Finally, to complete the disruption of paleolithic life and education, the new dampness in the air gave the saber-tooth tigers pneumonia, a disease to which these animals were peculiarly susceptible and to which most of them succumbed. A few moth-eaten specimens crept south to the desert, it is true, but they were pitifully few and weak representatives of a once numerous and powerful race.

So there were no more tigers to scare in the paleolithic community, and the best tiger-scaring techniques became only academic exercises, good in themselves, perhaps, but not necessary for tribal security. Yet this danger to the people was lost only to be replaced by another and even greater danger, for with the advancing ice sheet came ferocious glacial bears which were not afraid of fire, which walked the trails by day as well as by night, and which could not be driven away by the most advanced methods developed in the tiger-scaring courses of the schools.

The community was now in a very difficult situation. There was no fish or meat for food, no hides for clothing, and no security from the hairy death that walked the trails day and night. Adjustment to this difficulty had to be made at once if the tribe was not to become extinct.

Fortunately for the tribe, however, there were men in it of the old New-Fist breed, men who had the ability to do and the daring to think. One of them stood by the muddy stream, his stomach contracting with hunger pains, longing for some way to get a fish to eat. Again and again he had tried the old fish-grabbing technique that day, hoping desperately that at last it might work, but now in black despair he finally rejected all that he had learned in the schools and looked about him for some new way to get fish from that stream. There were stout but slender vines hanging from trees along the bank. He pulled them down and began to fasten them together more or less aimlessly. As he worked, the vision of what he might do to satisfy his hunger and that of his crying children back in the cave grew clearer. His black despair lightened a little. He worked more rapidly and intelligently. At last he had it — a net, a crude seine. He called a companion and explained the device. The two men took the net into the water, into pool after pool, and in one hour they caught more fish — intelligent fish in muddy water — than the whole tribe could have caught in a day under the best fish-grabbing conditions.

Another intelligent member of the tribe wandered hungrily through the woods where once the stupid little horses had abounded but where now only the elusive antelope could be seen. He had tried the horse-clubbing technique on the antelope until he was fully convinced of its futility. He knew that one would starve who relied on school learning to get him meat in those woods. Thus it was that he too, like the fish-net inventor, was finally impelled by hunger to new ways. He bent a strong, springy young tree over an antelope trail, hung a noosed vine therefrom, and fastened the whole device in so ingenious a fashion that the passing animal would release a trigger and be snared neatly when the tree jerked upright. By setting a line of these snares, he was able in one night to secure more meat and skins than a dozen horse-clubbers in the old days had secured in a week.

A third tribesman, determined to meet the problem of the ferocious bears, also forgot what he had been taught in shcool and began to think in direct and radical fashion. Finally, as a result of this thinking, he dug a deep pit in a bear trail, covered it with branches in such a way that a bear would walk out on it unsuspectingly, fall through to the bottom, and remain trapped until the tribesmen could come up and despatch him with sticks and stones at their leisure. The inventor showed his friends how to dig and camouflage other pits until all the trails around the community were furnished with them. Thus the tribe had even more security than before and in addition had the great additional store of meat and skins which they secured from the captured bears.

As the knowledge of these new inventions spread, all the members of the tribe were engaged in familiarizing themselves with the new ways of living. Men worked hard at making fish nets, setting antelope snares, and digging bear pits. The tribe was busy and prosperous.

There were a few thoughtful men who asked questions as they worked. Some of them even criticized the schools.

"These new activities of net-making and operating, snare-setting, and pit-digging are indispensable to modern existence," they said. "Why can't they be taught in school?"

The safe and sober majority had a quick reply to this naive question. "School!" they snorted derisively. "You aren't in school now. You are out here in the dirt working to preserve the life and happiness of the tribe. What have these practical activities got to do with schools? You're not saying lessons now. You'd better forget your lessons and your academic ideals of fish-grabbing, horse-clubbing, and tiger-scaring if you want to eat, keep warm, and have some measure of security from sudden death."

The radicals persisted a little in their questioning. "Fishnet-making and using, antelope-snare consturction and operation, and bear-catching and killing," they pointed out, "require intelligence and skills — things we claim to develop in schools. They are also activities we need to know. Why can't the schools teach them?"

But most of the tribe, and particularly the wise old men who controlled the school, smiled indulgently at this suggestion. "That wouldn't be *education*," they said gently.

"But why wouldn't it be?" asked the radicals.

"Because it would be mere training," explained the old men patiently. "With all the intricate details of fish-grabbing, horse-clubbing, and tiger-scaring — the standard cultural subjects — the school curriculum is too crowded now. We can't add these fads and frills of net-making, antelope-snaring, and — of all things — bear killing. Why, at the very thought, the body of the great New-Fist, founder of our paleolithic educational system, would turn over in its burial cairn. What we need to do is to give our young people a more thorough grounding in the fundamentals. Even the graduates of the secondary schools don't know the art of fish-grabbing in any complete sense nowadays, they swing their horse clubs awkwardly too, and as for the old science of tiger-scaring — well, even the teachers seem to lack the real flair for the subject which we oldsters got in our teens and never forgot."

"But, damn it," exploded one of the radicals, "how can any person with good sense be interested in such useless activities? What is the point of trying to catch fish with the bare hands when it just can't be done any more. How can a boy learn to club horses when there are no horses left to club? And why in hell should children try to scare tigers with fire when the tigers are dead and gone?"

"Don't be foolish," said the wise old men, smiling most kindly smiles. "We don't teach fish-grabbing to grab fish; we teach it to develop a generalized agility which can never be developed by mere training. We don't teach horse-clubbing to club horses; we teach it to develop a generalized strength in the learner which he can never get from so prosaic and specialized a thing as antelope-snare-setting. We don't teach tiger-scaring to scare tigers; we teach it for the purpose of giving that noble courage which carries over into all the affairs of life and which can never come from so base an activity as bear-killing."

All the radicals were silenced by this statement, all except the one who was most radical of all. He felt abashed, it is true, but he was so radical that he made one last protest.

"But — but anyway," he suggested, "you will have to admit that times have changed. Couldn't you please try these other more up-to-date activities? Maybe they have some educational value after all?"

Even the man's fellow radicals felt this was going a little too far.

The wise old men were indignant. Their kindly smiles faded. "If you had any education yourself," they said severely, "you would know that the essence of true education is timelessness. It is something that endures through changing conditions like a solid rock standing squarely and firmly in the middle of a raging torrent. You must know that there are some eternal verities, and the saber-tooth curriculum is one of them!"

Paleolithic Defense

I missed an important conference on education and defense yesterday because I encountered J. Abner Peddiwell on the steps of the Library of Congress where he is engaged for the duration of the summer in scholarly research. He pulled me into a dairy lunch on C Street, Southeast, and at the first sip of milk embarked upon the following dissertation.

I see now (said the eccentric educational historian) that there was more than one tribe on the other side of the mountain from our paleolithic community. The original jutting-browed, massive-chinned, breast-beating ruler who trained his people in purposeful club-swinging and rhythmic growling by the woof-woof method now had his imitators in the chiefs of various other groups. Indeed, one of the younger woof-woof chiefs, although seriously handicapped by less impressive facial features than those enjoyed by the original Bigness, made up for this lack by a certain imaginative facility and vocal virtuosity which in the long run out-woofed the woof-woof technique itself. For this younger leader not only woofed in standard style; he also perfected methods of mass teeth-gnashing, varied by sobbing, roaring, and mouth-foaming, which made the best efforts of his competitors look like substitute-Sunday-school-teacher stuff. This technique was so effective that the young sob-roar chief soon had his people out on the trails clubbing all the non-sob-roarers in sight.

The peaceful paleoliths in charge of affairs on the good side of the hill were first worried, then agitated and at last thoroughly frightened by these ultra-montane goings-on. They were so scared by the sob-roar chief's successes that they felt they had to hate him and copy him at the same time without of course losing any of the paleolithic gains which had made their tribe so great and prosperous in the past. They had to have a psychological technique for mass control like that of the evil foreign leader so that they would be successful in opposing him when he would cross the twenty-fish-eats-high mountain to club them, yet it must also be different from his technique so that they would not become evil like him.

Under the leadership of a democratically elected Head Paleolith, the good people of the cis-montane tribe hit upon the boo-hoo technique. This was not at all the evil and aggressive sob stuff of the vicious clubbers across the hill but more of a general, quiet, eye-rubbing weep which sank at times to a semi-reassured sniffle and then rose again to audible but dignified wails. It was a

This selection appeared in *School and Society*, Vol. 54, No. 1398, October 11, 1941, pp. 290-292.

democratic defense-crying rather than the insane and brutal attack-sobbing of the aggressor tribes.

The boo-hoo method got results. The Head Paleolith cried — in a nice way. All the big and little vice-Head Paleoliths, associate paleoliths and assistants to all the vices and associates promptly echoed the big 'lith's weeping — not in any such regimented or slavish imitations of the leader as were current in the sob-roar way of life but still sufficiently close to the boo-hoo line to indicate loyalty to the tribe and to the Head Paleolith. The people cried too, some of them, enough of them to get things started.

Everybody began to explain through their tears what they were going to do for defense. The big fish-chiefs said they would manufacture a lot of new nets, employ a lot of new fishermen, and catch a lot of fish for the defense workers, soldiers and boo-hoo experts to live on. They expected to make a lot of money, too, although of course they did not say so right out loud.

The big antelope chiefs said they would get heavy industry to build a lot of new hunting equipment, they would hire a lot of new snare-setters and trail watchers and they would produce a lot of meat and skins for the use of the defense workers, soldiers and boo-hoo experts. Naturally, without mentioning the matter specifically, they figured on making a lot of money too.

The defense chiefs said they would secure a lot of potential fighters, harden them up with a lot of discipline, sharpen them up with a lot of training and equip them with a lot of the finest throwing-rocks, clubbing-rocks, rolling-rocks and catapults available. They expected also, of course, that a lot of them who were only one-club-mark chiefs would gain two-or three-club ratings, and that some of them would actually get four-club status. They were too modest to say anything about those ratings, but their eyes shone as they thought of possible club-marks.

Then things began to hum. Everybody got busy. The fish chiefs built up their industry, employed a lot of men, caught a lot of fish — and made a lot of money. The antelope chiefs had the snare factories working two and three shifts a day, hired a lot of extra hands — and made a lot of money. The defense chiefs built a lot of camps (making money for the building chiefs as they did so), gave a lot of disciplinary training and got a lot of extra club-marks. The Head Paleolith was almost completely occupied in appointing commissioners to maintain boo-hoo, adminstrators of boo-hoo management and coordinators of boo-hoo activities. Ignoring petty political differences in this great hour, he appointed his boo-hoo experts without regard to party, creed or ability so long as they were members of the big-chief class and cried faithfully.

It was a thrilling effort and would have succeeded magnificently perhaps had conditions only been more favorable. Unfortunately certain conditions were terrible. There were un-paleolithic individuals who gummed up the defense program from the first.

There was the striker, for example, who would say, "Here we fishermen are still making only the same amount of money we made last year, but we have to pay higher prices for everything we need. In terms of what we need, our wages have been cut."

"It is not very much," the big fish-chief would say, "and you ought to be proud to offer it as your sacrifice to defense."

"But where is your sacrifice, your pay cut?" countered the striker. "After setting aside enough of the profits for depreciation, amortization and all the taxes, both real and anticipated, which may be levied on the company for defense purposes, you are still paying five times as great a dividend for the first six months of the present year as for the corresponding period last year."

The big fish-chief was hurt. He began to cry a little and to chant softly. At first he was unintelligible, but after a while he got into the swing and spirit of the chant and began to put words together very well indeed.

"Striker, striker! Defense piker! What's the reason you make treason?" he sang, sadly but pointedly.

"Whaddya mean, treason?" cried the scandalized worker. "Don't you call me a traitor, you big stiff! I swung a club in the ranks during the last war while you were a one-fish-a-year man!"

"That makes no difference now," hummed the big chief. "The principal point is one you miss; it's treason to strike at a time like this!"

"Time like this!" repeated the striker. "What time is it? Is it war time? Is it war time? If it is war time, when did the council of all our paleolithic chiefs put us into war? If it is not war time, but we find we are in the war without knowing it officially, then maybe you're right about there being treason around some place — a place higher than this picket line."

The big fish-chief's eyes flashed. "Don't you talk that way!" he warned sternly. "Don't you start name-calling, you tut-tut, over-the-hill mentality!"

Whereupon the striker really was ashamed of himself. He felt that he had gone too far — beyond the bounds of decency and loyalty, or at least beyond the bounds of polite conversation with a big-chief person.

There was also the un-paleolithic soldier (very rare, indeed, however, among such a thoroughly paleolithic class) who would say, "We could teach these recruits a lot better in my opinion if we had real wood-and-rock clubs for them instead of these grass-stuffed imitations. Where in the world are some of these big fine clubs which industry was supposed to make for us six months ago?"

Then a middle-sized industrialist would reply sadly, "We can make those clubs. We could have made them months ago, but we've got no contract yet. None of our vice-presidents can get on the boo-hoo expert list somehow, although they are willing to work for half a fish a year. In the meantime we have been making antelope snares hand over fist — twenty per cent more than we made last year — but we're going to have to shut down soon if we don't get a club contract."

Well that was the way it was going, so the Head Paleolith went up on the hill, found a nice conference pond up there and talked with a Good Big Shot from the other side, and then he came back and said, "Our clubs are going to keep the peace which will be won by a lot of heavy clubbing. We are no nearer actual clubbing than before."

"What does that mean?" asked a dopey little tribesman down by the creek.

"Those are peace aims," a minor boo-hoo expert told him.

"Peace aims? repeated the tribesman stupidly. "How come we got peace aims when we ain't even in the war?"

So it went. You can see the level of the tribe's morale was not getting any higher. The Head Paleolith recognized the unsatisfactory condition in a flash. He asked one of his best experts at lunch time what morale was. The expert said it was an educational product. So the Head Paleolith appointed a fish grabber to work up all the morale in the tribe.

Dr. Peddiwell finished his milk and fell into a constrained silence. "You mean a professional teacher of fish-grabbing?" I suggested gently. "Oh, no," he replied, "an amateur ichthyologist – a one-fish-a-year man, of course."

"That sounds a little off-center," I protested. "The boo-hoo was the morale-building stuff, wasn't it – so they got an amateur ichthyologist – why, your story doesn't make sense!"

"But you forget that boo-hoo was essentially amateur stuff," explained the professor kindly. "If it had been a real war effort with actual clubbing being done by this tribe, of course professional work of all kinds would have been necessary. But for boo-hoo defense – well, after all, don't be so critical."

"Look here," I said. "I don't like the moral of this story, and I am –"

"Just a moment!" the old man interrupted brushquely. "Any morals you get from this narrative are your own doggoned morals!"

We parted at the library steps with verbal expressions of friendliness but, I regret to say, a certain coolness of manner.

The Saber-Tooth Tiger Returns

When I called on my distinguished former teacher, J. Abner Pediwell, Ph.D., professor of education at what was once the Petalum State College but is now, of course, the Petaluma State University, he was seated on the porch of his cabin, staring at the Pacific Ocean. He greeted me with his usual absent-minded courtesy, shaking my hand warmly, pulling out a chair for me, and forcing a glass of beverage into my fist, all without the slightest idea of my identity.

I told him my name, and his eyes narrowed.

"Ah, yes," he commented. "Your're the man who put those paleolithic lectures, or rather those lectures on paleolithic education, into print."

I admitted that I was.

"Specifically," he inquired crisply in his old classroom manner, "what good did that book ever do?"

"Well-er-it-ah," I began hesitantly, overcome as always by the directness of his questioning, "quite a few people have read it."

"That isn't what I asked you," the professor said with a touch of pity. What good, what educational good did it do?"

That word "educational" saved the day for me. I knew the answer now. "It has caused my students and colleagues, returning from tourism in Baja, California, and elsewhere below the Border to bring me back over the years a total of gallons of tequila," I answered glibly.

"And you drank that stuff?" Pediwell asked.

"Certainly not," I said firmly. "I gave it to hospitals, nursing homes, and a few individual investigators for private research projects. The last liter was contributed to a local high-school science club as possible rocket fuel."

"Huh!" the old man mused. "And now, lacking creative stimulant for your own uses, you come to me for help on the paper you have agreed to give to the National Association of Secondary School Principals next month."

"How did you know?" I blurted out in astonishment.

"We have a secondary-school administrator in Petaluma who belongs to that organization," said the professor primly, "and I have intelligence contacts with his office."

"The Executive Committee did suggest," I explained, "that I might get you to-er-sort-of-er-prophesy about—."

Paper read before the 1958 meeting of the National Association of Secondary School Principals, Indianapolis, Indiana.

"Prophesy?" he interrupted. "Never! Impossible! Like any scientist I sometimes make predictions, but I never prophesy."

"I thought the two words meant pretty much the same thing," I suggested.

"The same thing!" The old man seemed outraged. "Of course, they don't mean the same thing!"

"Just what is the difference?" I inquired timidly.

"Difference?" Peddiwell snorted. "The difference is simple and big. When you prophesy you just reach into the air, often right after throwing sand over your left shoulder and repeating the Seven Cardinal Principles or other appropriate incantations, and wham! you have the prophecy full-blown right there in your hand. When you predict, you first examine the evidence, then you interpret it in the light of one or more hypotheses, and finally you track it into the future as far as it points. You see the difference? Is it not apparent to you?"

"Yes sir," I said slowly, "but would it be too much to have you demonstrate?"

"Demonstrate?" he blinked.

"Yes," I suggested eagerly. "Just predict, for example, the history of the American schools for the next fifty years, and I will have—"

"Your paper for the meeting in Indianapolis," he supplied the ending.

"Well, I could use it, with your permission, of course, in preparing my lecture," I said ingratiatingly.

"No," he snapped. "Don't put any of your own stuff in there. Quote me in full or not at all. And this is not a lecture; it is a paper. You should read it to those gentlemen and not add unscholarly comments or tell any of those maize-fashioned anecdotes to which you have become addicted, particularly that one about the psychologist who was studying fleas."

He spoke exactly as he would have spoken to me forty years ago. I should have felt hurt and told him to keep his flourishing views for his own papers. I should have said plainly and with dignity that I would compose my own lecture and that he could go if he wished to some hot, dry place that was full of professors of education. But I did not. I just promised humbly to do as I had been told. It was a coward's way, but it did save me the trouble of preparing a lecture for the meeting.

Here is what the old man said, as nearly as I can transcribe my notes. It is hardly necessary for me to add that I disagree profoundly with some of his implied views.

In 1958 (began Professor Peddiwell) the people of the United States were in great educational difficulties. They were well aware that they were in difficulties, but they were somewhat handicapped by not knowing what the difficulties were. They thought — many of them, at least — that they knew. They thought their difficulties were caused chiefly by personnel and material shortages, a lack of teachers, buildings, and money to supply them. Actually, their difficulties stemmed primarily from a shortage of beliefs.

The Americans did not know what they wanted education to do, and so they concentrated their attention largely on educational motions, processes, content, and methods without much regard to purposes. This made it easy for them to travel in circles, educationally speaking. When put under sudden pressure, as when they awoke abruptly to a fear that the Soviet Union was outstripping them in education, their circling was stepped up to near-hysterical gyrations. They whirled easily, because they lacked a basic belief to give them solid anchorage in educational matters.

Much of this gyration centered on the secondary school. The ordinary American citizen did not like to look critically at the elementary school. Brought up in a Momistic culture in which love for children and dogs was second only to reverence for Mother and the Flag, he could not criticize easily an institution performing so many child-development, child-welfare, and child-protective functions as did the elementary school.

The higher educational institutions, furthermore, overawed the American of 1958. For every situation, they had a language that subdued him. When he was not himself a college graduate, he assumed that he lacked the necessary schooling to understand higher education pronouncements; when he was a graduate, he knew he could not understand them. In his student days, he had heard about scholarly disciplines, humanities, liberal arts, and basic scientific concepts, but it had been all he could do to get through Zool. 5, Pol. Sci. 11 and 12, and the rest of those courses his adviser and the dean had made him take. He had almost failed Phys. Ed. 1 by not being able to meet the required standard in push-ups.

When the college and university professors and presidents in 1958 turned accusing eyes and voices on the secondary school, therefore, and the elementary school people gazed modestly but confidently at their solid floor of concern with child growth and development, the average American turned his critical attention too on the secondary school. He knew what driver training was; he knew that algebra was a process of finding out what x equalled. It was not long before he could say, almost enthusiastically as though he knew the facts, "Driver training? Hah! It may be all right, but it takes mathematics to put a sputnik aloft. Home economics, art, and music? Very nice if you can afford them, but physics — there's the stuff to make the Russians squirm."

This, then was the situation in 1958. From two main tendencies in that situation, I am going to attempt two different sets of predictions. The first of these I will call the Alpha Prediction because it is based on the Alph Hypothesis. The second is the Beta Prediction because it is derived from the Beta Hypothesis.

The Alpha Hypothesis holds that the Americans from 1958 onward did not acquire a basic educational belief and lacking that belief, they redoubled their efforts. The Beta Hypothesis supposes that the Americans did acquire such a belief and acted upon it. Let us consider the possible outcomes of these two hypotheses.

THE ALPHA PREDICTION, 1958-2008

In 1958 the Americans circled around one chief item of educational content; they sought to teach their young people more mathematics so that they could learn more science in order more nearly to rival the supposed Russian accomplishments in extra-terrestrial and other military technology. They increased the pay of the teachers of those subjects in high school and colleges, while taking care to pay less than the going wages in government and industry. They required courses in algebra, geometry, trigonometry, the calculus, physics, and chemistry. They established special secondary schools which emphasized mathematical and scientific instruction.

This development had several results. First of all, it did increase substantially the number of people with elementary training in mathematics or raise the quality of that research. Practically everybody, from the highest-ranking scientific and political leaders to the pundits of the mass media of communication, paid lip-service to the importance of basic research. "We must have scientists freely engaged in the pure activity of investigation for its own sake," they said; and then they increased the pressure for quick results in the perfection of missiles and other weapons. To those who made speedy, spectacular, and military applicaions of research, they gave generous recognition in the form of well-paid honors. To those engaged in basic, impractical research, they gave a condescending nod and a gracious, unpaid pat on the head. The only scientific people who ranked below the pure researchers in public estimation were the science teachers.

It did not take the students of science long to respond to these stimuli. They flocked to the standards of technology until only a few visionaries remained to work on basic investigations. Those who could not make the grade in either technology or pure research became teachers.

Other results of this development were changes in the teaching of subjects other than mathematics and science. Social studies became suspect; the Russian children studied history rather than social studies. The humanities, fine arts, and music were regarded with distaste; the Russians studied such subjects with Marxist-Leninist objectives, and the Americans had no substitute objectives. Anything that had practical, which is to say, military value received support as handmaidens of essential effort with mathematics and science. Geography and foreign languages were obviously practical; the Russians studied them. Instrumental drawing and design were practical because they were useful in planning weapons; and besides, the Russians studied them too.

For the most part, however, the areas of learning outside the fields of mathematics and science became second-rate territory. In purchasing power, the salaries of teachers in these second-rate fields steadily declined. Students and teachers who had failed in the first-rate fields drifted into the lower echelons. The social studies, the humanities, the arts, and music became more and more places of refuge for second-rate teachers and students who shrank from the pressures of technological achievement. If you were seriously concerned with philosophy, poetry, or drama as teacher or student, you were not only regarded as inferior; you probably were inferior.

After the war period of the 1970's the Americans changed the plane of their educational circling. Nobody won the war, of course, but China's rather successful bacteriological attacks on the two great nuclear-weapons powers toward the close of the conflict aroused great excitement in the United States. The chairman of the House Committee on Education saw the situation at once. "We are behind China in bacteriology," he said. "Our educators have been remiss. They have got to do something about it." College and university presidents and heads of zoology departments promptly made statements. "Ever since 1958," they complained, "the secondary-school enrollments in biology have been dropping. Students are being graduated from high schools today who won't know what a cell is. They can't even define 'life.' They waste their time in missile clubs."

The curricular wheel spun. Biology, botany, and zoology became required subjects in practically all high schools. Bug clubs flourished. Teachers of the biological sciences had their salaries raised until they were averaging almost eighty per cent of the pay of a second lieutenant in the Bacteriological Corps of the United States Defense Forces. Teachers of mathematical and physical science subjects began to slip into second-rate status. Those in social studies, humanities, and the arts — the few that were left — dropped even further down the scales of prestige and pay.

Then came the Olympic Games of 1988 with Indonesia winning first place in every event except the women's shot put and discus throw which went as usual to Byelorussia. The presidents of the United States and the American Physical Fitness Association immediately issued joint statements to the effect that physical education was at a low ebb. The American Association of Collegiate and University heads of departments of physical education, health, and recreation adopted resolutions demanding one half of the high school curriculum for the preparation of all youth in those studies. "Human beings are at least half physical," they said, "and thus need to spend at least half their secondary schooling in physical education and related activities."

The succeeding course of events was the familiar one already described in connection with the previous curricular reforms. By the year 2,000 the Americans had some of the best weight lifters in the world.

Throughout the period 1958 to 2008, except for training in the favored studies of the particular year and decade, the Americans abdicated more and more of their educational functions to non-school agencies. Attitudes were formed by the mass media of communication. The uses of slogans in place of reasoning, labels instead of argument, and conformity for its own sake combined to reduce differences among the people. Political decisions became merely questions of the relative popularity of personalities built up or broken down by advertising techniques. Instead of making economic choices, consumers merely responded to subliminal forces. In artistic and moral judgments, the Americans followed the same patterns. Questions of taste and ethics alike were answered automatically for them by agencies of the mass culture. The people who controlled these agencies, moreover, generation after generation became themselves less competent to make esthetic or moral choices. They relied more and more on a process of copying the choices of their supposed superiors. Their superiors naturally were the people, groups, or nations that they envied or feared. Thus, in a descending spiral, they merged into the lowest possible cultural denominator of their times.

When the Sagittarians landed in 2007, the cultural gulf between the invaders on the one hand and the Americans and other Earth natives on the other seemed to be even greater than the relative abilities of the two races warranted. Since the Sagittarians came from a planet about one thousand years older than the Earth, it was to be expected that they would have a considerable technological superiority over the natives. Their most spectacular skill, however, and the one in which they showed their superiority with greatest ease was not in mathematics, engineering, biology, physical fitness, or even in the arts, but in psychology. They could read an Earthling's mind like a book — only they had no books, relying instead on much more advanced means of communication. They could predict native behavior with great accuracy. This was a very practical and powerful skill. It was the toughest weapon the Americans and other Earth natives had ever faced. It reduced the whole world very quickly to the status of a conquered Sagittarian province.

The new rulers gave the conquered nations complete autonomy in matters of education. Early in the year 2008, therefore, as the half century with which we are dealing ended, the Americans entered a new curricular gyration. "Why," asked the president of the United States Chamber of Commerce, "has not psychology been taught in our high schools? The Sagittarian secondary-school boy and girl study psychology for six years. Besides the Sagittarian school day is 27 hours long, and the school week has eleven days in it. No wonder we are backward!" You can supply the remainder of this phase of the story.

THE BETA PREDICTION, 1958–2008

By the beginning 1958, a significant number of Americans, both laymen and schoolmen, saw that the first thing they had to do in trying to improve their educational systems was to find and agree on a central belief to which all their schooling could be tied.

They looked for this belief in their history. "Here is a nation," they said, "which was born in the rattle of revolutionary gunfire. Its national birth was announced in the noblest language of the eighteenth century enlightenment, listing the inalienable rights of the individual citizen. It fought the most devastating civil war of the nineteenth century to clarify and guarantee those rights for a poor and weak minority of its people. It won the status of a great power in the twentieth century as it fought again and again against tyrannies of whatever composition that sought to take away these rights."

"This is the greatest of all human causes," said the pioneers of 1958. "It is our American cause, the cause of individual human freedom. It is the heart of our national belief." We will organize our society around it. We will build and man and operate our schools in accordance with it. When it is challenged by opposing doctrines, we will support it and strengthen it with every possible peaceful measure and instrument. But if these peaceful measures and instruments be not enough and if the drums of war roll again, we will draw steel and strike again for our great American cause as our fathers did before us. And when in behalf of this cause we sheathe our weapons again, it will be for lack of argument. Let this be clear to a candid world."

"In the service of our national belief and its necessary processes of popular rule and equal justice under law," the Americans declared further, "we will organize and operate our educational systems to provide every citizen with the maximum opportunity to make wise choices in all the areas of public and private concern. We will seek to give him the greatest possible freedom to develop his abilities to the utmost in the service of himself and his people. We will do this with regard to the needs of our own people and of all people for the informed and disciplined freedom that we have envisioned. We will not be attempting to imitate the school systems of Russia, China, Indonesia, or any other nation. We know that their national beliefs are different from ours, and that is enough to tell us that our educational institutions and practices will necessarily be different from theirs."

The practice of this doctrine had as one effect a great increase in the number of people who studied mathematics and science. Basic research in these fields reached new levels, since it appealed to students who had strong individual preferences for particular kinds of scientific and mathematical problems.

Because the school became increasingly organized as an agency for the development of individual learners rather than as a storehouse of curricular wares or a factory of curricular divisions, the situation in the social studies, the humanities, and the arts developed in much the same fashion as those in science and mathematics. The number of advanced students in each of these areas was increased, and the amount and quality of basic research were also stepped up.

The schools and universities gave outstanding technological services in the development of weapons systems. Fortunately, they also gave to the United States and to the world historians, political scientists, economists, and sociclogists who played major roles in settling the 1970 crisis without war. They furnished writers, artists, philosophers, and religious leaders, furthermore, whose achievements more than any others made the United States the acknowledged leader in cultural advance throughout the world.

By 2008 the pattern of American education was being developed to the point of moving easily and surely with the times. It was obviously the greatest factor in inaugurating the twenty-first century's great era of world peace and progress.

What were the chief characteristics of this new American education? First, just as the Americans centered their theory of education around their belief in individual freedom, so their educational organization was centered around their guidance and counseling systems. They believed that every learner was unique, and they studied him with care to discover and understand his motives, interests, and abilities. In similar fashion, they centered their methods of instruction around what they knew about the individual learner. As a result, they had more discipline in their learning than was ever dreamed of in the days of the minimum curricular standards. They recognized that those were the standards which had often exacted little effort from the ablest member of a class and then had praised him and rewarded him for doing practically nothing. Those were the standards which had often asked the slower student to do work that was impossible. They discarded those standards for a scholarly discipline which was applied to the individual learner in terms of his capacities. Its ideal was a one hundred per cent performance in every subject for every student.

The second main mark of the new American education was its variety. The primary and upper elementary schools were of many kinds, and each of them had variety in its own program. The secondary schools were even more varied, providing as they did for work experiences as different as the communities in which they were located and as different as the abilities of the students who were members of them.

The research institutes, laboratories, workshops, and studios for the advanced practice of scientific research, creative expression, social investigation, and experimental innovations of many kinds were features of the new American education that made it most unlike its predecessor of a half century earlier. Although these agencies always had university students and teachers working in them, they also had secondary school students and teachers, other people who were not enrolled in any school or university but whose main vocational activity was related to the agency's area of study, and a few ordinary citizens, some of them beyond the usual working age, whose special abilities and interests were such that they desired and were competent to help in this particular kind of research. The entrance requirements to one of these institutes was ability to do the work, and the main pay was getting it done. This seems strange to us because it is contrary to our general 1958 educational practice. That it is not contrary to human nature, however, was discovered by pioneers of 2008.

* * * * *

The old professor stared at the Pacific, and, after a long pause, I could see that he had reached one of his baffling silences.

"Could you-er-give a little more detailed description of that new American education?" I began inquiringly.

"No," he said flatly. "I've given you enough. Fill in the details yourself."

"But these two predictions," I complained, "are so extreme. Is there not some middle way between them."

"No," he snapped. "There is not. If you try to get a middle way you will slide right slap-dab into Alpha. You can go to hell on the Alpha downgrade while you try to pussy-foot out of it."

"That is a harsh doctrine," I murmured.

He regarded me icily before answering. "It's a harsh world," he said finally, "but it has a clear-cut choice before it. It can head for a great educational revival, or it can head for the cosmic garbage heap!"

I reached out for another glass of beverage.

What Makes Schools Better?

As usual in a case of this kind, I asked my revered but somewhat disreputable former teacher, J. Abner Peddiwell, Ph. D., of the Petaluma State University, who is attending this meeting in disguise, for advice on what to say here tonight. "I was assigned the task," I told Peddiwell, "of speaking on the topic, 'What Makes Schools Better?"

"Better?" said Peddiwell.

"That's right," I said. "Better."

"Wrong approach," said the old man flatly.

"Wrong?" I cried. "Do you realize, Sir, that I got that topic from the executive secretary of the National Association of Secondary-School Principals, and that he represents ..."

"Yes, yes," interrupted the professor. "I know, but I don't think he would mind a change of one word in that topic. What you need is a positive approach rather than the negative one suggested by the question 'What Makes Schools Better."

"That sounds positive to me," I ventured. " 'Better' is positive, isn't it?"

"No," said Peddiwell. "It is negative. It assumes that what we have now in the way of schools is not so good — not, mind you, and *not* is certainly negative."

I remained silent, puzzled.

"Is not *not* negative?" he demanded.

"Well, yes," I began hesitatingly, "but ..."

"But nothing," he interposed scornfully. "What you want to talk on is 'What Makes Schools Worse?' There's a pretty positive approach. It assumes that what we have now is pretty good — *is*, mind you, and *is* is certainly positive."

I listened dumbly.

"This," he said impressively, "is what you should say."

After considering my own positive approach which he thought negative, and his negative approach which he thought positive, I decided to quote him verbatim without regard to plus or minus signs.

In order to make anything worse, (began Peddiwell), whether it is in a school, a government, a society, or a man, for that matter, it is first necessary to discover, study, and understand at least one crucial strength of the institution or the individual you are attacking. It is a mistake to start hunting first for a

Address delivered before the thirty-sixth annual convention of the National Association of Secondary-School Principals, February, 1952.

weakness in an organization or a peson that you wish to destroy or otherwise render ineffective or powerless. A boxer who starts blithely working on his opponent's notorious susceptibility to left hooks and knows nothing or pays no attention to the man's lethal overhand right is liable to find himself peacefully reposing on the canvas staring at a beautiful display of pyrotecnics in a vari-colored sky. A general who develops his strategy and tactics primarily on a basis of his foe's relative lack of armor and overlooks enemy artillery massed wheel to wheel is also riding for a fall. Similarly, a politician trying to win an election, a salesman endeavoring to break down a buyer's resistance, a lawyer fighting for a favorable verdict, or anyone else seeking an advantage against opposition must discover and study and solve the crucial strength of his opponent, or jury if he hopes to succeed.

You notice I say crucial strength. By crucial strength I mean simply a deep-seated characteristic that carries weight in the contest. The boxer may have fine curly hair or the enemy may have most resplendent uniforms but their crucial strengths are the right hand in one case and the massed artillery in the other.

So now the problem is how to make the schools worse, American schools worse. We look for the most crucial strength we can find in American schools, the most deep-seated, presistent strength.

How about the buildings and equipment? Are they not very important? Are they not strengths?

Well, yes, they are strengths but not crucial ones. It takes more than a gymnasium, auditorium, library, laboratory, superior floor coverings, and venetian blinds to make a good American high school.

Perhaps it is the scholarship of the teachers — how much do they know about literature, mathematics, science, and history? After all, the teacher makes the school.

Well, yes, that is a strength, but still it is not the most rugged one in American schools, not the one that ties most deeply into the structure of the institution.

Ah! Organization? The 6-3-3 arrangement?

No.

Administrative set-up? Department heads and assistant principals rather than ...

No, no.

Well, then. What is it? What is this crucial strength of the American school?

It is so simple that it is hard to see at close range. It is easier to recognize when you back off a ways — a century or two, for example.

The Americans began to build this great strength into their schools a long time ago. They set up their new nation squarely on the foundation of a belief in the unique worth of each individual citizen, that particular man right there, that specific woman yonder, that boy in that frontier cabin, that girl in that tenement house, that baby in that cradle. They based their new government on the proposition that each citizen had certain rights that no government or other man-made agency could properly take from him. They saw clearly that a government established by and for men with rights of this kind was not their master but their creature, and the proper education of such men was therefore a public concern of first magnitude.

So the Americans began to set up schools, first elementary schools then secondary schools and colleges, on a scale that astonished the world including themselves.

The astonishment of foreign and domestic observers of this phenomenal growth in the American schools was heightened by their ignorance of the great strength underlying this institution. They thought that when the United States doubled its secondary-school enrollment every decade for sixty years it was merely teaching secondary school subjects at a particular time to twice as many young people as ten years earlier.

Actually what the Americans were doing in these schools, sometimes more or less unconsciously, was changing the environment of its children and young people in important ways. They discovered that you did not educate a child merely by teaching something to him; that you educated him by changing his environment so that his total behavior would be different.

The Americans did not always accept this view easily. The elementary-school people grasped it early. The junior-high school teachers and parents got it a little more quickly than the senior-high school people, and many of the higher educational institutions have not got it yet, but the concept took hold, took root, went deep into the American educational soil, because it was needed and because American society as conceived by its people required an education of power and scope which could be secured by this approach and this approach only.

How did the Americans develop this crucial strength?

First, they invented various instruments for putting their schools in the lives of their people and their communities. Obviously, it was difficult to change a child's environment for educational purposes in a glass cage sealed off from the community. So the Americans invented the lay board of education; they developed parents associations; they utilized the interests of civic, professional, business, labor, patriotic, and other community groups to understand, counsel, and support the public schools.

Second, they broke gradually away from a curriculum of logically organized information, skills, and attitudes designed for the education-by-teaching-something-to-the-boy-period system. In the elementary schools they began to teach by modifying a whole phase of the learning environment. To be specific, the children were not merely educated that $2 + 2 = 4$, but they were educated in a play store, a modified environment, in which they learned, incidentally of course, that 2 + 2 did equal 4, and they learned it somewhat better thereby.

In the secondary schools, the Americans began to do the same sort of thing. They developed projects, activity programs, guidance facilities — all with the purpose of educating the boys and girls by wise modifications of their environment rather than by merely teaching to them the general formula for the solution of a quadratic or that verbs compounded with *ad-ante-con-in-inter-ob-post-prae-pro-sub-super* and sometimes *circum* take the dative, or *1066,* or *It is I.* And these Americans in their education capitalized on and developed this crucial strength by a continuing build-up of relationships of the school in and with the community.

How then would you go about making these American schools worse? You would attack that crucial strength. You would call the kind of education that seeks to modify a learner's environment significantly harsh names. You would call it progressive education and you would shout over and over again that progressive education increases delinquency. You would attack the social studies as being socialistic, insist that socialism is the same as communism and then scream in horror at the strain of the association you had just made.

You would set up self-appointed censors of school books and special "school" or "educational" councils or committees or commissions deriving their authority from their own destructive purposes, trying to nullify and cut the ground from under the great inventions of lay boards of education and parent-teacher associations. You would rally to your support those who do not believe in the American ideal of the unique worth of the individual.

This is the way, the most effective way, to make the schools worse.

At this point my impatience overcame me.

"Look, Dr. Peddiwell," I cried. "I don't want to make 'em worse!"

"You don't," he asked in surprised tones.

"No, of course not. I'm a teacher. I'm an American who holds that belief in the unique worth of the individual upon which you say the country was founded. I believe in that government of law which is the creature and the servant of free men. I want public education which has that crucial strength for such people in such a society. I don't want to tear down our public schools. I want to build them up. I don't want to make them worse. I want to make them better.

"Oh," said the old man. "Well, in that case, you just reverse the suggestions I have already given. An institution can be weakened or destroyed by a skillful attack on its strong points. It can best achieve greatness too by the development of its strong points."

"To make the schools better, then, we just build up this thing you called the crucial strength?"

"Yes."

"But our weaknesses? Shouldn't we look at them and protect them against attacks?"

"If you build your strong points high enough," answered the professor, "your weaknesses will take care of themselves, but if you retreat from your strong points in the face of attack to nurse and guard your weaknesses you too may suddenly connect your chin with a looping overhand right or find your tanks in a defile with massed guns on both flanks."

Protecting the Rights and Advancing the Responsibilities of the Teaching Profession

Recognizing that you all know more about the real details of defending the rights and extending the responsibilities of teachers than I do, it would be presumptuous for me to try to talk on the subject in any technical fashion. I am glad, therefore, to lay as much of the blame as I can for my remarks on J. Abner Peddiwell, Ph.D. Peddiwell is now professor emeritus at the Petaluma State University, and he holds a number of high-scounding titles from various universities, foreign and domestic. Sometimes I fear that those labels have tended to make him think that he is important, but really he is not important. I think I can say this since he is not actually present here except in certain unimportant ways. Another thing that worries me about the old man is that he has developed a spurious energy with advancing age. I recognize that with persons of his temperament this is one of the possible characteristics of incipient senility. It might not be very harmful to him or to society, except that he rushes around so much nowadays that he persuades himself a great deal of the time that he is busy.

Furthermore, Peddiwell has developed various new idiosyncrasies which bother me. Some of these traits may be desirable, but many of them are probably regretable. For example, he has stopped drinking alcoholic beverages except for minor medicinal or nutritive purposes. He does use rum in his afternoon tea, I notice. And he uses sparkling Burgundy at dinner on all national holidays of his own country or of other countries that he regards as being important. On St. John's Day, for example — Flag Day, Independence Day, Bastille Day, Dominion Day, San Martin's Day, O'Higgins' Day, and the birthday anniversaries of his numerous kinswomen and kinsmen in Oregon, and also the birthdays of various national heroes of the countries he regards most highly — the United States, of course, France, Argentina, Chile, Uruguay and Italy. He always has sparkling Burgundy on those days, usually at dinner.

When I met Professor Peddiwell yesterday at the Chicago International Airport, I braced myself for an explosion from the old man as I started to tell him about the dinner meeting where I was to talk on this topic. But he was surprisingly genial to me.

"Yes, yes," he said tolerantly, "I know all about it. I knew that you would be wanting a manuscript. But let us talk about the anniversary first."

"Anniversary?" I inquired.

Address before the 1962 convention of the National Education Association, Denver, Colorado.

"Why, yes," he said, "surely you have not forgotten that Sunday is the 272nd anniversary of the Battle of the Boyne."

"Well, yes," I replied, floundering a little. "County Kildare – yes – King William the Third on a white horse, and pipers, of course, and those Huguenot regiments."

"Right, right," said the professor approvingly. And then I noticed that bottle of sparkling Burgundy in the ice bucket. Well, I won't go into that. I did find, however, that Peddiwell had no speech whatever prepared for me, and he did not propose to prepare any. He demanded rather that I read the notes of my own ideas upon this subject, and I did so. The notes run in this fashion:

The half century from 1962 to 2012 was one of the most difficult and at the same time one of the most productive periods ever experienced by the teachers of North America and indeed of other countries generally. There was a time during and right after the great troubles of 1963-68 when it seemed as though the world was going to hell on a downhill grade and teachers instead of being leaders of their cultures in any important way appeared merely to be running frantically to keep from getting tramped on in the rush by preaching politicians, big hardware salesmen, space agents, and pseudo military mental giants who had become educational sciosophers overnight. The level of know-ledge artisans seemed to be in a hundred saddles at once, waving their disci-plinary banners and calling upon their followers to charge in all directions except forward. By 1968, however, it was apparent that most of this frothing came from surface eddies; that the deep current of human affairs was moving steadily in one direction – in the direction of a new period of progress and the freedom that must go with that progress – and the teachers of the United States were going to be the key leaders of the period unless they abdicated that role. The generation of 1968-2000 triggered the new era. (If that seems a long time to you I may add parenthetically that it is only one generation from now.) Until 1968 there had been relatively few periods in the history of mankind when progress occurred or, indeed was possible. In the 12,000 years of history let us say, before the yearr 2000 A.D., it was generally agreed by competent students of the subject that there had been only four such main periods. They were: first, the period in which pioneer groups of hunters and foodgathers became herdsmen and farmers – perhaps from about the year 10,000 to 9,000 B.C., in Central Asia, for example. Second there was the period when city-centered states were developed in the Middle East from 4000 to 3000 B.C. Third, the great religious, artistic, intellectual movements in the period 1000 B.C. to the beginning of our present Christian era. And fourth was the period of our own Western Civiliza-tion, which got under way with a swing only about 500 years before 2000 A.D.

These dates are just approximate and do not cover similar periods devel-oping at later times in isolated portions of the world, as in Mayan Mexico and Guatemala and in Guechua Peru under the Incan rulers. There were long stretches of stagnation in the intervals – 5,000 years between the first and second periods — 2,000 years between the second and third periods — 1,000 or 1,500 years from the end of the third period to the beginning of the current period of progress.

In those periods of stagnation, furthermore, extraordinary men acted and thought in ordinary, traditional, stuck-in-the-mud fashion. Individual freedom was usually not sought after and was never present in those periods to any significant extent. In the periods of progress, on the other hand, extraordinary men had extraordinary perception, and attempted daring innovations of one kind or another, but ordinary people still dragged along in their routinized ways, and freedom was extended only in special activities — activities sanctioned by the ruling society. For instance, when horses and cattle were being domesticated, men were generally allowed to attempt domestication of any useful animal, but they were not encouraged to build city-centered states, or proclaim new religious views.

Within the periods of progress there were more limited flare-ups occasionally of ability and achievement, usually lasting less than a century, and often confined to small geographical areas. In those short flare-up periods, not only extraordinary people but rather ordinary ones tended to think and act in an extraordinary manner. Human beings have usually been very proud of those brief explosions of daring activity and resourceful confidence when their fathers "bent up every spirit to his full height" and fought so well to extend the area of freedom and responsibility they often had to sheath their weapons for lack of argument at the end of those periods.

The peculiar characteristics of these flare-ups periods of human achievement must be very important to us for there are clear indications that we are now about to enter, if indeed we are not already in the beginning of, such a golden age on a planet-wide basis.

In the past, all these golden ages in their limited and varied occurrences displayed four necessary and distinctive characteristics. First, they always began only after a society, a culture, a people had been jarred loose from accustomed moorings by troubles, by conflicts, by wars, by threats, and by similar vicissitudes. There are few lengths to which the human mind will not go to avoid the pain of thought, or the labor of creative work. Men are natively slaves to tradition. Ordinarily they yearn for stupidity much more than they yearn for wisdom. But when a period of troubles is strong enough and lasts long enough to bat them out of the mud, but is not so severe or so lengthy as completely to exhaust them, they can think and act swiftly and decisively in new ways. When the dogs of trouble really hound them on and hang on their heels, they will look for new trails or they will make new trails where they need them.

In addition to this first characteristic of the golden age, you have the second characteristic, that the golden age or the brief flare-up period of creativity always has a new instrument of communication, or has discovered new uses for old means and old tools of communication. That is why such measures as poetry, drama, painting, sculpture, the dance, the novel, oratory, new systems of schooling — new ways whereby the people could inform and inspire each other were usually stepped up dramatically in any golden age.

Third, there were always special groups who served in key positions for each golden age. In Mogul India, for example, it was the Afghan horsemen riding down from the north; in Elizabethan England it was the new dramatists and the ocean-circling mariners; and in Grundtvigian Denmark it was the peoples' college founders and operators. Seemingly every such period has to have people who have special knowledge and special skills in developing the communication lines and instruments and understanding the drives that are the characteristics of the fourth phase of this.

In the fourth place, in addition to these three characteristics I have mentioned, there had to be a driving force of some kind, a creative spirit that took people who were already thoroughly shaken up by their troubles and showed them how to develop and use the new communication instruments and techniques — how to reach the goals that people now could see and want.

In the period 1968 to 2000 A.D., for the first time in human history these four factors were present on a planet-wide basis. For 70 years before 1968 there had been wars of world-wide implication and sometimes world-wide participation going on constantly. By 1968, furthermore, it was obvious that in the new education, the new electronic sorting, relating, storing, rearranging-of-data machines — the so-called electronic brains — would be the key instruments in any new flareup of progress. The mass media of communication which had been deemed very important — the press, the radio, the television, the cinema — were not nearly so important in the starting of the new world-wide golden age as were these relating, remembering, and computing machines that had been developed very largely in times of troubles. By the year 2012 it was a commonplace observation in the schools and universities of the free world that the best students were hypothesis makers. The professors were now saying to their students, "Anything you can dream up these hypothesis-testing machines can check out very swiftly. They can try in a matter of minutes or hours what would have taken you thousands of hours or even many years to test."

The new creative spirit was thus in the ascendance all over the world, and its greatest leaders were the North American educators. In 1962 the United States, for example, had more than 200 students attending higher educational institutions for each 10,000 of the general population. This was twice as many as in any other country of the world and 100 times as many as some countries had. The elementary, secondary, and technical school enrollments in the United States were similarly advanced.

By 2012 this ratio of higher educational enrollment to each 10,000 of the general population had gone from 200 to more than 500 in the United States, and in other countries from 50 or 100 to 300 and 400. By 2012 the chief aim of all education was to develop the attitudes and the skills necessary for the vast new areas of choice revealed and imposed by the achievements of the first global golden age. Children, adolescents, and adults all had to face rapidly developing situations with new problems every day, sometimes every hour, to an extent hitherto unrecognized, unimagined.

Instead of being overwhelmed by these new problems, however, the people of the free world were stimulated by them to new levels of insight; new levels of drive, attempts, and achievements, in education. Ordinary people now by the hundreds of millions thought and acted in extraordinary fashion under the leadership of extraordinarily artistic and socially daring educators. These were the same educators who 75 years earlier would have been only ordinary teachers giving ordinary instruction under the watchful gaze of stuck-in-the mud critics quick to pounce upon any signs of extraordinary thought.

* * * * *

Professor Peddiwell had sipped his Burgundy reflectively as I read this manuscript thus far, but when I came to this point he shifted a trifle uneasily an said, "Ha, hum, very pretty, very pretty — yes all about that artistic — what was that, extraordinarily artistic and socially daring educators — what are they, anyway?"

I had been the old man's student long enough to know that I must not give him a weak-kneed answer, so I replied bravely, "An extraordinarily artistic educator is one who has been so well prepared for his profession he doesn't have to fumble around for the applicable scientific principles in any situation. He knows what they are. His main problem is how to teach his pupils and how best to communicate with his people. This is always an artistic problem. A socially daring educator, furthermore, is not limited by this classroom here or this particular goal in this phase of a prescribed curriculum; he knows what his people want and need educationally, for he has talked with them, he has listened to them. His professional vision goes far beyond the classroom, laboratory, or library walls and his professional spirit is on a proud level because he is vowed by the ethics of his profession to wear his heart out after the unattainable."

The old professor listened to me curiously. "You have become an orator?" he asked cryptically.

"The word offends you?" I inquired.

"No," he said, "although oratory, if it means clear and simple expression, dramatically given, might well be offensive to certain groups right now that seem to be dedicated to muddying the understanding of the people concerning their schools by making the current race to various places outside this planet more important than education. You mean to tell me that only 50 years later most of the people knew that the single question of overwhelming import and one that had to be answered correctly before real answers to any question of government, commerce, industry, warfare, or international competition could even be attempted was that central basic question of education?"

"Yes, sir," I replied, "I believe that completely."

"You have a great faith in the future of the teaching profession then," he commented.

"Yes, I do," I said.

"Well," he said further, "if we do not have that faith we need not worry about the future of this country and of the free world because they have no future."

The Curious Case of Homo the Non-Sapient and His Seven Smart Sons
By J. Abner Peddiwell, Ph.D.

Once upon a time there was an organism named Homo on one of the sub-microscopic specks of cosmic dust in the multiverse. He was called the Non-Sapient because he was not very bright. But he had one saving characteristic. He wanted to be bright and he kept trying to change his ways in any direction which he thought might improve his condition.

When he was first observed by my reconnaissance agents he lived a rather poor existence. He huddled with his wife in a hole in a bank near the mouth of a creek running into the ocean nearby. He lived on shellfish which he picked up at low tide. His wife dug roots and gathered berries to augment the food supply. So the family barely survived.

Then Mrs. Homo had a baby, a little boy. Homo himself had more work to do now, more pressure on him. The population had increased by fifty percent and the work force was reduced somewhat because Mrs. Homo had to spend time taking care of the baby. Homo was up at the first glimmer of dawn, running along the beach looking for shellfish. When he had found as many as he could hold in both hands, he had to run back home and deposit his meager catch on a flat rock in the cave. Next he rushed into the woods, gathered berries until he had his hands full, and then rushed back to deposit them on the flat-rock larder; returned to the woods to dig up roots with his bare hands, and when his hands were full, resumed his running home again.

Homo seemed to spend most of his time running. The pack rats, which were numerous in the creek valley and which Homo never tried to catch since they were too fast for him, contemptuously watched his running to and fro. They gathered food too and packed it to their domiciles, but properly regarded themselves as being more efficient than the Non-Sapient. They overlooked one important difference between their way of life and that of Homo, however, they did not have the driving concern that he had to do things better.

Homo did not seem to find better ways until his son began to grow up. This boy was smart. When he was hardly more than a toddler he began to play with slender willow branches, weaving them together and criss-crossing them. His mother watched him, became interested, helped him, and finally the two of them discovered how to make mats and, most important of all, baskets. Now Homo did not have to run so much. He went out on the beach to gather

From the University of South Florida, *Educational Review*, Vol. 2, No. 1, Fall, 1963, pp. 1-7.

shellfish, Accompanied by his wife and son. Each of them carried a basket. When the baskets were filled they had enough food from just one trip to feed themselves for a whole day. The same technique applied to the gathering of berries and roots. The family was definitely on its way to more gracious living. The cave floor and walls now had mats as rugs and drapes. The family slept on mats and covered themselves with mat blankets, instead of shivering on the bare earth and rocks.

Then the smart son, observing the numerous pack rats, asked his father one day, "Are those creatures good to eat?"

"I guess so," said Homo, "probably better than shellfish, but the question is academic. You can't catch them. They run too fast. We have to stick to shellfish. They stay put so we can pick them up."

But the smart boy kept pondering the pack rat problem. He threw stones at the little animals, but he seldom hit one, and when he did the blow was insufficient for capture. One day he picked up a heavy stick which floated down the creek. Apparently it had been broken and bent by the fall of a tree so that it was slightly curved. He began throwing it, at first just for fun, and then he noted that it seemed to gather weight as it whirled in the air and that he could direct it with some accuracy. He tried it on a group of pack rats and with the first throw he knocked down three of them. Their meat was delicious. Thus pack rat hunting became a chief enterprise for the family.

At first the boy's mother just threw the skins outside the cave in a pile, but then the smart lad began to play with the skins, rub them together, tie them together with sinews, and finally he made a crude coverlet of pack rat hides and gave it to his mother. This was possibly the origin of Mother's Day.

This is enough to explain the origin also of the school's activity curriculum. Homo's first smart son was the originator.

In the meantime the population of the family was steadily increasing from the 50 percent the first year to a 33 1/3 percent increase the second year, 25 percent the third, 20 percent the fourth, 16 2/3 percent the fifth, 14 2/7 percent the sixth, and 12 1/2 percent the seventh, a new baby each year, all of them sons.

It might be assumed that the second boy would have been taught under the same activity curricular arrangements as the first, but Homo varied the educational procedure. When the second son got big enough to learn to participate in the group enterprise, his father sat down with him on the beach, threw sand over his right shoulder, then over his left, and chanted spells to make it easier for him to gather shellfish and berries, dig roots, make baskets, and catch pack rats. He taught the boy these mysteries, showed him how to make magic signs with a stick, and in general sought to turn him into a citizen whose schooling would be first of all evident in his mastery of symbols and ceremonies.

The second son grew up, learning the activities needed by association with his father and elder brother, but he was always slower, less efficient, less single-minded than his brother because he had to stop and throw sand over his shoulders and sing propitiatory songs to charm the shellfish, berries, roots, and pack rats. In this way the magic-subject curriculum developed.

When the third boy began his schooling, again the father sat down with him on the beach, but this time instead of throwing sand and reciting spells, he drew diagrams in the sand and spoke directly and practically. "Here is a sketch of our Valley," said Homo, "and up here is where the pack rats come down from their hillside homes. Your brothers can come in on them from this point, you and I will meet them here, and in an envelopmental tactic we will make a great haul of meat and skins."

The third smart son listened, enthralled. He followed the activity curriculum with its scientific-experimental hypotheses and applications, and he became the best-educated boy in the family thus far. It looked as though Homo the Non-Sapient now had his curricular problems solved.

When the fourth son came down to the beach to begin his formal schooling, therefore, it seemed obvious that his father would put him through the same practical-scientific curriculum which had just worked so well with his next older brother. But, alas, Homo had another mess of curricular fish to fry. He sat down with that fourth boy and began lecturing him, instructing him, explaining things to him. "This is a stick of the kind we throw at pack rats," he would recite, for example. "It was invented in the year 10, Valley Era, by your oldest brother." He droned on and on recounting the details of valley throwing-stick history. He taught the boy dates, rules, regulations, names, definitions, and language skills. When the fourth boy finished school he could talk and explain pack rat hunting, shellfish gathering, root digging, and berry picking better, more glibly, in greater detail than anyone else, but he was not very good at those activities. Even his magic-formulae-using brother could beat him in the practical pursuits the family needed to have done. The discuss-talk-explain-re-talk and re-discuss type of curriculum was even less efficient than magic-subject curricula. Of course, the activities-plus-common-sense-and-science-curriculum was the best, the plain activities approach was almost as good, but the second son's magic-subject curriculum and the fourth boy's talk-talk curriculum were clearly the worst.

When the fifth boy started his studies, his father and his older brothers had just returned from a long reconnaissance trip to look (from a distance) at the strange tribe on the other side of the hill. In their schooling these enemies taught some subjects which were familiar to the Non-Sapients, basket and mat weaving, shellfish and berry gathering, and pack rat hunting. There were also other subjects which the family observers did not completely understand, but they tried to memorize them. Back in the home Valley they set up a new curriculum for that fifth boy, a curriculum in which the newly imitated, poorly understood foreign topics held first place. This fifth boy got an education, but it was not as good as those received by any of his older brothers. He seemed to be fatally

handicapped by a belief that the more important a subject was the more mysterious, incomprehensible and useless it would be. Thus the foreign-models curricular idea had its origins.

When the sixth boy's schooling was just ready to begin the Homo tribe was
so busy preparing for an imminent invasion from the strange tribe across the hill,
that no one had much time to teach the lad. Everybody tried to give him a little
instruction, so he learned some practical activities from his eldest brother, a few
spells and rites from the second boy, a diagram and map or two from the third
son, some talk from the fourth, and a vague notion from the fifth that the
foreign tribesmen had something, *something*, **something** of importance in their
schooling. So the sixth boy was on his own. He had individualistic schooling. He
taught himself mainly. Because he was concerned about the possibility of war,
he studied the chief weapons of his tribe, stones and sticks. Finally, after many
trials and failures he took a strong, springy stick, strung it with a stout line of
pack rat sinews, bound a sharp rock on a straight slender stick, and invented a
great, new devastating weapon, the bow and arrow. When he showed his invention to his father the old Non-Sapient shook his head admiringly but sadly.

"Boy," he said, "this will end inter-tribal conflicts. I will never order it
used unless I have to do it — unless the pressure of life and death is upon us."

And just then the fifth boy came running down the creek shouting, "The
enemy! The enemy! They are over the ridge. They're invading our Valley with
their mysterious foreign abilities and techniques." Behind him came the fourth
boy talking rapidly and explaining. "I can tell you just how it happened," he
chattered glibly, but no one listened to him. Then the third son came running
back with some blood flowing from superficial wounds. He drew a diagram in
the sand. "The enemy column is coming here, down this side of the creek. My
two older brothers are trying to hold them at this point. Let us now cross this
little canyon and hit them all together on their exposed left flank." His father
assented and the maneuver began. They could see, down in the valley, their two
brothers' gallant rear-guard action. The oldest boy, practically, deliberately,
although weakened from wounds, was fighting to make every blow count. The
second son did almost as well, but he was somewhat handicapped by his education. He had to stop occasionally to throw sand over his shoulders and recite
spells.

And now the enveloping movement was completed. The reserves composed of the father and the third, fourth, and fifth sons fell on the enemy's
exposed left flank while the sixth son's deadly artillery attack spread havoc in
the strange tribe's ranks. When two of the enemy had gone down under the
horrible arrows the invaders broke and fled in utter confusion.

While the sons of old Non-Sapient were returning, singing songs of victory,
old Homo was trying to decide what curriculum he should use with his seventh
and last son, a boy of tender years but of great promise. As the victors neared
home, however, they heard their mother's high keening wail and they knew they
would not have to educate the seventh son.

What Should Our Children Inherit?
By J. Abner Peddiwell, Ph.D.

He fumbled with his Phi Beta Kappa key and peered anxiously through his thick-lensed spectacles. "I was looking for an answer," he said humbly.

"Uh-huh," said the Devil, "and then you were hit by a truck. That's why you're here."

"But I didn't see the truck."

"Of course not. That's how you got hit."

"Well — ah — I still need an answer."

"What do you want to know?"

"I want to know what should our children inherit?"

"Humph! Funny question. What were you, a lawyer?"

"Lawyer? Were? No, I *am* a professor."

"You *were* a professor. Professor of what?"

"Professor of education. But why do you say *were*? I'm still a professor, I hope."

The Devil smiled grimly. "Not here, you aren't. Since you crossed the river back there you're not a professor. You're just a soul, a soul stripped bare of the flummery and doo-dads which men use to cover up their ignorance — and their sins."

"What — why —" stammered the professor. "You mean I — I'm . . ."

"Sure," said the Devil, "you were dead before you hit the ground."

"But in that case I must be in . . ." The professor halted modestly. "You're here — at the gate. You aren't — are you — ah — St. Peter?"

"Oh, no," the Devil laughed. "Much obliged for the compliment. I'm the head man here — really only just a chairman, however. Thank badness this is one place where we still have true democracy. Of course we have to have an administrative head like any other organization, and I have been an administrator so long that I must take the lead in policy making and policy executing. You should see the committee on methods, committee on tenure, committee on the activity program, and a very fine committee on evaluative criteria — temperatures, you know — latest stuff."

The professor was visibly shocked. "You mean — you can't mean I've actually gone to . . ."

"Sure you have. Why not? It's no disgrace. We have some of the worst people here. Our entrance requirements are not so rigid as those of another place, but after all we do pride ourselves on our activities and on our democratic traditions and procedures."

The professor pulled a neatly folded handkerchief from his breast pocket and wiped his forehead. "I had noticed it was warm," he said agitatedly, "but I had no idea it was because I had gone to . . ." He paused, visibly embarrassed by his proximity in flesh and in language to a place which he never mentioned save under appropriate stress of anger.

"Why don't you go ahead and say it?" the Devil asked impatiently. "There's nothing profane about a mere place name, is there?"

The professor jammed his handkerchief into a moist ball. "Well — er — I suppose not — at least when one is there. But isn't there any way out? Do I have to stay here? I have a number of engagements — some studies I have promised to complete — and that question I mentioned to you. I wanted that for a speech I have to make."

"Now, now," said the Devil soothingly. "Don't take it so hard. I know this place has a bad reputation. Many people think it is just a prison, but actually it is much more than that. It is a clinic, a guidance center, a testing bureau, a division of research and — well, I sometimes say, more or less jokingly, of course, that it is really a lot like an adult education center or even a university."

"That's astonishing," commented the professor. "I always thought this was a — a . . ."

"A hell of a place? I know. Go ahead and say it, you can't hurt my feelings. And in a sense it *is* hell here. It should be. We have to provide that service too. You will see what I mean as you go through the grind. First of all we must examine some of your basic beliefs. If you were a doctor, we'd diagnose your difficulties. If you were a lawyer, we'd try you. Since you're a professor of education, however, we'll put you in a panel discussion. We do that with all men in your field."

"Ah, do they all come here?"

"Well, yes, practically all of them. Step this way, please. The panel is waiting."

"What do I have to do?"

"Just act as a member of the group. You know what a panel discussion is."

"Yes. I have served on them. In fact I have organized them, even presided . . ."

"All right, then. You know what to do."

"But — er — for this purpose — a panel discussion — isn't it liable to be — ah — vague and — maybe controversial and everyone exhibiting his pet prejudices — and no one having very many facts — and no real direction of the discussion and . . ."

"Why, certainly," admitted the Devil with a touch of asperity. "What do you expect? Remember where you are."

The Devil introduced his victim brusquely. "This man thinks he has an educational question," he announced.

The members of the panel rose from their seats around the conference table and, one by one, solemnly shook hands with the professor.

"An educational question?" said the man with the mathematical nose. "You have come to the right place."

The Devil waved the professor into a vacant chair, and they all sat down.

"Well, now," said the Devil, "unless somebody else wants to do it, I'll just act as chairman to save time. What's the question you have to propose?"

The professor swallowed embarassedly, "Why — er — I want to know what our children should inherit."

"There you are, gentlemen," explained the Devil. "That's his question, and I don't mind saying that it sounds funny to me. What should our children inherit? What *should* they inherit but what we have to leave them? That's all there is to it. That's a simple answer to a very simple question. I don't see what there is to discuss."

"Nonsense," snapped the man with the mathematical nose belligerently. "It is a very sound question and a profound one. It is not simple, but your answer, sir, *is* simple, so simple as to be ridiculous, if you don't mind my saying so."

"Oh, not at all, not at all," said the Devil beamingly. "Thank badness there is left one place where we can have free and untrammeled democratic discussion. Go right ahead and tell us what's on your mind."

"Thank you," said the man with the mathematical nose. "The question is an excellent one, and I am of course prepared to answer it. We do not want our children to inherit everything we have. We want them to inherit only our goods and not our ills. When men become civilized they know that a trained mind, a disciplined spirit, is the best inheritance they can give. So they establish schools by which they transmit the distilled wisdom of the ages. That is the answer."

"Ah, yes," said the man with the social expression, "but the question of what this inheritance shall be is not merely an academic, a pedagogical matter. It is society itself which has to answer the question; it is society which has to transmit the inheritance, and the way in which society answers the question determines in the long run whether its children are going to have good bread or ground up twigs to eat, whether they are going to live and learn, warm and secure, or die in mangled heaps with the grip of fear on their hearts at the moment of their extinction."

"Bosh," said the man with the mathematical nose. "Society! The next thing we know you will be talking about democracy. We must give our children the ability to use symbols — languages and mathematics. We must make them familiar with the words of the great men of the past. We must have them memorize poetry. Thus we shall discipline their minds, give them strong and keen instruments with which to order their lives. If they decide to have democracy, dictatorship, autocracy, communism, that is their lookout. We have done our part. Let them go where they will."

"But how do you know what will best train their minds?" asked the professor.

"The tried experience of the schools," answered the man with the mathematical nose. "That is why we should not teach them about current problems, the recent, the ephemeral things. To know what Plato said will help make them wise; to know the relief situation in their own city may help to make them only foolish agitators."

"It was the tried experience of the schools which perpetuated for men the worst forms of their ignorance," said the man with the social expression. "No school system which has been committed to teaching only the tried wisdom of the schools has ever escaped dry-rot."

"You are both wrong and both right," said the man with the artistic gleam in his eye. "It is true that we must use the old experience of the race, but it is false that we must use it in a traditional school fashion. It is true that we must make our children familiar with the problems of contemporary society, but it is false that we can show them how to change that society. We must allow and encourage them to grow freely, naturally, to express themselves in words, line, rhythm, tone, color, and form not for the sake of the training in expressional skills but for the sake of the personalities which are expanded and enriched in the expressional process."

The stubby-faced man said nothing.

The professor looked bewildered.

"Let me draw a few loose ends together," said the Devil, smiling impartially as a democratic chairman should. "Can't we agree on these three points: we should give our children trained minds, we should give them an understanding of current social problems, and we should give them well developed personalities?"

"You have a passion for simplicity," snorted the man with the mathematical nose. "It is this messing around with such questions as how the local fire department ought to be run that keeps the so-called progressive schools from giving the proper mind-training to their pupils. It is this dabbling with paints and projects that prevents children from knowing how to parse and diagram an ordinary sentence. Everytime you try to make a world-saver of a child, you seem to produce a sloppy thinker who can't learn trigonometry because he was never taught geometry. Every time you turn out a free and untrammeled personality, you seem more liable to get a dope or a criminal."

"I shall not address my further remarks to you," the man with the social expression said stiffly, "but rather to our friend here who asked the original question. I have no objection to a child having a trained mind. I am merely convinced that his abilities are best developed by attacking difficulties which he and his society want and need to have solved."

And I maintain," said the man with the artistic gleam in his eye, "that the child must not be developed at all, in fact, he cannot be developed. He is not developed — he develops. He is not developed by some school master with a nice, neatly ticketed and numbered set of distilled-wisdom-of-the-ages tools and devices or even by society. He develops himself, using the wisdom of the ages, the phenomena of social existence, anything, everything he needs in the process of growth."

The stubby-faced man said nothing. The professor looked more worried than ever.

The Devil smiled democratically and pulled his chair nearer to the professor. "They can go on like this for hours," he whispered, "and what's more, they will unless I stop 'em."

The man with the mathematical nose had started to repeat his arguments with a new vehemence. The man with the social expression was pretending to listen but was obviously rephrasing his next comment. The man with the artistic gleam in his eye did not pretend to listen but gazed idly about the room, waiting for his turn to make a statement which he knew so well that he did not need to rehearse it mentally.

The stubby-faced man continued to say nothing.

"Why doesn't that one man say something?" whispered the professor.

"Well, I don't know," replied the Devil. "I guess it's because he's got nothing to say."

"Is he always like this?"

"Oh, no. I don't even know that he is dead. He was sent down as a representative on this panel from the other place up there. They always have one representative. Those other three who are doing all the talking are local boys. They know their stuff, such as it is, but this silent chap–. Of course, I don't know. You want to hear him talk?"

The professor nodded. The Devil waited for a break in the flow of the argument and then cleared his throat for an opening.

"We have had a wealth of discussion here," he said, "and the issues have been clearly isolated and ably worked over. There is one member of the panel, however, who has not yet contributed to the discussion, and we all know he has a contribution to make. We'd like to hear from you, sir."

The stubby-faced man shifted uneasily in his chair and twisted his clasped hands without breaking them apart. "I — I don't rightly know the terms being used," he said apologetically. "I thought I might just listen and, you know, maybe learn a little — not that these gentlemen haven't been saying a lot but just that I was never a school master and so I can't understand everything."

"Oh, come on now," urged the Devil heartily. "Thank badness we're still democratic here, and every man has got to say his say whether he feels like it or not. Go ahead and give us your answer to this question of what our children should inherit."

"Certainly, go ahead," said the man with the mathematical nose. The man with the social expression nodded approval. The man with the artistic gleam in his eye leaned forward, waiting.

The stubby-faced man began slowly. "I have to tell the truth," he said, "without cover of even a single word that is not needed to make it truth. Where I come from there is no shelter from the glare of truth.

"I will not speak of schools; they are merely instruments. I will not speak of the wisdom of the ages; it is only mumbo-jumbo for pedagogical medicine-men. I will not speak of society; it is a false idol that demands human sacrifice. I will not speak of precious personalities developing as they may; they are the elements in an escapist game of psychological marbles.

"I will speak of men, young and old, men who can learn, men who can change their ways. For many hundreds of years they have changed their ways, sometimes with great speed and effect, sometimes slowly and fumbling, sometimes in the direction of the stars above their heads, and sometimes in the direction of the dirt beneath their feet.

"Nothing is sharper truth than that men change their ways for purposes, sometimes lofty, sometimes clearly seen, sometimes muddled and muddy. The greatest hoax of the last two thousand years has been that perpetrated upon the world by formal systems of education which claimed to have no purposes outside themselves. They claimed to give men education for its own sake.

"It is that kind of education today whose supporters say is not designed to prepare for citizenship in a democracy any more than in a dictatorship. Men who do not have purposes for their lives clearly enough in mind to know whether they want the masses of their fellows to order their own ways for their own benefit, certainly do not know enough to help change the ways of their fellow men intelligently.

"By education we give our people purposes, clear-cut and unshakeable. If we do not, we cheat them to protect ourselves from the pain of recognizing and accepting goals for changing ways. Do we want children to starve because they were sent by God to the wrong side of the railroad tracks? Do we want the maternity death rate to be far higher than we now have it? Do we want to kill our fellow men, sometimes in dreary economic stealth and sometimes to the proud accompaniment of drums and banners? If we do not want these purposes, we must set up the purposes we do want and follow them in the changing of our own and our children's ways.

"By education we give our people motives, driving desires, to achieve their purposes. If we do not, we are merely playing a game for gentlemanly exercise instead of fighting to reach real goals. It is a superstition, developed by those afraid of a truly motivated changing of human ways, that education must be always coldly calm, balanced, and unruffled by emotion. Learning that lasts, learning that shakes the foundation of men's accustomed ignorance, is a learning white-hot with motivation towards great goals.

"An education like this cannot be given by schoolmasters in pedagogical corners. It must be given by men, old and young men of all callings, men of all abilities, working together. The final and most priceless inheritance we can give our children is more willingness and skill in this working together to change their ways in the direction of clearly-seen and strongly-desired goals."

The stubby-faced man fell once more into silence. His fellow panel-members spoke briskly again, battling for the chance to repeat themselves.

"He made a speech," apologetically whispered the Devil to the professor. "I would have stopped him, only, you know, a visitor and everything."

"Certainly he made a speech," interrupted the professor testily. "But look what he said!"

"Ah, yes," agreed the Devil whimsically, "and that, my friend, is the hell of it."

II | INTERNATIONAL EDUCATION

When you consider that Benjamin has had illustrious careers as a public school teacher and administrator, university professor and dean, author, and soldier, it is astounding to realize that he is best known for his pioneer work in the field of comparative education. He assumed the leadership in this field shortly after World War I. As a specialist in international education he has been constantly in demand by other countries to assist in the establishment of improved school systems. In this capacity he has made studies and served as a consultant in many countries of Europe, Asia, and Africa, as well as the Canadian provinces of Manitoba and Quebec. Benjamin's most extensive research has been in Central and Latin America, as evidenced by publications ranging from a 1924 report on "University Revolution in La Plata, Argentina," to his most recent comparative education offering, HIGHER EDUCATION IN THE AMERICAN REPUBLICS.

In THE UGLY AMERICAN, William J. Lederer and Eugene Burdick succinctly point out that Americans not infrequently experience difficulty and hostility when serving on foreign soil because of their inability to communicate with the natives. Too often they fail to even try to learn the new language, other times they master only simple phrases which will permit them to express personal needs and desires. They seldom take the time necessary for the diligent study of language and culture which in addition to creating good will would allow them to better understand the problems of the country.

This criticism could never be leveled at Harold Benjamin; his facility in languages is truly phenomenal. He has made it a cardinal rule to study the linguistic, historical, and cultural patterns of every country he visits. In many cases he has learned the language well enough to deliver a lecture in the native tongue. Among other places, he has performed this feat in universities of Chile and Pakistan. On a recent trip to Illinois he mentioned that he was giving serious thought to visiting eastern Africa in a year or so and was studying Swahili. He then completely amazed me by saying, "Did you know that in Swahili the accent is always on the penultimate?"

To better understand the lengths to which Benjamin goes in order to establish a suitable rapport with the people he is working it is necessary to give a brief illustration. Let us assume, for the moment, that he is visiting Argentina for the first time. He has spent many hours studying the history and culture of the Argentine. Previous visits to other parts of South America have enabled him to speak the language (Spanish) fluently. Shortly after his arrival in Buenos Aires he changes into a strange costume and leaves his quarters. He is dressed in the garb of an Argentine Gaucho and, accompanied by a native Argentinian, heads for the poorer section of town. In spite of his companion's protests he visits several *cantinas*, some of doubtful repute, where he can leisurely talk with the people and gather their impressions. From meetings such as these and more formal gatherings with school personnel and education officials of the government, Benjamin begins to put together the pieces for his "scheme" of comparative educational research. He had long since decided that comparative education studies should be developed in terms of four main questions:

1. *What education does this people need? To make this determination the researcher must study the culture, history, and religion of the people. He must also make a careful investigation of their vocational and recreational activities.*

2. *What education does this people desire? The answer to this question required examination of the philosophy and statements of the people. (In many cases this examination will disclose what they think they need or to what desires they give lip-service).*

3. *What education does this people attempt? This information can be obtained by looking at all their instruments of education – schools, radio, television, newspapers, advertising, etc.*

4. *What education does this people achieve? This can best be assessed by looking at the products of the educational system rather than at what is taught.*

Graphically, we have:

The closer the needs to the desires (1) the greater the *insight* of the people into education. The closer a society's desires and their attempts (2) the higher their educational *drive*. The relationship between attempts and achievements (3) is the measure of educational *efficiency*. Finally, the relationship between achievements and needs (4) is the educational *significance* of the society. The final significance of a people's education in any area is a matter of how closely their achievements come to their attempts, attempts to desires, and desires to needs.

The selections included in this section of the collection are a representative sampling of Professor Benjamin's extensive work in comparative education.

Our People

What is the basic cause of war? How may that cause be removed? What can I do to help remove that cause?

I cannot consider intelligently the international aspects of teacher education, even in their smallest applications, without first finding some answers — however tentative and inconclusive — to these questions.

For myself alone, I state as a first principle that anything I do in the field of international education has one great purpose and one only — to help save my people from the scourge of war. If I do not have some hypothesis about what makes war and how education can help prevent war, my efforts in international education will fail to help make even a minor footnote in the history of education.

To me, one of the most moving passages in the literature of classical antiquity is that in which the great Athenian schoolmaster, looking death clamly in the eye, spoke to his people very simpley and directly about his feelings for them. He said:

"I love and respect you, Men of Athens, but I love and respect the truth of the immortal gods even more. Some of you have suggested that from fear of death and love of you I might retreat from what I consider to be the truth and cease to teach it, and then my life might be spared.

"It would indeed be strange if I who stood in the ranks on the battlefields of Potidaea and Amphipolis and Delium and fought for you under the command of the officers whom you appointed over me and did not in fear of death step back from the flashing steel — it would indeed be strange if now, cringing from death I retreated from the truth of immortal gods."

When I picture Socrates, I do not see him old and ugly as he is commonly described. I see him young and strong, a sturdy boy handsome in his armor, who started with a love for Athens, which he never lost even when Athens had condemned him to death, and ended with a love and understanding for all men, which to him was the truth of the immortal gods.

Could the Peloponnesian War, or any other war, have been fought among Greeks who had Socrates' grasp of the truth of the immortal gods?

Of course not, we say.

Why not?

Because to the teacher, Socrates, his people were all mankind.

From the *NEA Journal,* October, 1949.

   This, then, is the cause of war and of the things worse than war which go with it: the concept of MY PEOPLE. It is too narrow a concept for peace — MY FAMILY, MY CLAN, MY TRIBE, MY NATION, MY RACE, MY RELIGIOUS GROUP, AND MY SOCIETY, I will do good things for them, I will perform difficult tasks for them, I will fight for them, but I will not do these things for other people.

   All other explanations of war seem to me to be merely definitions of war in terms of its characteristics or its instruments, as though one might say, "War is fighting and killing," or "War is why we need armies." or "War is caused by men having weapons at hand," or "War is waged by governments," or "War comes because people are not friendly to each other."

   I have studied such answers respectfully. I have examined them in the quiet of libraries and in those greatest of all silences, which are punctuated by the roar of battle. I have thought them over, sometimes calmly, sometimes frantically, as I have remembered the boys who stumbled a little beside me in advance and fell forward coughing; the women with stricken faces along the line of pastwar parades; the babies with old-man wrinkles in their faces which only slow starvation can give; the mountains of frustration and torture piled so high that they benumb all normal sense of horror. I have thought of these answers under such circumstances and I have known that these answers were not true.

   War is as simple in its cause as in its degradation and misery. It comes from MY PEOPLE'S being less than all the people on this planet. It will be halted only when MY PEOPLE and YOUR PEOPLE are all the people.

   That is the truth of the immortal gods, and that is the truth of the God of my people and your people. That is the truth which our God has stated often enough through his prophets.

   "Well, now, wait a minute. What about nationalism?" It might be said.

   "Well, what about it?"

   "But if your people are all the people in the world, how can you fight for your people in time of war?"

   "Ah! That is the heart of the matter. If my people, if our people, are all the people of the world, I won't be fighting them, and you won't be fighting them, and there will be no war."

   "Ah, yes. You can say that in church. You can say that in a high flown speech as you welcome German and Austrian teachers to your campus. You can say that as you send CARE packages to undernourished children in faroff places. But do not say it in connection with war. It sounds sort of—well—unpatriotic."

   Yes, it does. As a matter of fact all basic effort to eliminate war is quite likely to appear unpatriotic in some respects, which is to say, unnationalistic, for war nowadays is largely, although not entirely, a national enterprise.

   Nations are born in war, they grow and develop in war, and they are buried to the funeral salute of a hundred thousand guns or the roar of two or three atom bombs. You are bound to be unnationalistic if you really try to eliminate the cause of war, just as you are bound to be unnationalistic if you really try to follow the teaching of the Great Galilean.

If I am going to try to attack the cause of war through international education, therefore, I might as well say "ALL right then, so I am unnationalistic. I do not want a baby in Siberia to starve any more than a baby in Kentucky. I do not want to have a mother in Bremen disemboweled by a bomb any more than a mother in Baltimore. I do not want my sons and grandsons twisted in mind and body, tortured, blinded, or killed any more than I want the children of any of my brothers so maimed or slaughtered.

"And I know who my brothers are. That is a truth which I have long confessed with my lips to my immortal God. Now I should put it in action or I should deny it with my lips."

"But wars are made by governments," it might be said, "and most of these teachers from Austria and Germany who are with us today will not go back to their countries and overturn governments."

I think that this too is something of a bypassing of the truth. Wars are not made by governments and they will not be stopped ALONE by establishing unions of governments, alliances of governments, or even a single great overall world government.

Wars are made by people. They are made by my people against your people, our people against their people, and whether or not those commending peoples are represented by governments, in the beginning at least, is more or less a matter of historical accident. We Americans know that.

We fought a war one time not so long ago. It taught us that truth. And it taught many people to know the bitterness and the in-growing hatreds of being a conquered territory occupied by victorious troops.

That war still remains for us the supreme test of our national effort and endurance, a war of staggering casualties in the lives of men and of even more horrible casualties in the enforced backwardness of conquered areas. That was a war of a people under one government. It is true that there was much talk of loyalty to state governments rather than to a national government, but this was the sheerest of political eyewash.

MY PEOPLE knew YOUR PEOPLE very well. There were many friendships, many intellectual exchanges, and much commerce between them. The great officers of the armies of both these people were trained in the same military college. They were often classmates and devoted friends and they led armies against one another. The men who followed those officers spoke the same language, belonged to the same families in many cases, and they fought the bloodiest, most savage and determined war of a bloody, savage, and determined century.

Why? Because they were not one people: they were not one society.

Let us examine this American Civil War a little further. Do I today love the people of Texas any more or less than did those kinsmen of mine who fought the people of Texas in that war? I think not. The men of my family did not fight on one side of the civil war because of love or hate. They fought for that one side because it was the side of their people.

I cannot fight a Texan today except, as I may become an individual criminal. Why not?

I cannot fight a Texan today because a society with a government, courts, a police force, an army, tells me I can't.

"These Texans are your people, mister," that society says to me, and if I try to get tough about it and say, "I don't care, I am going to declare war on Texas anyway," that society flashes its badge and touches the butt of its pistol and says to me, "No, you're not, mister, because this badge and this gun are your people speaking to you."

Now I can ask myself why do I want international exchanges of teachers? Why do I want international education of teachers?

Because I want teachers to build up a society like that society which speaks to me about my people in this country. I want teachers to build up a society like that for all the world. That means a government, of course, but it also means the other matters of communication, of economic efficiency, and of habits and attitudes which make up a cooperating society.

That is a great task of social engineering, which is to say a great task of education for a whole society. Can that task be done by Marylanders or Missourians or Americans or Europeans or Asiatics acting alone? Of course not. It has to be done by all our people.

For my part, I am going to try to help the teachers of MY PEOPLE acquire the skills and the wisdom for teachers in a great society.

Most of the teachers of MY PEOPLE with whom I deal will be Marylanders, but some will be Virginians and some will be Californians and a few will be Burmese. If there are not some from those latter groups of people outside of Maryland, it would be somewhat harder for us Marylanders and for us Burmese to see that we are one people and to learn how to construct our supporting society.

This is a rather danerous task. It is safer not to attempt it. It would indeed be strange, however, if the teachers of our people who have stood in the ranks in these wars of our times, both as civilians ans as combatants — and who have not shrunk from danger unduly in those circumstances — it would indeed be strange if they should now, to avoid danger, retreat from the true service of all our people.

I do not think they will retreat!

Interchange of Cultural Viewpoints

I remember clearly the occasion on which I first became professionally troubled about the educational meaning of culture. Sitting on the floor beside the local fuel merchant at the back of a crowded hall in a little Western city, I had listened to an Eastern university educator of current renown speak on the true end and essence of a liberal education. With many references to the thinkers of classical antiquity and with a series of apt quotations from their timeless works, he described his new system of educating young men for a true freedom of the mind. He conceived that freedom as something which had once been, which was not now what it used to be, but which could be achieved again by his own variety of pedagogical magic.

At the end of the lecture the fuel merchant and I walked away from the hall in silence. I was stimulated by the flow of oratory decorated with those academic tabs which I had learned to revere in happy, bookish hours. I strode along in a dream of a future education which would be complete in one logically self-contained bundle, or, better yet, which would be a sovereign remedy in one nice, big, neat bottle.

A remedy for what?

I did not think that far. As a matter of fact, the lecturer had not thought that far. If the question had been put to either of us, the reply, no matter how beautifully polished and verbose, would have had to be, "A remedy for the lack of that particular kind of education contained in this bottle."

My pleasant reverie was soon broken, however. "Nice words! Culture, *culture*! And what the hell has that got to do with the price of coal!"

I did not appreciate how devastating a criticism this comment embodied, and my reply was therefore inconsequential. It had to be inconsequential because I had been taught to regard culture as a complex of ornamental and magical processes which had nothing to do with the price of coal.

The first and greatest obstacle to a successful interchange of cultural viewpoints among nations in general and among the nations of the Western Hemisphere in particular is the prevalence of this concept of culture. It has the faculty of leading its followers into a variety of intercultural *cul-de-sacs*. It nurtures a reverence for certain "cultural" activities which is out of all proportion to their effects upon the true cultures of the Americas. It obscures the need for interchange of information and attitudes on basic cultural matters.

Phi Delta Kappan, Vol. 24, November, 1941, pp. 101-103. Used by permission of Phi Delta Kappa.

An old jest in comparative education used to appear in many forms, always starting with something like this: One Frenchman equals one dancing-master, two Frenchmen equal a literary problem, and three Frenchmen equal a political party; one German equals one corporal, two Germans equal a *turnverein,* and three Germans equal a *herrenvolk;* one Englishman equals a spot of tea — and so on in whatever desired series of facile comparisons the professor might wish to make. A recent Latin American ending within this framework runs as follows: One gringo equals a go-getter, two gringos equal a deal — perhaps new but more likely old — three gringos need another one for bridge, and four gringos — ah! Senor — four gringos equal a society for the promotion of Pan-Americanism.

Underneath this particular jest, there runs little or no malice. There is affection for the eccentric but good-hearted gringos, a perpetual astonishment at their *naivete,* some suspicion, too, that their sudden desire for better cultural relations with Latin America is non-culturally motivated, and a wistful admiration for their worldly success. The personal-appearance swing south of the equator by a Hollywood luminary, the swift printing and wide reading in the United States of books describing Latin American countries by the soul-of-a-people-in-three-weeks formula, and the steadily heightening conga-rhumba throb from the North American name bands do not change very much this general pattern of attitude toward the gringos' efforts to be cultural good neighbors.

For it is precisely in such matters as music, art, *belles-lettres,* drama, and philosophy that the Latin American is likely to have slight respect for Yanqui achievement. He will admit that the people of the United States are strong and skillful in many ways. They build railroads and ships and airplanes, smelters and refineries and power plants, and they make them run and they make them pay. But, although he will not commonly say so in public out of regard for social decencies, he is inclined to believe that their poetry is inferior, that their better music is stolen from the Negro and their poorer music is copied ineptly from European models, that their grasp of philosophical issues is most uncertain, and that their mores are well symbolized by the undeniable fact that their loud-voiced and highly-painted women go shopping in slacks. One gringo may be a cultured lady or gentleman, two gringos may be devoted and respectable friends, but 190,000,000 gringos may very well be a horde of barbarians whose innate savagery is a threat to continued cultural progress both within and without the boundaries of their own domain.

If to this picture we add the impression which the North American is likely to have of Latin America as a composite of comic-opera revolutionists, guitar-playing serenaders, and poison-dart Indians, the need for better intercultural understanding in the Americas is obvious. Upon what concept of culture shall that understanding be based?

The culture upon which better inter-American understanding and improved inter-American good will must rest is something which includes all the elements of the pictures already mentioned. It includes music, art, drama, and philosophy. It includes also the slacks and the cosmetics, the comic strips and the tease strips, the dance rhythms and the double features. It takes in the head hunters who live only in the Sunday supplements as well as those who reside on the upper Amazon. It involves *tortillas* and maté as well as the Krispy Krunchies which make athletes strong and those incomparable Skunko cigarettes from which dare-devil test-pilots and beautiful lady acrobats derive soul-satisfying and throat-cooling surcease after their nerve-shattering labors.

If such things were all that culture included, however, the chances for significant improvement of inter-American cultural relations would indeed be small. Fortunately, the true culture of any society includes much more than such things. The culture of a society is the society's ways of attacking its problems, achieving its goals, and translating its ideas into reality. The most important phases of its culture are those which relate to its most crucial problems, its most pressing needs, its most enduring ideals. It is compounded of the ways a people get their food, shelter, and clothing, of how they protect themselves from disease and accident, of how they create and operate govern- ments, of how they worship God and serve their fellows, as well as of how they make pictures, tell stories, and sing songs.

If we start with this concept of culture, the whole problem of intercultural exchange is seen to be more difficult than is commonly thought. In certain parts of the United States we have been teaching the Spanish language in secondary schools for a long time, and it has recently been thought in various quarters that extension of this teaching of Spanish to all secondary schools in the United States, to elementary schools perhaps, or the substitution of the Portuguese language for the French language in those schools where French and Spanish are now taught, somehow — no, not somehow but surely — would do a great deal to improve intercultural relations in the Americas. In almost all of the colleges and universities of the United States, Spanish is the chief foreign language in the curriculum in point of numbers of students enrolled in Spanish classes. In some institutions, more students are enrolled in Spanish than are enrolled in all the other foreign languages combined. Spanish is the language which the students desire to learn and which the parents insist that their children should learn. All this is good for intercultural relations but probably not so good as some of us would like to believe.

The logical and scientific tradition of foreign language teaching seems to clog the wheels of learning Spanish in too many instances. Young people in the United States are often required to devote so much attention to the logic and grammar of the subject at the very beginning of their study that they develop a marked aversion for its verbs and can only shudder impotently when asked to tell how many subjunctives it has. Yet there are teachers in growing numbers who, while recognizing the value of grammar and using it as an appropriate instrument of learning, know that language is made by the needs of men and grammar is made by professors. They know that the language a man uses best is usually the one in which he learned to employ a word, a phrase, a sentence long before he ever learned the place of that word, phase, or sentence in a grammatical system. They believe in the teaching of Spanish grammar only after there exists in the learner's experience something upon which grammar can be based.

The teaching of Spanish-American literature in the schools of the United States is carried out effectively in the case of the few students who learn the language well enough to read the literature. In the secondary schools, however, there is a lack of books adapted to the needs and interests of adolescents.

The greatest lack in the curriculum in this area is the absence of the teaching of Latin American history and geography in the secondary schools. For every graduate of a United States high school who knows a great deal about Napoleon, there are many who have never heard of Simon Bolivar. For every one who remembers that Hannibal won fame leading an army across the Alps, there are many who do not know of the crossing of the Andes by José de San Martín beside which the passage of the Alps sinks to the level of a bedtime story.

For our secondary schools we need a good many books in English which tell the story of men and events in Latin America. The person who can write a simple and interesting history of any phase of Latin American social, political, or economic development will contribute a great deal to better inter-American understanding.

The teaching of the geography of the Americas is almost completely neglected in the secondary schools of this country. It is taught very well in the elementary schools in the form needed for elementary school children. It is taught well in advanced form in some universities, moreover. In the high schools, however, where the need for good geography teaching is the greatest, it is taught practically not at all.

The exchange of teachers and students among the American countries is at present only in its first stages. The small beginning needs to be developed into a great body of cultural contacts among the American peoples. Compared with expenditures for many of our current efforts to promote hemispheric defense measures, the money needed to expand student-teacher exchanges in significant fashion is very small. In the long run it is likely to do more good than the expensive activities.

It is clear that the interchange of cultural viewpoints with the aim of developing the understanding which will help to make all the Americans a great and civilized people is a difficult task. The drumming of the guns from over the seas tells us precisely how difficult it is. Our ordinary methods of intercultural exchange are old stories in Western Europe. The teaching of foreign language, history, geography, literature, music, and art has been carried on in Europe for a long time. And now the crashing bombs and the coughing machine guns tell the Europeans that they have failed, at least temporarily, to teach international understanding by these methods.

It is possible that this task is also too difficult for the Americas, yet the need for the successful carrying out of this task is so great that the spirit of our people in the Western Hemisphere cries out that the task must be done. The spirit of our people has enabled them in the past to complete very difficult jobs in the face of tremendous obstacles. They have a tradition of achieving the impossible.

The peoples of the Americas can keep that tradition alive in understanding and guarding and bettering the culture of all the Americas.

Higher Education in Latin America

If early provision of higher education in a country were as important as many observers have claimed, Spanish America should be a very advanced part of the world. It has some of the oldest universities in the world.

In the period 1538 to 1624, when there were only about fifty universities in all Europe, Spain established ten universities in her American colonies. Two of these institutions were set up in what is now the Dominican Republic (1538 and 1558), one in Mexico (1551), one in Peru (1551), two in the present capital of Colombia (1563 and 1622), two at Quinto in what is now Ecuador (1568 and 1622), one at Córdoba in what is now the interior of Argentina (1613), and one at Chuquisaca, later to be called Sucre, Bolivia (1624).

It was 1636 before the English colonies of North America established their first higher educational institution at Cambridge, Massachusetts. Spain, there-upon set up three more universities, one in Guatemala (1676) and two in Peru (1677 and 1692) before the English started their second colonial college in Virginia (1693).

In the eighteenth century, six additional universities were established in Spanish America: one in Cuba (1721); one in Caracas, the present capital of Venezuela (1721); two in Mexico, at Guanajuato (1732) and Guadalajara (1792); one in Chile (1738); and one in Ecuador (1769).

Practically all the Spanish colonial universities were founded by religious orders, at first mainly by the Dominicans, but later by the Jesuits, who found one American university in the sixteenth century (1558) and became very active in the seventeenth century. The first four universities established in Spanish America in that century were Jesuit institutions. In the first half of the eighteenth century the Society of Jesus became increasingly influential in higher education, as in other phases of colonial life. When Charles III, the Spanish king, expelled the society from all his dominions in 1767, as the Portuguese and French monarchs had done eight and three years earlier, respectively, and when Pope Clement XIV followed in 1773 by complete suppression of the order, the higher educational systems of Spanish America received a devastating blow. Dominicans and Franciscans were at first generally rushed into the breach, but political and economic conditions were such that universities did not fare, in the last quarter of the eighteenth century, even as well as they had done earlier. They were singularly undistinguished institutions.

Phi Delta Kappan, January, 1964, pp. 178-182. Used by permission of Phi Delta Kappa.

The leaders of the 1810 and later revolutions against Spain were not ordinarily men who had received any significant higher education, even though they had sometimes attended universities. José de San Martín, greatest soldier of the revolution, was schooled between the ages of twelve and thirty-two only in the Spanish army. Simon Bolivar, most acute observer and analyst as well as leader of the revolution, could hardly be considered a university product. It should be remembered, however, that higher schooling in the eighteenth century was often lacking in the education of leaders. George Washington had no more formal schooling than had San Martín, and Benjamin Franklin's education was undoubtedly superior because his chief teacher was the cultivated Dr. Franklin.

When Pope Pius VII re-established the Society of Jesus in 1814, the Spanish American revolutionists were generally anti-clerical and rejected religious influences in higher education. The sixteen universities founded in the period 1810 to 1847 were mainly revolutionary products. The University of Los Andes in Mérida, Venezuela, was established in 1810 by the revolutionary junta of the Province of Mérida. The University of Buenos Aires was set up in 1821 by the Congress of the United Provinces of the Rio de la Plata. The University of Cartagena in Colombia was founded in 1824 under similar revolutionary auspices. The Peruvian universities of Trujillo (1824) and San Agustín de Arequipa (1825) were established by decree of Bolivar, the Liberator. The Universities of Benito Juarez de Oaxaca (1825) and San Luis Potosi (1826) in Mexico, the University del Cauca (1827) in Colombia, and San Andres de la Paz (1832) in Bolivia were also revolutionary foundations.

After the first revolutionary period was over, universities began to be founded to meet new national needs for the liberal professions. The University of the Republic in Uruguay was set up in 1833 as Montevedio swarmed with Argentine professors and students in exile from the Rosas dictatorship. El Salvador, Costa Rica, and Honduras established universities in 1841, 1843, and 1847 respectively. Chile set up her present national university in 1842 under the leadership of a great Venezuelan scholar, Andres Bello.

Originally the colonial universities had the one aim of training members of the four traditional liberal professions: theology, law, the arts, and medicine. Until the revolutionary periods, moreover, the training of priests was by far the most important of the university's tasks. The rectors were almost always clergymen; the universities were religious foundations; and theology, canon law, and philosophy were the disciplines of highest prestige.

The civil functionaries of the colonial regime were commonly trained in law. They were given a minimum of historical and political knowledge and a maximum of juridical theory.

The faculty of arts was usually errected upon the work of an earlier secondary school. It was primarily an agency for training secondary school teachers and giving preparation for students wishing to enter the theological faculty.

The faculty of medicine was considered important but was for a long time low in academic prestige. When Spain had started her colonial enterprises at the beginning of the sixteenth century, she had also driven out the two groups of her people, the Jews and the Moslems, who knew most about medicine as well as about the natural sciences in general. As a result the low state of medicine characteristic of Europe was even more characteristic of Spain. There was a great lack of trained physicians in all the American colonies. Many of the first universities had a faculty of medicine only on paper. Ecclesiastics could teach in theology, in law, and in arts, but they rarely attempted to teach medicine.

With the coming of the revolutions, the faculties of theology lost their pre-eminence and were generally suppressed. Those in law began to gain prestige, often changing their names to faculty of jurisprudence or of political and juridical sciences. Faculties of medicine were strengthened. Faculties of arts, philosophy, and letters now began to include mathematics and natural sciences, and sometimes new faculties were established in sciences and engineering.

By 1850 the second main aim of the modern university, scientific research, was just beginning to find a place in Spanish American universities.

Ten more universities were founded in Spanish America in the second half of the nineteenth century. Of these, only one, the Pontifical Catholic University of Chile (1888), was a religious foundation. The others, set up in Argentina, Paraguay, Bolivia, Ecuador, Venezuela, and Mexico (with two each in Argentina, Bolivia, and Ecuador), were state or national institutions.

In the nineteenth century, higher education suffered greatly from the grave political situations of the time. The gaining of independence from Spain was generally followed by dictatorships, wars, and various periods of near-anarchy. From Juan Manuel de Rosas in Argentina, 1829-1852, to Porfirio Diaz in Mexico, 1876-1911, the pattern of limited progress under a dictator was repeated again and again. In most cases, of course, only a would-be Rosas or Diaz was available for leadership. In the first sixty years of El Salvador's independence, for example, 1841-1900, there were sixty presidents or other chiefs of state exercising what the stately Spanish language calls *el poder ejecutivo*.

Under such circumstances, it is remarkable that universities developed or survived at all.

By the early twentieth century, however, there were a few Spanish American universities which were already modern in their teaching, research, and community service programs. The most notable of these institutions were founded or re-established in the late nineteenth or early twentieth century.

Up to this point we have spoken only of Spanish America, leaving out Brazil and Haiti. The reason for this is tied to much more than the fact that the largest Latin American nation uses Portuguese and the smallest one French. It is related rather to monumental differences in historical development.

Brazil had no universities until 1920. From 1500 to 1808 she had very little secondary education and only some professional training in theology at

Bahia and Rio de Janeiro. If a student wanted to study law or medicine he had to go to Europe, usually to the University of Coimbra in Portugal.

When the Portuguese royal family fled to Brazil in the Napoleonic period, separate courses began to be established in medicine, economics, agriculture, and the fine arts. Under the Empire, 1822 to 1889, the basic pattern of all later higher education was established that (1) everything connected with higher education, no matter how detailed, had to be specified by law; and (2) to carry the highest prestige, the law must be a federal one.

By 1889 there were faculties of law at Sao Paula and Recife, of medicine at Bahai and Rio de Janeiro, a polytechnic school at Rio de Janeiro, and a school of mines at Ouro Preto. But there was no university as such.

The Republic, before 1900, added three more schools of law, two schools of engineering, two polytechnic schools, and a faculty of medicine.

The University of Rio de Janeiro was finally set up in 1920 by combining a polytechnic school, a faculty of law, and a faculty of medicine.

By 1961 Brazil had twenty-seven universities and almost 400 other higher educational institutions as separate schools and faculties with a total enrollment of almost 100,000.

Haiti had no university until 1944, when the University of Haiti was established by grouping earlier schools and setting up new faculties. The faculty of law, for example, began as a special school in 1859 and was made a national school of law in 1890. The polytechnic school was started in 1902, the school of agriculture in 1924, and the faculty of medicine in 1938.

In 1961 the University of Haiti had an enrollment of approximately 1,000.

In 1961, the Spanish American republics had a total population of about 130,000,000 and total higher educational enrollments of a little less than 500,000, giving a ratio of about thirty-eight students in higher education for each 10,000 of the general population.

This ratio may be compared with about 200 for the United States, fourteen for Brazil, and three for Haiti. In the Spanish American countries these ratios spread from ninety-three for Argentina and forty-eight for Uruguay to five for Honduras.

Most countries with higher enrollment ratios are increasing their provisions for university education more rapidly than those with lower ratios.

Countries with lower enrollment ratios spend relatively more money on their universities and secure inferior results.

It seems reasonable to suppose that countries of greater potential and developed wealth will have more of their young people in universities. The facts do not always support this generalization, however. Brazil, with tremendous resources and many wealthy people, has an enrollment ratio of only fourteen, while Uruguay, with only modest material resources, has a ratio of forty-eight. Colombia and Venezuela have about the same ratios, thirty-five and thirty-one, respectively, but differ markedly in wealth.

The extent and quality of a country's educational efforts depend only in part on its wealth. Behind developed material resources and developed human resources, represented in the one case by wealth and in the other by education, is a national drive which makes both wealth and education possible.

In many instances the leaders of a country have curiously fragmented notions of the best way to advance its fortunes. They sometimes appear to think that wealth is independent of education and act accordingly. They develop industries, importing foreign directors to run them. They try to expand or modernize their universities without being concerned about the development of supporting elementary and secondary education.

The factor of overwhelming weight in determining the scope and quality of higher education or of education in general in any country is the extent to which the people exercising power believe in education. These people make choices between education and other activities. The cost of an aircraft carrier for the Argentine or Brazilian navy could build magnificent university cities in both countries. A much needed university laboratory in Chile or Peru could be built for the price of a dozen luxury automobiles imported from Europe or North America.

Latin American republics, as well as practically all other countries in the world, rich or poor, large or small, tend to ignore the truth that education always has to be bought with more than money. It must be secured with insight into the needs of the people, with administrative efficiency, and instructional competence. When these three primary elements are present, the secondary element — money — is readily found. When the primary elements are lacking, large amounts of money can be spent on education with the result only of deepening the confusion about the country's educational needs, lowering the administrative efficiency, and increasing the instructional incompetence.

Latin American countries are backward to varying degrees in their higher educational programs. They appear in many cases to make little effort to have university programs related to the needs of the people.

In Argentina, to take an example of the country with the largest university enrollments, both relatively and absolutely, in Latin America, the universities are presently preparing more people in law and the social sciences than those in Bolivia, Chile, Ecuador, Paraguay, Peru, and Uruguay combined — six countries with a total population 10,000,000 greater than the Argentine population. Argentina has not produced enough political leaders, however, to avoid the steady recurrence of military dictatorships, coups d'etat, and overthrows of legally constituted institutions, a chief mark of backwardness in law and social sciences.

Brazil has multiplied faculties of economic sciences, particularly in the last decade, at a rate far exceeding that in any other country of this hemisphere, yet its solutions for economic problems are among the most backward in the world — printing-press money and foreign loans never repaid.

Most Latin American countries have administrative inefficiency built into their universities. The typical ruling council of the university is composed of professors, students, and alumni, with the students and alumni representatives often outnumbering the professors. Even in the few cases, as in Brazil, where student representatives have no vote, the power of the students over university policy and procedure, mainly through actual or threatened student strikes, is very great.

The chief executive officer of the university, the rector, is elected for a short term, usually two years. Often he does not complete his term; he is forced out by a strike. Deans of faculties are similarly elected by comparable councils of professors, students, and alumni, and are similarly insecure in their administration.

Instructional incompetence is also often built into the Latin American university. In the University of Brazil, for example, an institution of relatively modest size with an enrollment of only 9,000, there were, in 1961, 533 autonomous chairs (catedras), including eighteen in mathematics, twenty-three in economics, twenty-eight in physics, and thirty-nine in chemistry. The elementary instruction in chemistry was given independently in the faculties of engineering, philosophy, industrial chemistry, pharmacy, dentistry, and medicine, with each catedra having its own laboratory, library, and autonomous team of professors and assistants.

The problem of preparing teachers for Latin American universities is a very difficult one. Graduate programs need to be developed in at least ten or twelve centers in Spanish America as soon as possible. Argentina, Chile, Uruguay, Peru, Colombia, Venezuela, Costa Rica, and Mexico are appropriate places for such centers. Two centers should be set up in Brazil and one in Haiti. The Brazilian centers should have particularly close relations with Spanish American and United States centers. The Haitian center should be developed in cooperation with Canadian and French institutions.

The improvement of university administration is another crucial problem in Latin America. Under a dictatorship, no real improvement is possible; the university always deteriorates. The longer the dictator holds power, the more the university becomes a mere courtier for his favor. Under constitutional regimes, on the other hand, the university tries feverishly to keep the rector or the deans from having any real power even for their brief terms of office. They are often elected, moreover, with bitter political fighting, so that each of them can count on having at least one defeated candidate on his staff to hate him and try to block his policies.

How then, under these conditions, can Latin American universities be given real help from other countries?

Let us admit at once that the first kind of aid which many United States leaders think of in this connection — money — is often of doubtful value and sometimes a real handicap to the Latin American institution. How many millions of dollars given to the University of Honduras, for instance, would counter-balance the arrangement which provides a student vote for every faculty vote in the board of control? How big a grant would the University of Brazil require to reduce its twenty-nine catedras of chemistry to fifteen or twenty?

To one who has observed these institutions at close range over a consider-able period, it seems obvious that no less than a change of spirit, of drive, of purpose, is the first great need of the Latin American university. This can come only from a new kind of teacher and administrator in the university. That is why the graduate centers mentioned above would be the most promising recipients of foreign aid. The aid should be primarily in terms of personnel rather than money; not for financial reasons but for reasons of the spirit.

It is lack of spirit rather than of purse which spells backwardness in any country's university. In this respect Haiti does not differ greatly from Harvard, Brazil from Berlin, or Chile from California. They all have as much and as good higher education as they have brains enough to want, heart enough to attempt, and guts enough to achieve.

Criteria for Judging the Worth of an International Education Program

In a certain sense, perhaps I am like the imaginative hobo who sat with a relatively unimaginative comrade on a bank overlooking the freight yard. This was in the good old days when a tramp could ordinarily get a hand-out in the morning and then find an empty boxcar going in his direction. But on this morning the good old days had temporarily disappeared. Unfriendly housewives had slammed doors in the faces of these two bums. Freight trains going east were all loaded, going west were sealed tight, and it appeared that these poor men, weak with hunger, would have to ride the blinds on an express train.

In these circumstances, the imaginative tramp spoke, "I wish I had a cocoanut cream pie as big around as one of them switch-engine drive wheels," he said dreamily.

The unimaginative tramp listened, greed welling in his throat.

"I wish," continued the imaginative bum, "that I had a deep-dish apple pie as big as that there water tank."

His unimaginative colleague swallowed convulsively but said nothing.

"I wish," said the dreamer, "that I had a great big juicy pumpkin pie as fur across and as deep as that there doggone' freight depot."

The unimaginative hobo could stand the recital no longer. "If you had a pie that big, you'd give me a piece of it, wouldn't you?" he asked.

"No," snarled the imaginative tramp. "If you want pie, damn you, wish for it yourself."

Here, then, is a pie I have dreamed up which may be called *Some Criteria for Evaluation of International Education Programs.*

I use the term *international education program* to include every organized activity which attempts to pass educational practices and concepts from one country to another. We want criteria that will be valid when applied to Horace Mann's collection of what he called "beneficial hints, for our warning or our imitation," from Germany, France, Holland, and parts of Great Britain, and Ireland.[1] We want the same criteria to be applicable to the most recent educational phases of the programs of the Agency for International Development. We want to be able to apply these criteria to all the international commerce in

An address before the October 23, 1964 conference on International Education at George Peabody College for Teachers, Nashville, Tennessee.

[1]Horace Mann, Seventh Annual Report, 1844, (4th ed., Simpkin, Marshall, and Co., London, 1857, p. 3).

educational ideas, procedures, and institutions between these two extremes, from the U. S. Army sergeants teaching in Cuba after the Spanish-American War, to the League of Nations Educational Mission to China in 1931; from Calvin E. Stowe's 1837 report to the governor and Legislature of Ohio on *Elementary-Public Instruction in Europe* to the most recent education missions of UNESCO.

First, we need to examine the purposes of education in a country to which educational ideas and practices are being exported. Suppose there are main purposes to which the would-be exporters do not and perhaps cannot subscribe. For here is a country which seeks to use education to keep an oligarchical dictatorship in power. It wants a school system to train the lower classes for efficient service to the dictatorship and make them content in that station of life in which it pleases the dictatorship to hold them.

It can be stated at once that the exportation to such a country of ideas seeking to change these educational purposes has built-in guarantees of failure. Of course the country ordinarily will welcome the transaction since it brings prestige and sometimes actual money, especially when it comes from the "paymaster of the western world," the United States. Educators in the country will often say earnestly that they agree with the purposes of education in the exporting country. As soon as the real purpose of keeping the oligarchy in power and the lower classes in their proper places is really threatened, however, all horses are suddenly of a different color.

Perhaps the most common way of avoiding this issue is for the exporters to come into the country with their wares and work to improve educational instruments, programs, and institutions without bothering the sensitive areas in which purposes reside. Thus we have had magnificent efforts to improve higher educational facilities in Indonesia, to establish basic educational programs in Haiti, to upgrade teacher education in Peru, and to develop effective secondary education in Bolivia, with results that are painful to contemplate.

Sometimes, nevertheless, the exporters try to meet head-on this problem of elevating the purposes of education. They set up an administrative and supervisory complex in the national capital which is, in effect, a second ministry of education. The usual effect is to split the country's educational leaders and their political supporters into warring camps. After the next revolution, whether from right or left, imported educational concerns of any kind are likely to get trampled in the rush for political insurance with the new regime.

The first criterion of a program of international trade in education, therefore, may be stated as follows:

The educational purposes of any country must be the products of the people's own wants in that country. The one best way to help the people improve their educational purposes is by helping to educate their leaders. Examples of profound changes in national educational purposes, from the Danish cultural renaissance in the last quarter of the nineteenth century to the school reforms of the Mexican Revolution in the second quarter of the twentieth century, show very clearly that this is the part of educational change that must be homegrown. No conceivable amount of foreign educational advice or other aid would have been likely to improve the educational purposes of Nikolai Grundtvig, Christen Kold, Moises Saenz, and Raul Ramirez. Foreign aid, even in the supposedly cheap form of advice, would have handicapped if not ruined any one of these men's efforts to re-state and re-vitalize their countries' educational purposes.

The importing agency, therefore, will find that it has more important work to do than trying to persuade a people to change their fundamental educational purposes to fit a foreign pattern. This is emphatically a job for their own people.

What would be the effect on United States' enterprises of educational aid to other countries if this criterion were generally followed? The first result would be a considerable reduction in the number of countries aided by the United States. A second result would be an intensification of aid to countries which are solving their problems of purpose. The latter countries can be aided without the political and cultural handicaps imposed by an outside agency trying to mess with their educational purposes.

The second criterion is applied to a country's importation of educational facilities and institutions. Does the country's educational purpose require changes in its programs? Can the exporting agency provide skills and technical knowledge that will help produce such changes? Do the importing country's leaders, supported by substantial elements of its population, request this help for educational reasons as contrasted, for example, to reasons of prestige or monetary aid? A negative answer to any of these questions simplifies at once the decision concerning how much and what kind of aid should be given by an outside agency.

I shall not multiply examples of how this criterion operates in various situations, but I cannot resist remembering and mentioning the earnest request from an outstanding South Korean secondary-school administrator in 1954 for aid in setting up core-curriculum programs in his war-devastated country. Many schools had been destroyed, and of those which remained standing a large number were still occupied as barracks and administrative offices by the South Korean Army. Those which were used for school purposes were unheated with broken windows in the dead of winter and were shockingly overcrowded. A room designed to hold a maximum of forty would have ninety or one hundred pupils packed into it in sardine-like rows. Books were almost non-existent; teachers were scarce, untrained, and so underpaid as to be almost working for nothing but public esteem.

Of all the changes required in the country's educational program, the adoption of the core-curriculum would have appeared to merit a rather low priority. There was certainly also a question, moreover, as to whether the education teams of the United Nations' Korean Reconstruction Agency possessed the requisite skills and technical knowledge to help the Korean secondary schools set up the core-curriculum. Why, then was it requested? The answer, I think, is simple. The core-curriculum would give prestige. In the face of problems that appeared at the time insoluble, here was a short cut. The teachers and pupils were hungry and cold and frustrated. With a core-curriculum they could at least starve, freeze, and despair in high-toned manner.

Of course, the request for the core-curriculum did not have general support among the country's educational leaders, much less among the general population. Yet where did it originate? I will give you one guess, and I know you'll hit the mark the first time. There was a core-curriculum expert from the United States of America who had been in a previous educational aid enterprise in the country, an expert in persuasion as well as in the core-curriculum.

The third criterion for evaluating the exchange of educational ideas and practices is concerned with the importing country's educational personnel. Are the teachers and administrators of the country's educational programs skilled enough to carry out the country's educational purposes? If so, they need no outside aid. If they need additional skills, how can they best acquire them? Are the political and cultural leaders of the country willing to have their educational personnel get those skills from an outside agency? If so, the method of furnishing the skills becomes very important.

This problem of up-grading personnel is best solved when attacked cooperatively by the aided country and the outside agency. Generally speaking, professional training in the aided country is superior to that secured in other countries. It is also more economical of time, effort, and money. It helps develop pride in local institutions instead of an attitude of superiority nurtured in foreign parts. It provides field experience in situations like those in which the trainee will eventually work.

Here, therefore, is my sketch of these three main criteria for helping us determine the direction and rate of international trade in education. There are inadequate and imperfect systems of education all over the world. Certainly we have many of them in the United States, and we have limited resources for improving them. We have to be prudent and practical in exporting and importing educational aid. There are obviously boundaries which must be set in our attempts to move all the world ahead in education.

In this paper I have suggested criteria for determining those boundaries under the three main headings of purpose, program, and personnel. The potentially most fruitful of these areas for international trade in education is personnel.

III | FOUNDATIONS OF AMERICAN EDUCATION

The selection of a title for this section was an extremely difficult task. The word "foundations" does not completely connote the idea I wish to convey. The foundations of which I speak are more closely akin to community attitudes or values. The esteem in which a society holds its educational system provides a good insight into what that society considers important.

At various times during the history of our young nation public education has been the pawn of different special interest groups. In the early schools of the 17th and 18th centuries the guiding force was the Church. The first settlers had come to this land in search of religious freedom; their first act was to establish churches and build schools. In the schools the people were taught to read the Bible so all could worship God. New ministers had to be educated to lead the people in the tenets of John Calvin. The religious motive permeated all levels of the early Puritan schools and served to enhance the "true faith."

Just prior to the Revolutionary War there began to occur a decline in the strength of the religious motive. There were several factors contributing to this decline: the "westward movement" had begun and settlers were migrating to new communities which were not so close-knit; as cities began to grow new problems appeared; the existing educational systems no longer fulfilled the needs of the citizenry. The War and its resultant victory for the colonists gave rise to the second motive – a political one.

As soon as their independence had been won the thirteen separate colonies became a new nation, tottering to be sure but a nation nevertheless. The political motivation was a natural result of the situation in which the colonists found themselves. Whereas the early Calvinists used education to maintain the status quo, the post-revolution leaders found it the natural vehicle to perpetuate the ideals of liberty and a democratic form of government. Since government was to be by popular consent an enlightened populus was a necessity. The idea of free-public education was conceived and pursued to its culmination in the mid and late 1800's.

The third so-called "base" for public education in America came from an old idea which found new support in the 19th century. This was sometimes referred to as "preparation for life." The school must be functional, practical,

67

utilitarian. The student who intended to go on to higher education attended the classical high school where he underwent a college preparatory course. The technical high schools offered curricula to prepare students to join the labor market. During this period the federal government offered incentive in the form of grants for agricultural and vocational (both practical) training.

A natural by-product of the practical or functional motive in education was a stress on economy. Some school administrators attempted to apply business principles to the management of public schools. Time-and-motion studies were made in the teaching of certain subjects in an effort to conserve time and, therefore, save money. Some courses, which had small enrollments, were deemed impractical because they were not self-supporting (i.e., there wasn't enough demand for the subject to justify employing a teacher for it).

The final movement strongly influencing education is the one in which we find ourselves today — to provide equal educational opportunity for all people. Inherent in this ideal is a respect for the human worth and dignity of every individual. This respect and an unshakeable faith in the American people is the keystone around which Harold Benjamin has built his foundations for education in this country.

Historically, on occasion, the fundamentals of an educational system have been determined by custom or habit, or perhaps by a statement that embodies the philosophy of, "It was good enough for me when I was in school, so it's good enough for kids today." Benjamin envisages education as a behavior-changing process, one which allows people to asses how they are living, determine what changes should be made in their lives, decide whether they want those changes (this is extremely important but often overlooked), and discover what means can be devised to bring about the desired changes. The purpose of the behavior-changing is to help the students develop the skills and attitudes which will enable them to better serve the needs of the community and nation. Hence, their behavior will be altered for the benefit of all.

Education is at the same time the world's greatest problem and the solution to its problems. To this belief Professor Benjamin holds steadfastly. He feels strongly that education can help to alleviate the major military, political, social, and economic ills of the world. To accomplish this the public must be made aware that education is an asset rather than a liability, is a worthwhile investment rather than a drain on the pocketbook, and above all, it pays a high rate of return. It pays in better goods and services.

This section includes an address which adequately illustrates Benjamin's great ability to communicate with his audience. In "Dimensions of Educational Policy," he combines an imaginative style and humorous presentation with a forceful and dynamic message. "Dimensions of Educational Policy" was delivered as the 1964 Sarah Olive Rush Lecture at the University of South Florida. The Lecture is an annual affair sponsored by a well known educator who prefers to remain anonymous. He is identified only as "a teacher, an ex-soldier, and a veteran of three wars, . . ."

Whose Fundamentals?

"I only took the regular course," a great analyst of fundamentals has his spokesman say.
"What was that?" inquired Alice.
"Reeling and Writhing, of course, to begin with," the Mock Turtle replied, "and then the different branches of Arithmetic — Ambition, Distraction, Uglification, and Derision."[1]

This classic colloquy might well be used as a chief item in some yet-to-be-constructed test of educational insight. Those who read it with only an amused chuckle could be marked as innocent professional bystanders. Those who accept it with a puzzled look would probably be scholarly conservatives. But those who read it and re-read it with mingled smiles and frowns should be branded forever as dangerous radicals.

These last are likely to be temperamental innovators who recognize and approve the Mock Turtle's deep heresy in suggesting that any true educational fundamental always belongs to the learner. They know the orthodox view that fundamentals are set by custom, by habit, by tradition, and by past values, real or imagined, rather than by current or future uses, but they are natively inclined to be suspicious of habitual custom and traditional values. To the question, "What good are fundamentals?" they reply, "Fundamentals are good for him who learns, good for him in his present society and in the better future society that he needs and wants, or else they are good for nothing."

The Persian boy, according to Herodotus, was required to master three fundamentals. He had to learn to ride, to shoot, and to speak the truth. No doubt the old historian recognized that in any horseless and bowless situation the youth so educated would have to use the third ability to confess his practical illiteracy. The Persian fundamentals were for men who had horses to ride, bows to bend, and true words to speak. It must have been obvious to all save the most reactionary that two of these fundamentals were ephemeral and that a different weapon or means of transportation could at any time require drastic curriculum revision.

The professinal horse-raisers and bow-makers of ancient Persia probably never accepted this view. The king's treasurers and tax collectors, the landed lords, and most men of material substance were also undoubtedly among those

[1]Lewis Carroll, *Alice's Adventure In Wonderland,* chapter 9. From the *Phi Delta Kappan,* October, 1951, pp. 87-89. Used by permission of Phi Delta Kappa.

opposed to new fundamentals. The old fundamentals could be taught without maintaining schools. Why put an extra burden on the tax-payers to teach non-essential folderol? It was obvious to these critics, moreover, that the old and tried fundamentals were not being well taught. Horsemanship, bowmanship, and truth-telling were all deteriorating. One can hear across twenty-three centuries the plaintive cry, "They don't even learn to tie a cinch strap or notch an arrow correctly nowadays, and as for giving a plain statement of unvarnished fact, that is apparently a lost art. What are the boys coming to? Let's go back to the fundamentals?"

Herodotus does not tell us whether any suggestion was ever made that to invision boys of the future without horses and bows was to be un-Persian to the core, but it is likely that this ancient accusation was already old in 400 B. C. Certainly, since that date, anyone suggesting changes in the fundamental branches of education has been immediately vulnerable to the three basic charges of ignorance, extravagance, and subversion.

The proponent of new fundamentals is probably antagonistic to the old fundamentals because he has never learned them correctly, it will be said. One who knows how to reel and writhe will love and revere those disciplines. The iconoclast is a tax-eater, moreover, because new subjects always seem to cost more money than old ones. Frills like uglification require laboratories. This innovator is subversive and atheistic, finally, because he is attacking the educational foundations of our society. By their very names, Distraction and Derision are revolutionary and treasonable concepts.

The re-shaper of fundamentals commonly faces another barrier in the path to what he regards as progress. The three natural divisions of fundamental skills and attitudes are those that relate to (1) communication-transportation enterprises, (2) tool-instrument-weapon techniques, and (3) character-personality traits. In most primitive societies, formal schooling is given only for the third fundamental; in most "civilized" societies, instruction tends to become more and more centered on the first and second fundamentals. To step up instruction in riding and shooting, piling requirement on requirement and technique on technique in eager profusion, while leaving the teaching of truth-telling more and more to the family, a political organization, a religious group, or other agencies, some of which may be weak, formless, or socially disintegrating in effect, is the usual tendency in a society that is discarding its bows and horses.

For the last 200 years the world has been busily discarding old means of communication and transportation and old tools and weapons. The development of industrial machinery, the utilization of fossil fuels, the extension of first the printed and then the spoken word over wide areas at accelerating speeds, and finally the basic discovery of a means of releasing atomic energy have set the stage for the greatest changing of educational fundamentals the world has yet known. How well have these changes been made?

So far they have been made poorly. Undeveloped countries are still struggling to teach the barest elements of reading and writing, often in two or more obscure and difficult languages, to people who will seldom have even a newspaper to read, who are doomed to death by starvation or disease at an early age from controllable causes practically unmentioned in their fundamental schooling, and who could be taught better agriculture, sanitation, and other conservation of human and material resources by radio and motion pictures within at least half the time and with at least twice the effect now obtained by customary illiteracy-eradicating campaigns. Nations with untouched hydroelectric potentials roaring down their mountainsides, with millions of fertile acres uncultivated, with mineral and forest resources undeveloped, and with disease-ridden and under-nourished children dying in droves will often be found educating ten doctors of laws for each doctor of medicine and a hundred writers of poetry, makers of philosophical "systems," and composers of "serious" essays for every trained engineer in the country. A clear measure of their understanding of fundamentals can well be gained by their usual response to such a statement as the one just made. "Don't you believe in lawyers?" they will demand scornfully. Don't you think we need the joys of poetry, the solace of philosophy, and the dignity of humane letters just as much as you crass materialists devoted to the worship of the dollar?"

An answer is hard to give in brief, simple terms. It cannot be the either-or response the inquiry poses. It is not a matter of law or medicine, of poetry or the development of natural resources, and of philosophy or irrigation systems. It is a total problem of how these people are living, what changes they need in their lives, whether they want those changes, and what instruments can be found or made to produce the changes. These are the stuff of which fundamentals are made. These are the bases from which the three C's of communication-transportation skills and instruments, craft and combat tools and weapons, and character-personality traits are derived.

A basic principle of comparative education is here suggested. An educational system whose fundamentals are taught and defended primarily for their own sake is a backward system. It teaches riding without horses, shooting without bows, and truth-telling without reference to the main truths of its time. It reaches the nadir of insight when it argues for its fundamentals because they are good in themselves.

What are the proper educational fundamentals in these United States. They are three in number, as always.

First, the total pattern of modern communication and transportation must be examined to determine the fundamentals of education at every level of maturity and skill from the nursery to the graduate school. To teach cursive writing in the first grade just because it is a "mark" of education is not simply useless; it is dangerous. To put an advanced student in any field through communication paces just for academic respectability is equally dangerous.

Throughout the current system of schooling in the United States is the recurrent emphasis on communication skills for their own sakes. This is what produces in great profusion curricular lags and anomalies. If one-half the energy now expended over the idiotic *ie* and *ei* problem in spelling, for example, were devoted to devising and teaching some rational modern symbols for vowel sounds, one could observe the first truly realistic instruction in this fundamental since the formation of the language. If one-tenth of the energy now spent throughout the world teaching hundreds of other native languages were given to developing and teaching a single world language for all communication between groups with different mother tongues, the communication achievement would be so profound as to put the release of atomic energy in a secondary rank among the discoveries of the last thousand years. The one is a great advance in the control of physical elements; the other would be a great step in the self-control of men and nations, elements far more dangerous than uranium and its variants.

Second, the instruments and weapons demanded by the shifting, swelling tides of new opportunities and dangers following the development of new sources of physical and social power must be studied and analyzed for the determination of fundamental schooling on every level. There are no sacred skills of computation and reasoning. There is no tool of craft or combat that must be acquired for its own sake. Every device and technique of the current world or of the desired world which education must envision is good for the learner and his society or else good for nothing.

In the third fundamental, the schools of the United States, as those of other countries, have neglected most seriously the necessary examination of the social pattern, real and ideal, for which character and personality need to be developed. In a welter of superstition and priestcraft, talking vaguely but heatedly about teaching morals, and coming out with such puerilities as attempts to inculcate a reverence for God through catechisms, a veneration for country through flag salutes, and love for fellow man through competitive drills, the formal educational system has staggered and blundered along this road almost as much as have the home, the church, and the community. The main difficulty to overcome here as elsewhere is to establish the ownership of this fundamental by the learner. It is the student's moral standard that is to be developed for his society and not that of a church for a society of the Middle Ages. It is the student's honesty, truthfulness, generosity, and honor which are to be taught and learned in the student's actions, and not those of his parents or the members of the union or civic club. The third C must be acquired in broad, intensive practice in the society for which it is designed. The program of activities in a modern elementary or secondary school, against which proponents of the old virtues are most wont to inveigh, is precisely the most important and often the only real teaching of this fundamental in modern education.

Are Reeling and Writhing ever proper fundamentals?

It depends upon who needs to reel and writhe in what situation. The modern school man must be a scholar and engineer of those needs in those situations.

Is Distinction never a virtue?

Who can say until he examines its uses for men and women, young and old, here and now, and predicts them as best he can for there and later? Atomic fission may be followed by atomic fusion, but the fundamentals of education will still belong to the learner.

The New Subversion

The United States of America was not founded on corn, wheat, cotton, or cattle. It does not derive its peculiar character from coal, timber, iron, or petroleum. Its spirit does not even reside in telephones, refrigerators, bathrooms, and automobiles, advertisements of these boons to the contrary notwithstanding.

This country was founded on a belief. It was an old belief in 1775, but it was given new application then. With efforts as diverse as the radicalism of a Boston pamphleteer, the suave genius of a Philadelphia printer, and the flaming steadfastness of a Virginia planter, the Americans established their new country upon the rock of a single main concept.

That rock was the old belief in the unique worth of the individual, the value of a particular man, the quality of a specific woman, and the potentialities of one child anywhere. It was the relatively new belief with respect to government that each citizen had dignity in himself and possessed rights which no government could properly take from him. It held that the government was not the master of people but only their creature and could operate rightfully only under rules which they imposed.

It seemed clear to the men who established this country that public education was indispensable to popular government of the kind they envisioned. They held that only educated men could successfully govern themselves. They reiterated their conviction that popular government without popular education was an invitation to disaster.

Slowly at first and then with increasing tempo and sweep, the Americans put this concept into practice. In the 176 years of their independence they have built and operated the greatest collection of public school systems in the world. They have developed elementary schools designed not merely to teach a child a particular knowledge, skill, or attitude but to change his environment to fit his capacities and the needs of his community and his country, so that his total behavior will be changed for the benefit of himself and his people. They have invented and spread to every village in the land the comprehensive American high school with its unique pattern of guidance, group activities, and instruction adapted to individual needs and abilities. They have established and supported public systems of higher education unparalleled not only in size but more importantly in their contribution to the nation's productive capacity and cultural achievements.

From the *Journal of the American Association of University Women*, March, 1952, pp. 151-153.

All this was not done without grave and determined opposition. From the first days of independence there were people in this country who rejected the foundational belief in public education as they rejected the concept of popular government. They opposed universal education for the same reason they opposed universal suffrage. They did not believe that all citizens should be equal in opportunity. They fought every effort to make the American schools public, free, non-sectarian, and compulsory for the same reason that they resisted every effort to increase the measure of democracy in the United States. They did not believe in a government of equal justice under law but rather in a government of "right" people over "wrong" people, with rightness and wrongness to be determined by race, color, religion, wealth, location, and above all by docility and agreement with their views. Their aim was always subversion. They struck at the foundation of the American system of popular government as at the educational instruments without which it could not endure.

In recent years and particularly since 1945, a few of these people led by "experts" on public education who received their training in curiously assorted places not connected with public schools, have made determined attacks on public education, attacks that have had effect out of proportion to the numbers of people involved. One obvious reason why these attacks have been so effective is their skillful use of the half-truth — always difficult to refute.

In most cases the attacks were repulsed, but in some instances they were successful. Playing upon the dislike of all citizens and especially older citizens without children in school for paying taxes, these attacking groups have allied "progressive" education with "progressive" taxation. To the tremendous increase in pupil enrollment and the pressing need for school building construction and repair, these groups have sneered, "A lot of nonsense. Let 'em use the buildings they have, or better yet go back to the little red schoolhouse."

This financial objective, it seems to the present writer, is the chief reason why the "attack" organizations get substantial support. The other and usually more spectacular features of their attacks on the schools are smoke screens behind which the work of knifing the public education budget is carried on. The persistent attempts to drag racial and religious feelings into discussions of public education, the frothing patrioteering, and the cursing of the public school for "increasing delinquency" are all designed to cover up the real attempt to reduce spending on public education.

The new subversives are shrewd. They know that the great mass of the citizens of the United States believe in spending money for public education. So the attackers of the public schools shout about patriotism being endangered by UNESCO, about giant conspiracies to teach communism, and about atheistic teachers — and all the time their eyes are on the tax levies.

The Americans long ago discovered the proper defense against such attacks of their schools. They invented the system of the lay boards of education when they first started public education. They developed such unique agencies for keeping a free people in touch with their free schools as the Congress of Parents and Teachers. The great voluntary associations, the labor unions, the civic organizations, chambers of commerce, and many other American groups have had a large part in the development of the public school system by studying it, criticizing it constructively, and strengthening it with their counsel. The National Citizens Commission for the Public Schools, headed by Roy E. Larsen, was founded in 1949 to assist nationally in this constructive effort, particularly by helping form local committees to work for better public schools.

With organizations like these to help determine what our schools should be and do and how we should support them, we Americans do not need hate-mongers, religious fanatics, racists, and racketeers to throw sand in our eyes concerning the cost of public education.

The 8,000,000 more children who will be in our schools ten years from now will have to be educated, we Americans think. It will take money to do it, a lot of money to do it right. We aren't taken in by the outcry about communism and delinquency. We'll find the money.

The Place of the Secondary School in American Society

The life of Girard College and that of its founder have more than covered the period of our nation's history. When Stephen Girard was still a young man, the American Revolution burst in the faces of George III and his tory counselors. As Stephen Girard passed well into middle age, his adopted country fought the Barbary States in the Mediterranean, the French on the high seas, and the British once again. When Girard College was born, the new country ended a brief but territorially profitable clash with Mexico. The College was a mere infant when the tragic Civil War opened, and she was still young when the Sioux made their supreme bid to halt the white man's encroachment on their lands. She had passed the half-century mark when the United States emerged from its war with Spain as a world power with a colonial empire. She was in her seventy-fifth year when American troops returned from their full-scale partici- pation in a great European World War. She had encountered the last decade of her first century when the country took decisive part in the most extensive war yet fought on this planet.

During this complete period of our national history, we Americans have seen a vast panarama of warlike and stirring events. We have taken part in many of those events, always lustily and sometimes carelessly; prodigal of our efforts, our material resources, and the blood of our sons; speaking face to face with kings abroad yet sometimes cringing before local "trigger-men" at home; and always talking of a beautiful peace of the highest kind and at the same time arrogantly looking for trouble of any grade or character. We Americans like to have the Europeans continue to think that we are a young people, but acutally we know better. We have seen too much, we have been mixed up in too many events since 1775, to be properly regarded as young any more. But, we insist, we are young. We still like color and conflict. We cannot be less than young; we are still strong and confident.

We saw the embattled farmers at Concord Bridge and Colonel Warren, with delicate lace on his wrists, strolling like a gentleman of leisure along the ramparts at Bunker Hill. We saw General Washington on his white stallion before the stacks of surrendered arms at Yorktown. We saw the Highland line dissolve in the flame of Kentucky marksmanship at New Orleans. We heard the fife play "Come to the Bower," as the rifles and bowie knives went into action at San Jacinto. We saw the flower of the Confederacy withering in the volleys of grape

An address given on May 20, 1948, at the celebration of the Centennial Year of Girard College.

at Gettysburg. We saw the broken Spanish fleet lie in a blackened ring at the end of a Manila Bay Day. We saw the gleam of steel beneath the trees at the Bois de Belleau and heard the high staccato cough of the Nambu light machine guns at Bataan and Buffalo Head. We saw the littered beach at Anzio and the shattered tanks in the Bulge. We heard the cosmic roar at Hiroshima and Nagasaki.

Yet in all these experiences we were not unique. Other peoples of our own times saw the same sights and heard the same sounds, drew their swords in like causes, put their guns and ships and warplanes into battle for similar reasons, and equally mourned their sons *tombes au champ d'honneur*. Here is no true mark of great national distinction. We must search elsewhere.

Where? Shall we look at the churches we have built? Shall we seek American uniqueness in the marts of trade? In commerce and industry? In art, music, or the theater? In agriculture and forestry? In health and medicine? In the skills of government? In the techniques of laboratories?

No. We must go further. We must go behind our highest technical and scientific achievements, our greatest advances in arts and the humanities, and our most effective practices in social and civic affaris to find the characteristic achievement which has set the people of these United States emphatically apart from their fellow peoples of other countries and continents.

When we make this search, we come upon the American school. At first glance it may seem to be a little, drab structure, set on a stony patch of poor land at the edge of the people's habitations, training the young in the dry but useful tricks of number and alphabet and their companion facts and skills on higher levels of literacy.

The citizens of the United States had a unique faith in this school. They dreamed a unique dream. They dreamed that their school could be a great gleaming structure, set in the heart of their community, giving more abundant life to all the children and all the youth and all the people of all their land.

Now, this dream was hard to realize. I should say, it *is* hard to realize; for the people of the United States have not yet made it come true as they have envisioned it in their hearts. For one, two, three generations —for a hundred years after the new nation's liberty was proclaimed — the people of the United States worked slowly toward the goal of giving education to all their children on their dreamed-of scale of national generosity and richness of spirit. Slowly they worked, slowly they improved their school for children, until, finally, in the last quarter of the nineteenth century, they were ready to display their unique dream in what I regard as the most colorful and dramatic achievement on their national history. They began to build the modern American secondary school with dazzling speed. Every ten years, from 1880, they doubled the enrollment in their secondary schools. They started with such small numbers, however, that it was 1900 before they began to have large enrollments. By 1920, their high-school populations began to soar. Communities built new high-school buildings to house a thousand pupils and found fifteen hundred waiting to enter when the building was finished and two thousand clamoring for admission a year later.

The increase in general population was responsible for this growth only in a small part. In 1900, for example, one person in two hundred of the general population attended high school. In 1940 one person in twenty was a high school pupil. Therefore, in 1950, it will probably be close to one in fifteen. In 1910 the twelfth-grade classes of high schools had less than 1 per cent of all pupils enrolled in public schools; in 1940 those classes had 5 per cent of all pupils; in 1950 it will probably approach 7 per cent. This was the single most dramatic achievement of the American people. To establish, for the most part within a period of thirty years, a total of thirty thousand public secondary schools with three hundred thousand teachers and administrators, was an effort of the most transcendant and striking character. The people of this country said in effect, "We are going to educate in formal fashion all our sons and daughters, not only when they are children, but also when they are fourteen to eighteen years of age." They said this not in words but in schools and teachers.

The American people made these tremendous increases in secondary education with necessary accompanying changes in higher education. In 1910, for example, there were fewer pupils in the secondary schools than there are teachers in the elementary and secondary schools of the country today. Since 1910, teachers' colleges and schools and departments of education in universities and colleges have been developed in the same rapid fashion as were the high schools themselves. There are more students in the colleges and universities of the United States this year than there were in all the high schools in this country in 1920.

When the depression of the 1930's hit the Americans, they continued to send more and more of their children to secondary schools, although at first they sharply curtailed expenditures for public education. Teachers went unpaid, buildings fell into disrepair, and the whole educational service was weakened.

Then the federal government stepped into the situation, establishing two federal agencies for the education of youth, the Civilian Conservation Corps and the National Youth Administration, spending on them more than three billion dollars during the ten years beginning about 1934. Large grants of federal money were also made to public schools for new buildings.

The depression was long and hard. Most of its pressure did not begin to ease until the war arrived, with its insatiable demands for employment. Since the end of the war, secondary school enrollments are again burgeoning, and the American people are once more engaged in the race to provide teachers, buildings, and equipment for all the young people to whom they want to give secondary education.

How many of these young people of secondary-school age do the Americans propose to educate in secondary schools? If we ask our fellow-citizens to answer this question in words, they will give us various answers. Some will say 75 per cent, some will propose 50 per cent, and some will estimate that only 15 or 20 per cent of our young people should be given formal education to the age eighteen. Through their actions, however, they answer almost unanimously. Practically all of them give their answer by trying to send their own children to secondary school. Practically all of them, working within a given community, will try to provide education for 100 per cent of the boys and girls of secondary-school age in their community. There are many communities in the United States today which send more than 90 per cent of their youth of secondary-school age to secondary school. There are some communities which do not come within hailing distance of that figure. Yet the people in a community which gives secondary education to only 50 per cent of its youth differ only slightly from those in a community which gives schooling to 90 per cent. In both cases, you will commonly find men and women who are determined that their own children shall have secondary education on a 100 per cent basis and that the children of their near neighbors, the children of the own local community, shall have such education on practically the same generous level.

It would be wrong to assume that the tremendous expansion of secondary education in the United States was a simple result of a simple belief in the value of secondary education on the part of the people of the country. Actually both the expansion of secondary education and the belief in its value are complex results of an intricately involved skein of social, political, and economic factors in the history of the United States.

Why does Seattle have more of its youth in high school than does Baltimore, Fort Worth more than Richmond, Lincoln more than Lexington? Why do the Mormons and the Congregationalists send practically all their children to high school? Why do people of Scottish or Swedish descent almost always go to high school? How much more likely is a child from a family with a yearly income of twenty thousand dollars to go to high school than one from a family on relief?

No simple answer can properly be given to such questions. We can say that the recency of frontier conditions make men eager to increase the educational opportunities for their children, that certain religions require the utmost possible intellectual development of their individual members, that Scotland and Sweden are advanced countries which naturally require secondary education from many of their people, and that parents who are in the twenty-thousand-dollar-a-year level are convinced that practically no one can qualify for that bracket without a secondary education.

Still these answers are all too simple. What is the "frontier," for example? It is nothing which can be generalized to fit a pattern of education from Butte in 1890 to Nome in 1948. The only way to assess the influence of the frontier on high school education in Alaska in 1948 is to study in detail the secondary-education beliefs and practices of the people of Alaska in 1948. They will differ between Ketchikan and Fairbanks; they will differ between the farmers of the Matanuska and the officials of the great salmon-packing companies; and they will certainly differ between the school teachers of Juneau and the board of the Alaska Steamship Company.

Similarly with the Mormons, it is not enough to say that their religion requires them to go to high school if possible. The frontier — a frontier very different from that of Alaska — has worked on them too. Moreover, they are a prosperous people. To what extent does their interest in education merely accompany their higher incomes?

So, too, we can study the people of Scottish and Swedish descent, the people of various incomes, and many other groupings of citizens who have varying tendencies to want secondary education for their children.

Some of these studies have been made. More of them need to be made. I believe that those which have been made and the general facts of the history of secondary education in the United States both suggest clearly that economic interests constitute the first and foremost reason for the American development of, and belief in, secondary education. The emphasis on preparation for college training, which is widely supposed to be of great economic worth; the vocational developments in the secondary-school curriculum; the almost universal belief, on the part of parents, teachers, and pupils, that a high-school education increases a person's earning capacity; the tendency of employers to set high-school graduation as a prerequisite to jobs; and the overwhelming fact that practically all the desirable jobs, as well as many of the less desirable ones, are held by high-school and college graduates — are all clear signs of the main reason why the Americans believe in secondary education for all their youth.

When we contemplate the inescapable fact that these 140 million people who expanded secondary education so dramatically, who first set themselves the objective of giving secondary education to all their children, and who have come closer to achieving that goal than any other people, also have at least twice the productive capacity of any other group of 140 million people in the world, we suspect that the Americans are fundamentally right. Secondary education on this 100 per cent basis pays. It pays materially. It pays in more and better goods and services. Its relative presence is a real reason why Santiago, Chile, is poorer than Sacramento, California, as well as a real result of that difference in prosperity.

What the Americans believe fully and practice partly with respect to the uses of secondary education in developing material wealth is precisely as true with respect to the development of what may be called a wealth of the spirit, but this fact is harder for them to see and to put into effective action. They feel it; hence their high-school bands and orchestras, their high-school art studios, their groping for better teaching of intercultural relations in secondary schools, their search for improved experiences in preparation of high-school pupils for local, national, and world citizenship; but they are far from being sure of their efforts in this area. Richard T. Ely told them long ago that "there are two kinds of poverty — one a lack of goods for the higher wants, the other a lack of wants for the higher goods,"[1] and that, of these two, a poverty of wants was by far the more terrible, but they have never fully believed the great economist's dictum.

The extent of the Americans' lack of belief in the value of secondary schools for the area of higher wants and, to a certain degree, for the area of higher goods is indicated in several ways. During the depression of the 1930's, for example, when the federal government gave billions of dollars for the education of youth, the established secondary-school system was very largely by-passed. Today many members of the Congress of the United States and millions of other citizens are seriously contemplating the establishment of a program of disciplinary, physical, health, and civic education for eighteen-year-old boys under the name of universal military training, at an annual cost of ten times the proposed federal aid to the schools of the country. Why? Is it because we Americans lack faith in our established system of youth education?

With three billion dollars a year, a conservative estimate of the cost of universal military training, a million-dollar high school could be built in each of three thousand counties of this country. With three billion dollars a year, a half-million high school teachers could be employed at an average annual salary of six thousand dollars. Does anyone doubt the tremendous increase in the quality and quantity of youth education to be secured by such expenditures?

In fact, the following paraphrase of the computation of the late Donald DuShane of the National Education Association shows that, with three billion dollars, the United States could accomplish all these things:

1. *Construct a ten-room school building in every county in the United States each year.*
2. *Construct a $50,000 library in every county in the United States each year.*
3. *Construct annually a $150,000 hospital in each county.*
4. *Employ ten full-time school and public-health doctors and ten full-time school and public-health nurses in every county.*
5. *Purchase ten new modern school buses in each county each year.*
6. *Maintain one psychiatric and behavior clinic in every county.*
7. *Provide ten recreational and juvenile guidance workers in every county.*
8. *Bring all schools of the county up to a reasonable standard of efficiency.*
9. *Provide free education for the three million children under eighteen who are now not attending school.*
10. *Meet the payroll of one junior college with ten instructors in every county.*

[1]Richard T. Ely, Thomas S. Adams, Max O. Lorenz, and Allyn A. Young, *Outlines of Economics*, p. 3. New York: Macmillan Co., 1929 (fourth revised edition).

11. Pay the expenses of a three-year graduate course for ten-thousand selected students each year.

12. Pay the full maintenance and tuition at college or technical school for one year of nine hundred thousand boys who would be conscripted under universal military training.

13. Erect a $750,000 trade school in each congressional district each year.

14. Still have a residue of fifteen million dollars each year to give each of fifteen thousand young reserve officers one thousand dollars worth of training each year.[2]

The improbability that the American people will make any such effort to give increased support to the secondary schools indicates clearly that the place of the secondary school in American society is not so secure as we commonly like to believe.

There are two main phases of this insecurity. First, the people of the United States do not fully understand what the modern secondary school can do, what it is trying to do, and what it should do educationally for the youth of the country. Second, the teachers of the secondary schools, as a group, are not professionally educated to conduct skillfully the program of a modern secondary school and to inform and lead the public in understanding and supporting such a program.

These are the two great gaps in the line of advance for those of us who are secondary-school teachers, for those of us who are professionally charged with the education of secondary-school teachers, and for all of us as citizens of a country long since pledged to the best possible education for all its youth.

How are these gaps to be plugged? I believe that they can be, and must be, met by two closely associated reforms in the practice of secondary education and in the preparation of teachers for the secondary schools.

The first reform is a program-building reform. The program of every secondary school — and by "program" I mean the secondary curriculum and all other youth activities of a behavior-changing nature — must be built up by and within the communities in which the young people live. A "good" program of secondary education in a community, most of whose people do not know that it is good, do not know what it means, and do not want it, is actually a bad program. Let us start with that principle and see what we can do. Let us have no more of this building a marvelously modern school in an intellectual and emotional corner.

In 1943, as a soldier in the field, I heard of the *New York Times'* investigation of high-school graduates' lack of knowledge of dates and great events in American history. I read one night a letter from the United States telling me of the *Times'* "proof" that the high schools were not teaching functional citizenship. I read that letter with a sense of aching loss in my heart — loss that day of a

2"What 3 Billion Dollars Would Buy," *National Education Association Journal,* XXXV (February, 1946), p. 109.

boy from New York, a high-school graduate who had gone down in what seemed to me the most brilliant display of intelligent and devoted loyalty to his country I had ever seen. I said to myself bitterly, "I wonder if the sergeant could have met the *Times'* test. I wonder if he knew when the Constitution was adopted."

Two years later, as the war ended and as I pondered on the boys I had seen under great pressure for great national objectives in 1917-18 and those I had known in 1942-45, recognizing clearly that those of the younger generations were incomparably better educated than were their fathers, for citizenship as well as for technical efficiency of all kinds, I heard about the patriotic New Jersey legislature's passing a bill requiring the study of American history for two years in the high school. Again I found myself wondering, "Would the boys whom we left in Massacre Valley of Attu, on the beaches of Anzio and Kwajalein, on the plains of Normandy and the slopes of the Rhine — would they have learned to love the United States as well as do New Jersey law-makers if they had studied American history in high school for two years instead of only one year?"

These questions are not to be construed as an attack on the *Times* or on the legislature of New Jersey. They are merely reflections on the gap between the modern secondary-school program and the ideas of the leaders in the community which the secondary school must serve, of which the secondary school must be an integral part, and without which the secondary school will fail to perform its function. The program of the secondary school must be understood, developed, and sustained by all the community — the pupils, the parents, the civic organizations, the religious groups, the professional and business associations, the labor unions, the nonschool educational agencies, the government, and the teachers.

I mention the teachers, because they are the most important of all these groups — much more important in the modern secondary-school program than in the older high school. A new education for teachers is, therefore, required to fill the second great gap in the line of advance.

The secondary-school teachers of this country are still being educated largely in academic corners. Their preparation is generally far inferior in quality to that given to elementary-school teachers. Prospective secondary-school teachers are too often trained to be minor specialists in history, French, or mathematics, and nothing much of anything else. Some of the persons who train them, furthermore, commonly cry that anyone who wishes to educate secondary-school teachers more broadly, more comprehensively, and more thoroughly is trying to make them less scholarly, less respectable, and less intellectual.

It seems impossible for some of these anxious defenders of the sanctity of subject-matter compartmentalizations to recognize that secondary-school teachers could, and should, know more about history, French, mathematics, science, homemaking, industrial arts, music, or any other disciplines related to their special work in high school and at the same time could, and should, know something else. They should know about the growth and development of young people, the nature and dynamics of group and community living, and the ways – outside of history, French, mathematics, and the like – in which young people may best grow up in groups and communities and work for their own objectives in most intelligent and effective relation to the objectives of the groups and communities.

A teacher educated in such a manner will not be less of a specialist than one who knows only an academic field and a few devices for instruction in that field. He will be a much greater specialist in the field of individual-and-group behavior engineering who, because he regards a subject as a useful instrument in his professional task, will have an academic and scholarly advantage over one who thinks his subject is an end in itself. Teachers educated in such a manner in the teacher-training institution and on the job will find the task of informing the community and of using the community's abilities in building the secondary-school program a difficult but a satisfying task and one which they can do.

The education of such teachers and their placement and support will give our great new secondary school a secure place in American life because the school will serve American life by being itself a central and powerful part of American life.

Dimensions of Educational Policy

Once upon a different time from the present and in a different place from any on this particular satellite, there was a planet about the same size as ours, rotating on its axis about as fast as our earth does, about as far from its parent star as we are from our sun and having the same length of year; in short a planet very much like ours in all the ways important to life like ours.

Let us call this planet, the *Island Planet,* to emphasize one way in which it was very different from the earth. It had only 58 square miles of land surface; all the rest of the planet was water. If the island which gave the planet its name had been regular in shape it might have been a little over seven miles wide and eight miles long. Actually it was very irregular in shape. Because of this irregularity and unusual patterns of ocean currents and winds, moreover, the small land mass on the Island Planet had many different kinds of climate running from very hot to very cold.

Only 33 square miles of the land were fit for farming. About 20 square miles more were dry plains on which a few animals could graze. The rest of the land was covered with desert — some of it hot and sandy, the rest of it cold and icy.

There were people on this island planet. Were they human? That is a hard question to answer. They looked like us. The had language, culture, personality traits like ours, but they were of course nowhere nearly so intelligent as we are. Let me attempt to prove that they lacked our level of ability.

At the time our observation of these Island People begins, we find that there are 3,000 of them. They have a history, as people who seem like us and like our ancestors, which runs back about 602,000 years. In that period of time, only 77,000 of these beings have lived on the Island Planet. It took the first 600,000 of these 602,000 years for the island population to reach the 250 mark. They were a mere handful of people. Then it took them more than sixteen centuries to reach a total of 500 people. It required another 200 years to reach the 1000 mark. Then in eighty years the population again doubled reaching 2,000. In thirty-two years it reached 3,000. In forty years more, the experts who observe these people say that the population will have doubled again. It will be 6,000 and then 12,000 about thirty-five or forty years after that, and so on, with populations of 24,000, 48,000, 96,000, 192,000, 384,000, 768,000, and so

The Sarah Olive Rush Lecture delivered at the University of South Florida, February 7, 1964.

on piling up every thirty, forty, or fifty years. How are these people going to feed all these thousands on only thirty-three square miles of arable land? Or suppose they distill the ocean water and irrigate the twenty square miles of dry plains and steppes? Suppose they cool and water the hot deserts? Suppose they utilize every acre of the total land mass — fifty-eight square miles — a total of approximately 37,000 acres? It is only a matter of two or three generations until there will not be room enough for these swarming thousands to sleep on their little acres, much less raise enough food to furnish even a minimum diet for them.

But are these people on the Island Planet doing something about this? Is their Island Government concerned about it? Do they have an island policy to meet this one great problem of over-population? The answer to each of these questions is negative.

These Island People have no island government. The present 3,000 of them are divided into about one hundred different family groups, ranging in size from large families of 200 to 300 or 400 to families down to one or two persons, although the average size family is 20 to 40. The theory is that every family group is politically independent although every one admits that economically they are interdependent.

Do they not quarrel, even fight among themselves over the small amount of good land? Yes, they do, and they have done so in the past, especially in the recent past. In the first 600,000 years of Island history there were so few of them that they did not fight very much. When the total population was 250 or even 500, the island seemed pretty large. But for the last 200 years, the land has been shrinking rather rapidly, and the families have been fighting rather steadily. Most of the time they have been fighting over land ownership.

No doubt we should stop worrying now about these insignificant Island People on their sub-microscopic speck of cosmic dust and turn to larger problems. For the moment, however, they are fascinating in their wrongheadedness. Obviously they have got to change their ways significantly to survive, but they seem determined to change their ways so that it will be difficult for them to survive.

Let us look more closely at just one of the family groups of the Island People. It is one of the largest families, although there are several that are considerably larger, and it is by far the wealthiest family on the island. It has 190 people on 3.6 square miles of land or 2304 acres. The gross family product, reduced to our U. S. currency, is approximately $600,000 per year. This family has about six percent of the land and six percent of the people, yet it can and sometimes does produce more goods and services of various important kinds than all the other 2,810 Island People combined.

Now we have gone far enough in this story so that its source is unmistakeable. The number of square miles on the island, the number of people, the figures concerning the richest family's productivity – all these are derived merely by dividing figures for this planet by one million.

Why can we see the Island People's problems and their possible solutions more clearly than we can see the problems and possible solutions for the earth's population?

It is because we have reduced the dimensions for the Island People's problems. Let us examine the nature of those dimensions. We are using the word *dimensions* here to mean the elements that combine to indicate the magnitude of anything. When that thing is an ordinary physical body, we use such ordinary physical dimensions as length, width, thickness, area, and volume. When it is an event in history we must add the dimension of *time*. When we come to human personality and character whether in small or large groups, we have to handle and understand even more complex dimensions.

In order to measure a society's greatness or smallness, we must include those key elements that make the society great or small. These are the society's dimensions. What are they?

First is the dimension of *scope*. How much territory does the society cover? This includes not only the extension of the society over physical areas, but also over social, economic, and cultural areas. To determine that a nation has 190,000,000 people is only a beginning of the measurement of its scope. How much productivity do those people have? How much security are they given? How much cultivation do they achieve?

Second is the dimension of *drive*. How far will a particular society go against obstacles to the improvement of its people's security, productivity, and cultivation? When it comes to a roadblock, will it lie down and stagnate; or will it bring up its mortars and demolition squads and remove the obstruction? When it is counter-attacked, will it fight or will it run? This dimension of drive adds substance to the society's territory.

Third is the dimension of *style*. By this is meant the methods and content of the society's main patterns of action. In giving its people security, in developing their productivity, and in furthering their cultivation, is the society elegantly precise or crudely bumbling in its efforts. The importance of this dimension should not be underestimated because of superficial appearance. Real style goes deep beneath the surface of a society's life. In the field of security it is style that makees a democracy work in some countries and fail in others. In productivity it is style that makes labor unions achieve reforms by orderly, non-revolutionary means in many cases and turns them into racketeering goon-squads in others. It is style rather than the externals of academic organization and regulatory mechanism that makes some school systems outstanding instruments of education and develops others that are detriational in their effects.

Now let us examine these three dimensions of *scope, drive,* and *style* in that little Island-People situation. Does the scope of these people's social concerns include the population explosion? Well, yes, we say calmly. After all, the Island People are really fictitious. Do these people have the drive, the courage, the guts to do something about it? Well, so far, not much. Finally, is their style of action, including their style of thinking, such that it can develop the necessary cultural solutions of the population problem? This is the crucial question; it lies at the heart of their educational policy making.

Now that we have these three dimensional concepts in mind, as applied to the small society of the Island People, let us apply them to educational policy making in the United States of America. What is the real magnitude of our behavior-changing systems in scope, drive, and style?

Taking each dimension in order, what is the scope of educational policy making in the United States? Let us look first at the learners. We know well that a child's education starts at birth, and that the period before the age of six has behavior-changing effects of overwhelming importance. Thus the baby, the two-year-old, the nursery-school toddlers, and the pupils of kindergarten age, all need an environment for effective learning. The importance of good learning experiences at those ages is as great as at any later age if not indeed greater.

Yet we still tend to plan our systems of schooling primarily for the years eight to sixteen or eighteen. At the same time we have little children spending their babyhood and their other so-called pre-school years in conditions unfit for human beings. Little children enter the first grade unable to talk in sentences, not primarily because of low native intelligence in many cases but simply because they have lived their brief lives in slum tenements or in rural shacks under circumstances which taught them the meaning only of such bits of language as, "Shut up!" "Get outa here!" "Cut out that _____ _____ yowlin'!" "What's that _____ kid doin' in here?"

Is this the proper scope of early childhood education for a proud and wealthy people? To ask the question is to laugh. We can send multi-million dollar shots to the moon and shrug off failures due to sloppy supervision by men who measure education in terms of geometry in the fifth grade. We can build atomic-powered submarines and sometimes sink them under the supervision of self-appointed educational experts who are so educationally naive as to think we can measure United States educational efforts in Swiss and British terms. We have self-appointed revolutionists who believe they can solve educational administrative problems by reaching for the protective arms of the law with one hand while flouting it with the other. We have all these and more, but we have very few people who can look this matter of the scope of our schooling in the face and say, "We can and will provide kindergartens, nursery schools, and nurseries for these little citizens of the United States of America. While we are seeking to give our planet more satellites than Jupiter possesses, while we try to land space craft on Mars and Venus, and while we are planning to run new rings around Saturn, we will develop an early childhood environment that will run rings around anything yet envisioned on this planet."

What has been said here about the scope of schooling for the pre-school citizens can be repeated for the fourteen to twenty-year olds. In a country like ours, it is a disgrace not to have schooling for all our young people to the age of twenty. Its pattern will have to be different for many of them. We will have to build many new secondary-school systems including junior and community colleges with work programs attached. We will have to prepare many thousands of new teachers for these expansions of our systems.

Higher education of greatly extended scope is also necessary for a country that in many ways is the most advanced, and in all ways should be the most advanced in the world. It is hardly necessary to detail this fact to an American university audience.

Will this expansion of scope cost more money than we can spare? Again to ask the question is to laugh. In a recent publication I have stated the issue in these words, "It is a lack of spirit rather than of purse which spells backwardness in any country's university. . . (All these countries) have as much and as good higher education as they have brains enough to want, heart enough to attempt, and guts enough to achieve."[1]

Of course, at this point we are already looking at the dimension of *drive.* Throughout the nineteenth and well into the first half of the twentieth century, the United States had a better record in this dimension than had most other countries attempting to reach similar developmental levels. By keeping the schools close to the people with decentralized systems of control and support, our fathers and grandfathers demonstrated again and again that there were no reasonable lengths from which they would recoil in developing what they considered to be good schools for their children and young people. The key word here was *reasonable.* The people had to be informed concerning proposed educational improvements before they would regard them as reasonable. No other country invented and operated a more efficient and varied complex of organizations and practices for interpreting its schools to its people than did the United States. It is no historical accident that the great parent-teacher movement originated in this country; that state, regional, and national associations of schoolboard members were developed here; and that woman's organizations, men's and women's service clubs, and many special-interest groups running along the political-social spectrum from the International Ladies Garment Workers Union to the United States Chamber of Commerce regarded educational concerns as basic in their programs.

But we are not measuring *drive* in the making of educational policy in the United States in 1884, 1904, 1924, or 1944. We are considering this dimension in 1964 and estimating what it will need to be in 1994. The best schooling for our people in 1964 is very different from that needed in 1934 or 1944, and the

[1]Harold R. W. Benjamin, "Higher Education in Latin America," *Phi Delta Kappan,* January, 1964, p. 182.

mechanism of our drive toward that school must be different or it will falter and perhaps even grind to a halt.

First of all we need to retain and improve the drive in localities and states and at the same time develop an increased educational drive of national and international proportions. The young American in the 1964 schools is going to engage in national and international enterprises and is going to have to understand them and support them to a hitherto unimagined degree. The changing communication and transportation patterns impose this requirement upon our society, and our drive must be shifted and intensified to meet them.

The drive displayed by any group is the social equivalent of individual courage. In military units, for example, we call it morale. We know how it is developed. It comes from pride in the group's ability, from confidence in the group's leadership, from devotion to the group's job, and from knowledge of how that job is to be done. The group has high morale in the same way that a man is not afraid when he is proud of his role, dedicated to carrying it out, confident of his ability, and skilled in its performance. In the individual and in the group these qualities come from education and only from education. A system of schooling not based squarely on the cultivation of these qualities need not be much concerned about the future of its educational policy making; it will never have a future in which to carry out the policies it formulates.

In comparative education studies, this principle can be documented almost endlessly. Many countries have elaborate constitutional and legal prescriptions for school systems with carefully detailed course descriptions, administrative machinery, and supervisory staffs, but have practically no discernible schooling for its people for the simple reason that educational drive is lacking. Educational authorities in such countries rarely admit this lack. They will usually instead say, "We are a poor people; we just do not have the money to implement our compulsory education laws; we need massive international help." As they talk, furthermore, fighter airplanes roar overhead ostensibly to protect their frontiers but actually to keep a landowning oligarchy in power. That oligarchy has plenty of drive for retaining power but practically none for education.

It is in the dimension of style, however, that the final shape of a society's schooling is determined. All education is a result of communication. A school is a very special and crucial communication instrument. All good teachers, no matter what their subject, are communication specialists. Style is the heart of communication. The word itself in many of our Indo-European languages comes from a term meaning an instrument of writing. Style is a mode of expression of communication. In that specialized institution of expression, of communication, which is a school, therefore, style means the whole pattern of the institution's operation. It covers method and content of teaching but even more it covers the entire complex of attitudes displayed by the teachers and pupils.

The non-school behavior-changing agencies in our modern society often have, indeed usually have, a style very different from that of the school. I have only to say, "Us Stencho smokers will fight before we'll switch," or "Glopsughs taste good like a cigarette should," to make the point. To labor it with examples from all the dreary by-paths of advertising, from whiskey that guarantees distinction to greasy kid stuff that blights teen-age romance, is unnecessary and conducive to nausea in the sensitive hearer.

Far more important educationally are such massive assaults on community style as newspapers that concoct events in order to have something to report, community leaders who are more concerned about their public image than their public services, and whole societies devoting major effort to self delusion.

Only a generation ago we wrote letters by hand to one another. I treasure a letter from Professor John Dewey which he beat out himself on his ancient typewriter; now I occasionally receive letters from people who could not differentiate John Dewey from Tom Dewey, with the final information at the end, "Dictated but not read by Dr. Gloop."

We are taught by extra-school instruction that money is a magical element easily obtained from a friendly loan office, that all houses are homes, that most "doctors" agree on the intestinal necessity of Whosis Pills, that a writer must be significant because he "dares" to transfer four-letter words from the walls of public privies to the pages of a novel, and a thousand other marks of self-deluding and gutter-snipe features of our society that run squarely athwart the style of the schools. It is our style in schools to teach our pupils to think; a skill which if practiced very extensively would send large numbers of our political office holders back to private life and would wreck considerable areas of our economy. It is our style in schools to teach children to understand their work and respect it for its results; and ability which could create difficulty in more extra-school affairs than one cares to contemplate.

In our educational planning we need to recognize this dimension of style and give it the support it deserves. We need to see clearly that it is much more than a question of whether to teach intuitive geometry or French by the direct method in the seventh grade. It is a question of putting the best ideals of our society into a complex of behavior-changing experiences. This is a task which requires high professional skill and even greater professional dedication. I have heart and faith that our teachers generally have that skill and dedication, if we will but give them room according to their size and strength.

I have further faith that teachers of such style, of such skill and dedication can help our people extend the scope of their educational enterprises over the areas which the next two, three, or five decades will demand; and that they can raise the cultural banners and sound the trumpets to which our people will have drive enough to rally. This can be done; it should be done: and by the splendor of God's grace, I believe it will be done.

Preface to UNDER THEIR OWN COMMAND

It is currently fashionable to be pessimistic about the future of mankind. Gloomy voices cry that humanity is standing at the most momentous crossroads of its history without brains or spirit enough to take the right turning, that this is an hour of great decision with few elements of greatness in those who have to make the decision, that new weapons of war call imperatively for an achievement of world unity which men do not know how to achieve and would not want to achieve if they did know how, and that in general this earth and the inhabitants thereof are in a frightful mess.

I do not share this pessimism. I do not believe that humanity is standing at a crossroads of any kind, momentous or otherwise. I believe, rather, that it is moving steadily down a broad highway toward gracious, humane, and truly civilized goals. I do not look upon this hour as being one of particularly great decision. I believe that every hour in the life of man is an hour of great decision. I do not regard a new means of human slaughter, however swift and efficient, as calling suddenly for world unity. I hold that call to have been just as clear and just as compelling in the days when the outstanding weapon of organized and disciplined violence was the short sword of the Roman legionary and a Galilean carpenter walked upon the earth preaching a gospel of the brotherhood of all men.

Men have come far enough along this highway to glimpse vistas of peaceful and effective living on the road ahead. They are equipped with better information of their past routes than ever before. In making decisions, they can call upon greater resources of developed intelligence than they ever possessed in earlier days. They now have, within practicable reach, instruments for making the great Galilean's dream come true, instruments for changing their own ways in the direction of their own ideals, instruments beside whose power and scope the latest atomic weapon sinks to the level of a paleolithic warclub.

I am confident that in the future, near and far, mankind will develop and use these instruments of education with greater and greater skill, for higher and higher purposes, and in fuller and fuller accord with the ancient yet ever-new vision of peace and good will to all the world.

At a time when men seem to be ridden by fear and obsessed by the power of their weapons of flame and steel, it is well for them to remember their heritage of courage and their weapons of mind and spirit. So equipped and so armed, they will win this struggle against the ignorance which underlies all their ills.

Under Their Own Command was written by Dr. Benjamin, in 1947, as part of the Kappa Delta Pi Lecture Series. Appreciation is hereby acknowledged to Kappa Delta Pi, An Honorary Society in Education, for permission to quote from the lecture. The portions used are the Preface and those sections titled, "Nationalism in War and Education," "The Nature of a People's Education," "What Education Do and Should the Peoples of the World Attempt?," and, "What is the Leadership Role of Teachers in the World Community?"

Nationalism in War and in Education

Man usually regards war as his most colorful and significant enterprise. He does not deck it with banners or sound its coming with trumpets to hide its ugliness from himself or his fellows but simple to symbolize the glamor and importance it actually holds for him. He has long denied that he thinks war is the most meaningful and dramatic activity in which he can engage. In oratorical moments, he declaims his hatred of war. In somber, morning-after moods, he periodically swears off war. Then he proceeds systematically and passionately to do everything and hold fast to everything that makes the next war inevitable. When war comes, furthermore, he serves it with all his might. He puts his life, his fortune, and his sacred honor into the balance. In our gaming idiom, he shoots the works.

Man's attitude toward education has been the reverse in many respects of his attitude toward war. For generations, he has piously protested that education is one of the greatest, if not the greatest, of all human tasks, that its values transcend almost all other goods, that its effects upon the prosperity and happiness of a people are incalculable, and that there are no reasonable lengths from which he will recoil to make education fully operative throughout his domain. Then he proceeds cautiously to confine education to a little book learning in the schools, doles it out in bargin lots to groups privileged in various economic and social ways, and leaves the bulk of its work to be done by agencies and individuals with special behavior-changing goals of their own. He serves education timidly, giving it occasional handouts and pledging it a carefully limited literacy. He does not shoot the works. He shoots two bits and then complains that his winnings are small.

These contrasting attitudes are all the more remarkable in view of certain similarities between national conceptions of war and those of education. As worshiper of God, artist, scientist, philosopher, or sometimes even as buyer and seller of goods, man often does not seem to mind being considered one with the rest of religious, artistic, scientific, philosophical or trading mankind. In matters of war or education on the other hand, he is commonly nationalistic to the core.

The reason for this nationalistic intensity for war purposes is easy to see. It is the nation today, as it was the tribe yesterday, that possesses the supreme power to wage war. The nation is born in war; it lives in a continuous process of carrying on war, recovering from war, and preparing for war; and at the end it dies in war. It is ushered into the world with a roll of drum-fire. It passes from the stage of history in a blaze of burning cities to the funeral salute of a hundred thousand guns or of one shattering atomic roar. A nation never dies in bed. It dies with its boots on, a smoking weapon in its hand and bitter hatred in its heart.

Not the religion which bids men love one another in conformity with the accepted design of a great Providence, not the economic necessity which increasinly demands their cooperation and interdependence throughout the world, but the constraint to aggression and ill will of their nationalistic boundaries in time of war still remains for them the duty to which they are set to give the highest measure of devotion.

In a similar though not so easily recognizable fashion, education is tied closely to nationalistic feeling. It is the nation today, as it was the tribe yesterday, that possesses the supreme power over schools and all other ways of changing human behavior by reasonable and emotional means. Nations are born, live, and die as a result of educational influences no less than in response to bomb, bullet, and bayonet. Classroom, library, and laboratory; press, radio, and cinema; forum and market place; home and confessional; it is such agencies as these that determine a nation's birth, the mode of its existence, and the time and manner of its ending. These are the true forces of final command. These are the real captains and kings. These are the generals who put the armored columns across the frontiers. These are the admirals who send the gray warships steaming beyond the headlands. These are the marshals who order the death-laden bombers into the air. These are the drivers behind the dictator's every strut and bellow. These are the lance and shield, the bow and buckler, without which wars cannot be made.

While war is often a condition of national existence, education always determines national behavior. War is a sympton and a result of conflict. Education can be either a cause or a cure of conflict. War is a surface phenomenon. Education is a volcanic force far beneath the surface.

That man will destroy himself through war is a too-simple fear. If he decides, through educational processes, to destroy himself, he will certainly find modern war to be a most suitable and effective instrument. The thing for him to fear, if he shuns self-destruction, is not war itself, but that kind of education which makes war inevitable. To attempt to save himself from his suicidal mania by seeking to abolish war through international agreement alone, without tremendous reforms in the behavior-changing practices which now underlie and require war, is like trying to stop murder by laws prohibiting the individual ownership of firearms. It is at best a surface attack on the problem, and at worst a device whereby honest citizens are disarmed to fall before the guns of the killers in the community.

Every competent policeman today knows that provision of good schools, playgrounds, libraries, athletic clubs, recreational centers, and other community educational services keep more boys from crime than all the anti-gun laws on the statute books. Statesmen the world over have yet to learn the principle underlying this simple fact as it relates to war and nations.

The world today is generally said to be in a dangerous situation. National groups regard one another as the chief sources of this danger. National leaders exaggerate their importance among their peoples by accusing one another of being menaces to peace. Reporters of international conferences, who appear almost uniformily to subscribe to the great-man-great-devil theory of world affairs, breathlessly describe a foreign minister's beetling brows, a diplomat's aggressive walk, or an ex-prime-minister's florid phrases as though they were the very warp and woof of coming war.

All this is to betray a remarkable naivete. Such ignorance of the facts of international life may have been credible in days when absolute sovereigns moved their subjects as pawns upon a power-chessboard — although that assumption is open to sharp question. But this generation twice saw ninety per cent or more of the people of a powerful and cleverly-schooled European nation throw all their weight for world war behind leaders whose chief distinction were their abilities to pose and to froth. To this generation the principle of *Führer*-answerability is a patent absurdity. The *verantwortlichkeit* of a Hitler — the responsibility of any national leader of our times — is merely a symbol and a summation of the obligations of all the people who hold the leader aloft. A strutting and insanely egotistical *Führer* means above all a strutting and insanely egotistical people. They acquired that strut and that egotism by education. Let them cry now that most of this bad education was imposed upon them from above, that it was under the direction of their evil leaders and not of themselves, but let them also remember that the central responsibility for the nature and end of their education is their own and only their own, that they cannot evade the duty to take command of all their own behavior-changing devices, and that the essence of the democracy for which in defeat they claim to be striving is that a people shall not merely order their own ways for their own benefit but shall also change their own ways in the direction of their own ideals.

A people who have under their own command only a small part of the forces which change their minds and thereby alter the direction of their ways can be only in small part democratic. All the forms and trappings traditionally associated with democracy may be furbished and paraded for and by this people, but they will never advance one step further along the road to democracy without a corresponding advance in the control of their own education.

The peoples of the world today are in a dangerous situation. They are always in a dangerous situation to the extent that they are being directed into new ways by forces over which they have no conscious control. Their great danger arises not from a war of rifles or nuclear fission launched by evil nationalisms but from the savagery and ill will which a misdirected education gives to an ignorant people.

Not only for teachers but also for soldiers, not only for students but also for statesmen, the first problem in the world today is not primarily a military, political, or economic problem. It is first of all the problem of how the people of the world shall assume command of their education.

To hazard the fate of the world on a conviction that the people themselves, when fully informed of all the consequences of all their behavior-changing ways, will know best how to modify and direct those ways, will appear very dangerous to many leaders in various quarters of the world. That conviction of the people's final wisdom in the educational as in the more narrowly political sphere is, of course, a matter of faith and not susceptible to formal proof. Its supporters can say for it only that it is a faith which has heretofore removed seemingly impassable mountains from the broad highway down which mankind is marching; and that if it be found unjustifiable in the event, the people can at least go down fighting under their own colors.

The Nature of a People's Education

The first requirement to be met by a people desiring to take command of their own education is that of finding out how their ways have been changed in the past and are now being changed.

How are the ways of any people changed? They are changed by an inter-action of internal and external, controlled and uncontrolled forces. The people whose ways are being changed are conscious of some of these forces and unconscious of others. When they select, control, and apply behavior-changing forces in the direction of their own desires, they have a consciously directed system of education, whether they call it schooling, training, advertising, recreation, propaganda, or any other name. They still continue to be educated, how-ever, by all the behavior-changing forces of which they are unconscious, and which they do not select or direct.

One of the first measures of the nature of a people's education, therefore, involves the determination of the area of behavior-changing which is not under their own control, and the discovery of those persons and groups who may be called the schoolmasters of this *terra incognita.*

These schoolmasters are often effectively disguised. Sometimes they assume priestly robes. Sometimes they wear the habiliments of war. Sometimes they sing songs and tell stories. Sometimes they sit in the counting houses and marts of commerce. For every schoolmaster who openly practices his trade in classroom and laboratory, press or forum, there are many who disdain the title but labor daily at the craft.

To know the education of a people, it is hence necessary to know who all their schoolmasters are and in what disguises they operate.

In this connection let us consider the case of a people moving from the northeast into the upper Missouri Valley some two and one-half centuries ago, one of the tribes of those Indians who came to be known as the Cheyennes. They were poor savages, driven toward the setting sun by forces which they could feel but could not understand, driven partly at times by pressures from other tribes who had acquired guns from white men of whose very existence the Cheyennes were unaware, driven from their woodland and agricultural homes further and further into arid, treeless plains.

This people traveled in fear and want. Their starving dogs dragged scanty loads on short travois poles. They pitched their little dwellings at the height of these dog-drawn lodge poles, and crawled in to sleep in hunger on the many days when their hunters were unable to get game by patient stalking. Their children snared rabbits and knocked down birds to eke out the family livelihood. Their women grubbed for roots and berries.

The old men and priests of this people did some small teaching of the boys. The old women taught the girls. There was an area of education over which the tribe exercises conscious control. It was directed mainly to survival by hunting game, fighting enemies, gathering food, and — above all — by right songs, right fasting, and right conduct where rightness was defined in terms of behavior acceptable to the spirits and to the tribe.

By 1700, a new schoolmaster was approaching the Cheyennes, bringing them the materials of a new and vastly-changed life. He had landed on the coast of what is now Veracruz in Mexico in 1519. He had entered what is now the United States in 1541. In 1680 he had left New Mexico, where he had been residing in the Spanish settlements for three generations of men. He was now coming steadily toward the Cheyennes, probably passing from Ute to Nez Perce along the west side of the Rockies, going from tribe to tribe, rocking the foundations of their culture, bidding them learn new ways or die. Early in the eighteenth century he crossed the mountains and came into the northern plains territory, and there he wrought hardly less than a miracle.

That schoolmaster was the Spanish horse. The Cheyennes were among his aptest pupils. He found them poor, and he showed them the ways of wealth. He found them hungry, and he taught them to have and enjoy rich feasts. He found them meanly clad, and he dressed them in magnificence. He found them in miserable little hovels, and he placed them in spacious lodges whose poles were measured by his own superiority over the dog. Where they had been afraid, he taught them to be brave. Where they had been incurious, he taught them to go and see. Where their imaginations had been earth-bound and pedestrian, he taught them to sing songs and tell stories befitting men whose minds and bodies were elevated by his service. He even taught them new prayers by declaring unto them features of a Great Spirit whom scurrying grubbers for food had less time to seek.

The old men and the priests now had more to teach the boys of the tribe. They expanded the area of consciously directed education to include skills, magic, and wisdom which the horse culture demanded. They pictured the history of the tribe in winter counts on the finest of buffalo robes. The young men took over direct educational activities by developing the rituals and programs of new secret societies of horsemen. The very code of battle was changed as its practice came to include this new and overwhelming factor of strategy, tactics, and logistics. The war bonnets were heavy with coup feathers, and the horses themselves carried decorations for every enemy they had run down.

Few changes in any society have been so complete, so spectacular, and so rapidly taken into the area of consciously directed education as the change made in the lives of the Cheyennes and the other Plains Indians by the coming of the horse. Not even at Hiroshima was a new weapon of war more dramatically displayed by a people than on that day, in 1868, before Beecher's Island in the Arikaree River, when Roman Nose rode along the Cheyenne line, chanting soberly, "My friends, I think this is a good day to die!" He ended his song, and then he swung his big bay horse against the blue-clad entrenched soldiers who could not be flanked but had to be charged head on through water to a horse's knees. The big bay charged, and the line charged behind him through the hail of lead from new fast-shooting weapons, up into the rifle pits and over the soldiers. It was the culmination, for the Cheyennes, of their use of the horse as a weapon.

The rest of the story, so far as the Cheyennes' nationalism, warfare, and education are concerned, is short and well known. We know today that the horse was only incidentally an instrument of war. He was primarily a means of communication and transportation, a source of economic power, and above all a bearer of new hopes and new dreams. What he gave to the Plains Indians in food, shelter, and clothing was very great. What he gave to their minds and spirits was even greater.

We know today that the Cheyenne effort at Beecher's Island was useless. The white man had caught up with the horse. The white man had the horse and other instruments of war, and he had also the superiority of numbers and education which the Indians lacked. In the ensuing conflict, the Indians were obliterated.

White men could easily see the inevitable outcome of this conflict. It was clear even to the most poorly schooled among them that the Indians could not win. Many of the Cheyennes and other Plains people were also aware of the hopelessness of their struggle. Their most distinguished chief understood enough of the factors involved to see that they must finally accept defeat. They fought on proudly, desparately, hoping for a miracle which they knew in their hearts would never come.

The men who fell at Beecher's Island were as completely dead as those who were destroyed at Hiroshima and Nagasaki seventy-seven years later. In each case, a force was employed whose meaning was outside the current conceptions of the peoples involved. The greatest danger to the Cheyennes in 1868 and to the Japanese in 1945 was not a danger from weapons of war to be countered by weapons of war. The greatest danger they faced was the danger of their own ignorance, the danger of changing ways over which they had no control.

What Education Does and Should the Peoples of the World Attempt?

In the field of science and technology, it can be said that peoples in most countries of the world attempt everything they believe will be of sufficient importance to them. The determination of what constitutes importance is of course a matter of relative values. Most countries, perhaps all of them, do not attempt enough education in the field of health, for example, to give all their people the kind of health service supplied to their upper economic, social, or official classes. Even in a country like the United States, which makes more attempts to educate dentists, both absolutely and relatively, than any other country in the world, a program of giving most needed dental surgery to all children of high school age only could not be carried through by all the dentists in the country working twelve hours a day, seven days a week. In countries inhabited by at least one billion persons, to supply the barest minimum of modern medical care would require the education of physicians, nurses, dentists, and pharmacists in numbers and on a scale undreamed of in any of those countries today.

In most of these countries, prospective officers of the armed forces are given free instruction and are supported while in training by government grants in the form of pay and allowances, while prospective physicians and nurses support themselves and pay high fees for instruction. The educational drive in the one case is much higher than in the other.

Why? Is it because the health of a people's children is considered less important than the defeat of their enemies in war? Possibly this is the answer in some countries, but in others it appears to be a matter of tradition. National defense has long been considered a government function; health has been considered a private matter except in the armed forces.

The attempts at education in the field of social relationships are equally varied. Practically all peoples seek to inculcate loyalty to the government, usually by reliance on ritual, symbolism, and rote memory to the virtual exclusion of activities which involve the practice of loyalty.

Attempts to educate children in schools for skill in cooperation, tolerance among groups, and understanding of other cultures are relatively few and ineffective. Political parties, the press, and other non-school educational agencies, in many countries, work directly against the teachings of the schools.

Attempts to teach international cooperation and understanding have been made increasingly during this century. Perhaps the most conclusive comments on these attempts have been made by the two world wars which have occurred in the first half of the century.

The League of Nations was established at the close of the first world war without provision for an education section or office. This oversight was later corrected in part by the establishment of two agencies, now known as the International Bureau of Education, with headquarters in Geneva, and the Institute of Intellectual Cooperation, with headquarters in Paris. Both of these organizations did excellent work within the limits of their assigned functions and their scanty budgets. Their distinguished directors would probably be the first to admit that the efforts of both organizations were totally inadequate to the tasks which needed to be done in the intervals between the wars.

The functions of these two international agencies are now presumably being assumed by the United Nations Educational, Scientific, and Cultural Organization. This organization has now been fully launched. The educators, scientists, and cultural leaders who are responsible for operating this organization are aware that it could succeed with other machinery and that it can fail with its present machinery. While the machinery is necessary and important, it is not so important as the drive which the organization receives from the support of national and local education systems in every part of the world. UNESCO will not succeed or fail in Paris; it will stand or fall in every crossroads community of Kansas, in every hamlet of Chile, in every village of Norway, and in all the other cities, countries, provinces, departments, prefectures, and regions of the world.

An example of a problem which is confronting UNESCO is that of providing university education for international services.

The United Nations, the World Health Organization, the Food and Agriculture Organization, the International Court of Justice, the International Labor Organization, UNESCO itself, and other international agencies need the best abilities available for their staffs. The tasks they have to perform will require services of the highest order. Men and women who perform these services will need technical education of a kind superior to that provided in most if not all universities in the various countries of the world. They need to acquire some of that training in an international university.

Many employees of national governments, as foreign service officers, need education on a similar high technical level in an international university. Students of international relations, international law, and international trade will also benefit by training in such an institution.

It has been suggested by those who regard an international university as unnecessary or impractical at this time that the world already has a number of great universities which are truly international in character, as the Sorbonne, Oxford, and Harvard. It is true that such institutions give the highest type of education for many of the international tasks suggested above, but they give that education mostly to the nationals of their own countries. When a foreigner comes to Harvard, he comes to an American institution, in some respects a New

England institution, and he is conscious of his foreign status. When he comes to Oxford he is in a British, and English, university and is still conscious that he is a foreigner. In the Sorbonne or in the great universities of any country, he is similarly a foreigner in national preserves.

The University of the United Nations would be as much the home school of the Englishman, American, or Frenchman, as of the Saudi-Arabian, Iranian, Indonesian, Swiss, Filipino, Finn, or Egyptian, and no more.

Universities and other higher educational and research agencies all over the world might well hold institutional membership in the international university which would give them privileges of voting for certain members of the board of governors, sending their professors and advanced students to the university for study and research, and receiving students and professors of the university coming to their campuses on similar missions.

The international university would not necessarily have its constituent faculties and institutes in one city or even on one continent. Its faculty of social sciences might be in Geneva, its astronomical observatory in South Africa, its school of medicine in Minnesota, and its meteorological stations in Greenland and Antarctica.

This university's budget, even after it has expanded fully, will look insignificant in comparison with the military expenditure of one of our smaller nations — an expenditure confined largely, if past experience can be trusted, to training and arming the country's forces for past wars. If our attempts to wage peace by education even approach our efforts in war, we shall have no difficulty in securing all the financial support we know how to use.

In the fields of art, letters, and philosophy the international university could play an equally significant part by furnishing services and opportunities of a kind which are very difficult if not impossible for national agencies to offer.

One of the divisions of the university might be an institute of linguistics where, in cooperation with world associations of scholars, the development of a second language or languages for international use could be carried on with an impartiality and authority hardly possible to any private or national institution or organization.

In the field of communication the present efforts of the peoples of the world are impressive in their extent and volume. Many of them are beginning to use the cinema and radio for school education, and practically all of them are beginning to see the educational possibilities of those new media of mass communication. In a very few years radio has advanced from the status of a scientific toy to a position where it has been used to change the ways of whole nations in a matter of months compared to the years that would have been required to produce comparable changes by means of the printed word. The cinema has been developed on a tremendous scale, not for conscious educational purposes very often, it is true, and yet having an impact on whole societies in a matter of years where generations would have been required to effect comparable changes before the days of the motion picture.

The world is on the threshold of the widespread use of television for educational purposes. This instrument, combining two great media which have shown their great potentialities in the last quarter-century, is a force which will be used for educational purposes within the next twenty years to an extent and with an effect probably much greater than is now commonly believed. Universities and schools will be slow in using television; the history of education does not warrant a prediction that academic institutions will ever be quick to adopt new instruments. Other agencies with behavior-changing purposes of their own will be quick to use television, as they now use the radio and the motion picture, with profound effect. Consider the possible impact on the voters of the United States of a weekly television of the President's press conference.

The attempts of the world in the field of teaching languages have undoubtedly been increasing in recent years. In the first place, linguistic nationalism has been growing. Within the present century, many languages, formerly dying out or existing only as dialects or primitive tongues without literature, are being revived and developed into national languages, used for school instruction, and otherwise given official status. The Norwegians have been developing Landsmaal, largely, so far as an outsider can see, for local patriotic purposes. The Flemings have been cultivating their Dutch dialect, when German, French, or Dutch itself would have made their educational activities more effective. The people of Eire have made heroic efforts to revive their particular Gaelic language (Erse) as a patriotic substitute for English which had long ago become the native language for a great majority of them. The Filipinos in 1937, as though to celebrate their coming independence, adopted Tagalog as the basis of their national language, inspite of the fact that to a large number of the inhabitants of the Philippine Islands Tagalog is a foreign tongue. This list of instances could be greatly extended. In Europe alone, an area containing only one fourteenth of the total land surface of the earth, there are at least forty separate languages (not dialects). Languages like Albanian, Basque, Breton, Slovak, Esthonian, Frisian, Galician, Romani, Lettish, Lithuanian, Maltese, Manx, Ruthenian, Welsh, and Wend are examples of separate tongues of peoples with their own additional educational burdens imposed by speaking a minor language.

Wend is spoken by only about eighty thousand people in Prussia and Saxony, with a German-speaking population all around them. Ruthenian, on he other hand, is spoken by thirty-six million people, most of them in the Union of Soviet Socialist Republics.

It is hard to tell whether the speakers of languages like these are increasing or decreasing. In some cases, as in Eire, the number of people knowing the minor language is undoubtedly increasing. In many other cases, as among the Catalan-speaking people in southern France, the number is steadily decreasing. One thing, however, is certain in this connection. The multiplication of languages and the necessity of teaching additional languages to children in secondary schools and often in elementary schools is a considerable burden in many parts of the world.

There is no greater educational reform needed in world education today than the adoption of one language to be taught as a second language in all schools of the world. The world needs this language not only for formal education but for purposes of carrying on activities vital to its peace and security.

The adoption of this language would not only leave the home languages untouched, but it would reduce the burden under which people in the minor-language areas now have to labor. Every child and every adult could and should learn and cling to the language of his home and community, because he would have available for all communication outside his community the world's second language.

This solution will not come rapidly or easily, but it will come. It will probably come by continuation of the process which is now definitely under way of developing a few great international languages to be used over wide areas. These languages are now being changed by their uses as international languages. They are tending more and more to acquire a common vocabulary. Technical, scientific, and sports words are surprisingly alike in English, Russian, French, Spanish, and many other languages at the present time, and the number of such words in increasing.

There is a growing tendency in the secondary schools of the world to teach at least one of the great languages in addition to the native language. In most of the English-speaking countries this place as second language goes more often to French than to any other language. In the United States the first place goes to Spanish. In Latin America it probably still goes to French, although English is increasingly rapidly. In northern Europe the second language is more often English, in southern Europe, French. In central and eastern Europe it is now probably Russian. In the Near East and Middle East it is French or English. In the Far East it is more often English. In Africa it is English and French. This is to generalize sweepingly, of course, and to ignore areas in the United States where the second language is Italian, German, or Polish, in the Middle East and Africa where it is Arabic or Persian, in the Far East where it is Chinese, and many others. The bonds of both patriotism and nationalism are so closely tied to language, however, that no matter how many claimants to linguistic internationalism may be recognized there is always a supporter of one more language to take the floor and cry passionately, "The ancient Sagittarian tongue was a civilized language when English was only a primitive jargon. Sagittarian has been used for centuries as an international language by all the tribes along the borders of this great empire."

For all practical purposes, however, the world now has only about four or five chief international languages. It is possible that this number will tend to diminish in the next fifty years. Perhaps by the end of this century only two or three main languages will be used generally throughout the world.

It seems probable, moreover, that instruction in these world languages will be given not only in "language" classes in the schools but in classes in other subjects, as is now done with good results in various parts of the world.

What Is the Leadership Role of Teachers in the World Community?

The term "teacher" as here used includes superintendents, directors, and principals of schools; professors, deans, and presidents of universities; secretaries, commissioners, and ministers of education; and all others charged with professional responsibilities in the field of education broadly conceived.

What is the leadership role of teachers in the world community?

For present purposes, a community will be regarded as a group of persons with common educational objectives and common institutions for attaining these objectives.

The first job of the teacher, therefore, is to help his part of the world discover that all peoples of the world have certain common educational objectives and certain common educational institutions. He has to help the world community discover the elements of its common life. He has to aid the world community to recognize its educational needs and state its educational desires. He has to show the community how its desires can be carried out in educational programs. He has to lead the community in carrying out these programs. He has to teach the community how to judge the worth of its own educational efforts.

These are tremendous jobs, but like most big enterprises they can be broken down into little jobs and attacked with confidence. To break them into little jobs, however, requires detailed knowledge of them. This knowledge must be amassed by the teachers of the world. Indeed one of the first tasks of the teacher is to inform his community concerning the abilities a modern teacher requires. The community, world or local, will not learn such things spontaneously. It will have to be taught them with all the verve and skill characteristic of the best classroom instruction.

Absolutely, teaching is at its highest level in modern history. There are more teachers, better educated teachers, and better equipped teachers than ever before since modern school programs were begun.

Relatively, teaching is at one of the lowest, if not the lowest, levels in its history. The educational desires of the world community have been increasing faster than the teachers' education, equipment, and numbers.

The responsibilities imposed upon teachers today are therefore very heavy. The personal and professional qualities required of them by the very nature of world events are greater than ever before. The truism that modern methods of speedy transportation and practically instantaneous communication have made the world smaller than ever before has a reverse side. Modern transportation and communication have also made the world vastly larger than ever before. Only a generation ago a teacher could stay well within his local valley, his state, or at most his own country in much of his teaching. Anything outside the local community was heard of slowly and scantily. Today a teacher in the same local valley deals with people who hear news reports daily from all over the world and often have more definite views on the policies of the Communists in Southeast Asia than on those of their county commissioners.

These responsibilities cannot be carried by men and women who have been educated meagerly or in a corner. The cry is inevitably raised at this point that teachers who are paid the same as laborers and waitresses can hardly be expected to have an education much more extensive and powerful than that given to laborers and waitresses.

This is a defeatist cry. The most effective way to increase the respect a community has for its teachers and consequently the support it gives its teachers is to improve the educational services the community wants and has the drive to attempt.

The kind of education needed by teachers of more effective international understanding may be suggested by the experience of the United States in educating teachers for cooperation among the many relatively independent school systems of this country.

It is very hard for a foreigner to understand to any degree of completness the local organization of education in the United States. A European observer of education in this country, even one who considers himself well informed, is very likely to talk about the "American school system" as though it were a single unit operated from Washington. When he is told that there is no United States school system but that there are rather fifty state school systems, three great territorial systems, and many hundreds of city, county, parish, district, and other local education systems within states, often quite independent of state prescription and state control, he will commonly say, "Oh, yes, I know – we have many local education authorities too, I know." But he is often mistaken in that conclusion. He merely thinks he knows. He thinks the United States Office of Education is like the Ministry of Education in London. He thinks that a national system of education in Europe which allows some latitude to local units is comparable to the "American school system," and he is inclined to feel ill at ease when told that if a ministry of education is comparable to anything in the United States, it is more like one of the state departments of education than like any national agency in this country.

This difficulty in understanding the organization of schools in the United States arises from the fact that what we actually have in this country is a great international organization of education. The states of this Union are as independent as sovereign nations in educational matters, and practically all the school men and women of this country, along with the other citizens, are determined to keep the states independent educationally. We can see many places in our schools which need improvement. We know our educational programs and institutions are far from perfect. We are convinced, nevertheless, that we have progressed thus far in large measure because we have had many systems of education competing with one another, stimulating one another, and trying out various kinds of programs in relatively untrammeled fashion.

The foreigner looks at our schools and sees that they have a certain surface uniformity. Their teachers are similarly educated, their legal requirements are often alike in many respects, their curricula contain many common elements, and therefore the foreigner believes he is looking at a national system of education. What he cannot see without long familiarizing experience is that such uniformity as we have, as well as the even more important dissimilarities and experimental variations, is not produced by national prescriptions of any kind but by exchanges of teachers and administrators, by agreements among voluntary associations, and above all by the free communication among the school men and women of the United States. These teachers go to national meetings together, they belong to the same professional associations, they read and contribute to the same national journals in education, and thereby they appear to have achieved about all the educational unity they need or want.

Notwithstanding the obvious fact that this agreement and cooperation among the school men and women of this country are dependent in large measure on their common nationality, it seems that a consideration of their experience is very instructive to the school men and women of the United Nations. For better education service to the world community, what these teachers need is not an international system of education but a variety of means of getting acquainted with one another's professional problems and activities. They do not need a bureaucratic control of textbooks in various countries of the world, a type of control which would not be tolerated for an instant in the United States. What they need instead are many discussions and investigations of the proper type of textbooks and other materials for instruction in good international relations, discussions of such problems in international education conferences called by the World Organization of the Teaching Profession, investigations sponsored by UNESCO, studies carried on in the University of the United Nations and in member universities of that institution all over the world, and many opportunities for teachers to visit and study the school systems of other countries.

The teachers of the United Nations should note well that the country which seems to them to have one of the best developed and strongest educational systems got that way by cooperation, persuasion, and argument over a long period of working together, studying together, visiting one another's schools, and teaching in one another's communities − not by governmental prescription; in fact, as compared with European practice, not by very much prescription of any kind, even from state governments and local school authorities.

With respect to my advocacy of a University of the United Nations, it may be pointed out that the United States attained the degree of cooperation and understanding among its teachers, mentioned above, without having a University of the United States. There are two comments to be made in reply to this condition. The first is that the United States did have a university, several of them, that played a large part in the education of teachers in all the states. It is neccessary only to refer to the role of Teachers College, Columbia University, to recall the influence of such institutions. The second comment is that the University of the United States envisioned by Washington and supported by him in characteristic fashion was one of the greatest educational possibilities this country ever met — and fumbled. If that University had been established at the beginning of the nineteenth century and supported with half the money wasted on various other Federal projects which could be named, the educational gains to the United States would have been incalculable. Harvard, Yale, Princeton, Rutgers, Columbia, Johns Hopkins, Cornell, Chicago, Stanford, Wisconsin, Michigan, Minnesota, Illinois, California, North Carolina, and the other great private and state universities of this nation would not have been diminished in their stature and effectiveness by the University of the United States. Their stature would have been increased. An examination of the relationship between state and other universities in practically any section of the country lends support to this view.

It is hoped that the United Nations Educational, Scientific, and Cultural Organization, the World Organization of the Teaching Profession, the University of the United Nations if and when that institution is established, national governments, and national and local teacher-education institutions and teachers' organizations all over the world will inaugurate and carry through a program of world education for teachers which will make all previous efforts in this area appear prehistoric.

The United States has a program of teacher exchange with the United Kingdom which involves a few hundred teachers. What the United States needs in any year is to have at least one thousand American teachers in various other English-speaking countries and at least nine thousand teachers in other parts of the world. If these numbers seem large, consider the fact that they total only about one percent of all the teachers in the United States. They are probably far too small.

Contribution of Education to World Security Through Improved Communication

A chief contribution that education can make and is making to world security is in the field of communication. The improvement of world communication is a chief requirement for the improvement of world security.

The chief instrument of education is, and always has been, communication. Without communication, indeed, children grow up almost as inarticulate and brutish as certain other mammals. This has been fairly well demonstrated by cases where association of children with other human beings has been very limited. The educational need for processes and tools of communication has been recognized for a long time. Probably for as long as men have carried on education at all, they have seen that attainment of a certain level of communication skills was required to move the individual effectively into the small group of family or village. At some later time in their development, they came to see that another and higher level of communication was required to move the small group effectively into the larger group of clan, tribe, state, or nation. Today, all over the world, they are beginning to search for those communication facts and skills which will help move states and nations into effective membership in a world society.

In this paper, I shall try to examine some educational phases of the search for improved means of communication, with particular regard to the objective of securing and maintaining world peace and security.

The primitive savage saw that a child had to be directed, rewarded, admonished, punished, practiced in skills, and given patterns of socially approved behavior by words, gestures, demonstrations, symbols, signs, and other means of communication. The child could and often did learn all by himself, but what he learned alone was infinitesimal beside what he could learn with others and was less likely to be socially desirable.

From primitive societies to modern national systems, therefore, education has been increasingly tied to communication skills, devices, and patterns. The relationship has been so close, indeed, that whole structures of education have been organized around particular instruments of communication, and communication vehicles have become again and again the actual objectives of elaborate systems of schooling.

The Chinese, for example, developed ideographic writing as an instrument for communication among groups with different spoken languages. It was and is

A paper read before the March 27, 1947, meeting of the North Central Association in Chicago.

a truly international means of communication in that it transmits ideas in any languages which the writer and readers happen to know. Thus the ideograph for *horse* means *cheval, caballo, pferd, sunka wakan*, or any other word for that animal which any people in the world wish to employ, without any regard whatsoever to differences among the languages. "Chinese" writing is not Chinese at all in the sense that it conveys the description of any Chinese speech. It is Chinese only because the Chinese have developed and used it.

The ideographic writing was extremely useful to a people like the Chinese who were trying to have peace and security in an association of peoples with widely varying languages. It was an indispensable instrument in particular to the leaders of this association of peoples. It was a great aid to those who had to direct the economy, administer the laws, and organize the defense of the Empire.

It was not because the Chinese were just peculiar, therefore, that they developed the system of long study of classic literature in the ideographic writing as a preparation for the imperial civil service. It was because, having discovered and developed a valuable communication instrument for holding varied groups of people together, they had a practical need for educating leaders in the use of that instrument.

Of course, as is well known, the Chinese stressed this particular communication instrument until the process became the goal of education, and even in the activity of reading and writing the ideographic symbols, form and technique assumed greater and greater importance over the dwindling values of content and purpose in communication until the whole system of Chinese education as viewed by foreign eyes was startling in its sterility, formalism, and uselessness. What had once been an educational instrument of great sweep and power for people seeking security in larger and larger groups had been reduced to a burlesque of learning by educators who, having forgotten their goals, redoubled their efforts in each succeeding generation.

The tendency of a particular communication instrument to be fastened upon schools and to become the objective rather than the tool of education has been demonstrated in many parts of the world other than China. Over a period of twenty-five centuries, European education passed from the schools of Athens where reading was much less important than songs, recitation, dialogues, and athletic games to schools where the study of printed books was the all-dominant feature of instruction. Most of the bookish schools of the world today have hardly yet recognized the development of the radio, the phonograph, and the motion picture. With the more recent development of television and the recording of language by such methods as magnetizing a wire or the iron oxide surface of a plastic ribbon which can be played back without needle contact, or wear, the relative importance of printed books in education may well decline.

To move local and national groups into improved relationships with one another, these and other new, direct, and fast means of communication are available. The most effective education for world security will test and employ every possible instrument of communication without falling into the ancient pedagogical pit of believing that one method or means of conveying thought has of itself more educational force than some other device or instrument. There is nothing in a "comic" strip which makes it inherently a poorer instrument than a book for teaching history, geography, morals, manners, or international understanding. What book? What kind of comic strip? These are the important educational decisions, rather than convictions that books are educational and comic strips are not, that a library is always a university of knowledge and a movie theater is merely a place of entertainment, and that in general any one form of communication has higher educational values in itself than does any other form of communication.

The greatest world educational need in the field of communication is one of which men have been aware for many centuries. It is the need, not for learning how to transmit ideas by new mechanical devices, but for education in the improvement of language itself as a means of world communication.

The notion of a "universal" language is very old. Both practical men of affairs and impractical visionaries have been attracted for centuries to the idea of developing a common tongue for purposes of improved understanding among cooperating groups. The idea, furthermore, contrary to popular opinion, has been successfully worked out in a number of instances. Of course, it has more often been unsuccessful. When it has been successful, relatively large numbers of people, acting under the spur of great historical movements, have made and spread the "universal" language. English, Arabic, Greek, Latin, Spanish, French, Russian, Turkish, Persian, and other tongues in certain times and places have become world languages in their respective "worlds." They have been taught and learned as second languages for purposes of commerce, travel, diplomacy, war, socal ornamentation, and all the other uses to which people put a language which crosses local or national boundaries. Such languagues have often risen from the status of second language to first languages, supplanting the original native tongues among peoples who discovered the advantages of adopting them.

These facts are mentioned here because there seems today to be an unusual amount of pessimism abroad in the world concerning the possibility of developing a second language for all the world so that all men could talk to one another directly, as they can see one another today by motion pictures. To every suggestion for the development of a second language these pessimists cry, "Impractical! It can't be done! Visionary!" The peoples of England once made such a language and then made it into a first language of such relative simplicity of grammar, wealth of vocabulary, strength, vitality, and flexibility that today only its incredible system of spelling keeps it from being the most popular choice of half the population of the world for a universal language.

On the other side of the picture, there is a tendency for all spoken languages to split into dialects and then into separate languages. In fairly recent times, for example, in spite of common literatures, Dutch has become Netherlands Dutch, Flemish, and Afrikaans; Norse has moved away from Danish and is now dividing itself into Riksmaal and Landsmaal; Canadian and Parisian French have drawn apart; and American and European forms of English, Portuguese, and Spanish have become differentiated.

Everybody in the world has a need for command of a language or of languages which are international in use. Obviously if there could be one of these languages agreed upon for everybody in the world, the educational advantages for teaching world cooperation would be very great.

At the same time, people all over the world need mother tongues, as distinct and local in words and accents as any group, however small, may desire. That need is present with all of us. It is why some of the Norwegians have been developing Landsmaal; it is why you and I say *schedule* and *again* though all the weight of Oxford may be thrown in favor of *skedule* and *agayne*. We just want to talk a home talk, and in this respect we are like the speakers of Bantu, Basque, Breton, Esthonian, Frisian, Galician, Lettish, Maltese, Manx, Romani, Ruthenian, Tagalog, Welsh, or Wend.

It seems clear, therefore, that everybody needs to learn and use two languages, one a "universal" language for general communication, the other a home language for local communication.

There was a time in Europe when this situation was approached. Latin was the universal language. It was taught in all the schools. University students and professors, for example, could transfer from Salamanca to Bologna, Paris, Oxford, Uppsala, Heidelberg, or Prague with no linguistic difficulty. Church services and law suits were conducted in Latin everywhere. Scholars from the tiniest countries with the least known home languages published their works and communicated with their fellow scholars in other countries as easily as those whose vernaculars were French or Italian. Comenius could be a world figure in education though his native tongue was a minor language, because he could use Latin and everybody of schooling knew Latin. What would Comenius use today? He would have to decide to learn to write Russian, English, German, or French, and whatever language he might select he would leave out of his readers a large number of scholars.

We say this world is smaller today than ever before. Actually, in many respects, it is today bigger and its parts are more isolated from one another than in the days of Comenius. From the standpoint of world security alone, the problem of teaching a second language is one of the most pressing problems of our time. The greatest obstacle in the way of selecting and teaching such a language is not a technical problem relating to the difficulties of any language. It is rather a problem of political jealousies, racial antagonisms, religious differences, and linguistic loyalties. Every person would like to have a world language if it could be his native language.

It was for this reason that various languages have been made up specifically to meet special inter-group needs, like the *lingua franca* of the Crusades, the Chinook jargon of the northwest American coast, and the various modern "artificial" languages, so-called.

One of the greatest international services that could be performed by UNESCO would be to set up an institute of lingusitics where, with the help of world associations of language scholars, the improvement and development of some second language for international use could be carried on with an impartiality and authority hardly possible to private or national organizations.

Such a solution of the world language problem will not be made easily, but I think it will be made. It will be helped by the process already under way whereby the world has developed its present four or five chief international languages. It is possible that this number will tend to become smaller in the next fifty years, and that by the end of this century two or three main languages will be taught as second languages throughout the world.

* * * * *

Among the various objections which can be made against the establishment of such an institution, there are two which seem to me to be of prime importance.

The first of these is the objection of cost. Such a university would presumable require a budget which in time might equal that of the University of Chicago, for instance. One reply to this objection would be that, although this would be a large budget for a university, it would be a trifling amount compared with the annual military expenditure of even a single small country. In the present state of world affairs, most of us would understand why any country, large or small, would wish to spend considerable amounts of money on its defense. Such expenditure would have a possible value for its future security. The expenditure of a comparable sum on a university of world significance would also seem to have a possible value for future world security.

The second of these objections is that students and professors might come from narrow national situations to the international university and there be exposed to ideas not current or even acceptable in their own countries. The reply that many citizens of a country like the United States would make to this objection is that we believe with such of our distinguished countrymen as Benjamin Franklin, Thomas Jefferson, and Justice Oliver Wendall Holmes that the truest test of the worth of any idea is its ability to get itself accepted in the market place of free competition, in the arena of intellectual and reasonable combat with fairness to all and favors to none, and that our undying hostility is not directed against any product of thought and imagination as such, but against "every form of tyranny over the mind of man."

If the international university succeeded in becoming only in small part such a free market place of ideas, such as arena for the fair testing of the products of human intellect, such a bulwark against tyranny over the mind of man, it would help move the practice of communication for world security to levels of which we do not now commonly dream.

"*If, if,*" you may say. "If it succeeds! But what if it fails to achieve all or even a small part of these great objectives? What then?"

Why, then, I should say, we will modify it or discard it and seek other effective means to attain these high purposes — means which we shall better know how to select and operate because of our earlier experience. We shall then at least be men who have dared greatly for great goals and not men who have humbly confessed we were whipped before we began to fight.

Education in a Democracy

The men who wanted to establish a high school in a little Western town forty years ago seemed to have the weaker arguments that day.

"If we set up this high school," they said, "we will attract a lot of new people to this town. We will increase property valuations. We will bring more trade to our local merchants. In spite of increased taxation, this high school will make our town more prosperous."

They said these things earnestly but somewhat abashedly. They were obviously ashamed to have to make such materialistic appeals to the voters at the school meeting, but at the same time they seem fully convinced that only such appeals had any chance of affecting the final vote.

The opposition's arguments sounded much more effective.

"Sure we need a high school in this town," they said, "but we need paved streets more than we need a high school. Look at that mud out there. You can't drive a buckboard through some of it in the spring now, and in the summer the dust is fetlock-deep. We need an electric light plant too — probably more than we need a high school. Are we going to use coal oil forever? We need new fire equipment. You get a blaze started here in a high wind and this town will go up like a powder box. We need a new courthouse. Lane County's got a new courthouse, and we never heard Lane County is better than this county. We need all these things and more. Where are we going to get the money for what we need? We're taxed now more than we can bear! Sure we need a new high school. We need a lot of things, but we have got to use some common sense. Where are you going to get the money for all these things this town needs?"

The outlook for the high school was admittedly very dark. The only doubt possible appeared to be the size of the majority in opposition to the proposal for the high school.

Then the Old Rancher got to his feet, twisting his battered hat nervously, seemingly so embarrassed that he could hardly be heard as he first addressed the chair.

But this seeming embarrassment was only an uncouscious pose. This man had great prestige. He had worn the mantle of that prestige so long that he was unconscious of it, and his seeming humility was merely that of a man who did not want to be thought uppity, high-toned, or too big for his breeches. He had

The Annals of the American Academy of Political and Social Science, Vol. 265, September, 1949, pp. 10-16. Used by permission of the American Academy of Political and Social Science.

not been a humble man when he had ridden into the valley at the head of his wagons, a rifle under his left stirrup leather, and the end of his .44-40 holster tied to his right leg for an easy draw. He had not been a humble man as he built up his herds and broke the land for his field. He was not humble today and not embarrassed even though his voice trembled at the beginning of his speech.

"I hear the boys tellin' what this town needs. This town needs this and that, they tell us. I'll tell you what this town needs more'n it needs anything else. It needs better and smarter folks, and the only way I know to get 'em is to educate 'em up to it. We've always figured in this valley that one man was as good as another, and sometimes a damn-sight better. How are these boys goin' to have a chance to be a damn-sight better unless we give 'em the best education we can?"

The old man's final sentences were cracking like pistol shots. His neighbors looked at one another with slight grins and voted for the new high school.

This scene was repeated many times with many variations but always with the same direction in the history of the American frontier. It was characteristic of the frontier that the men who walked or paddled or rode into new lands believed that democracy was not old but new, that its structure was not set long ago but was something which needed remodeling and sometimes drastic repair, and that its functions were *not* the same yesterday, today, and forever.

Men holding such beliefs were compelled to build schools – not replicas of something back in the old settlements, but schools that were new in their purposes and practices. They had to be new in their purposes and practices if one man was going to be given an equal break with another man so that he could demonstrate his individual worth, so that he could be as good as another man and sometimes better.

In this sense, the American concept of democracy was based squarely on the American concept of public education. Notions of government and schooling on this continent, European at first, came to be very un-European.

In Europe, if a people were ruled by an aristocracy, whether of blood or of brains, it seemed all right for them to set up a double-barreled school system, with "higher" education for the higher classes to give them the special skills and the wisdom needed for good government, and "lower" instruction for the masses to train them in patters of diligence, docility, and devotion, to their divinely appointed leaders and institutions.

If, on the other hand, as in America, a people believed that they themselves should rule themselves, and if they sought to put this notion into practice, they were forced into militant support of a single system of free, public, compulsory, universal education. Only thus could they help to give all children equality of oportunity to be as good as anyone else and as much better as the development of their unique capacities permitted.

The difference between European and American concepts of education and democracy was steadily widened throughout the nineteenth century. "To bring up the children of the poor in the principles of the Established Church and to make them content in that station of life to which it hath pleased God to call them" was an English formulation of the objective of mass education which was accepted by many Americans in 1800. By 1900 it was rejected by most of them with brusque contempt.

In 1798, a great English supporter of improved public education argued in dignified fashion that one of the blessings of schooling for the masses was that it set up a bulwark against the inroads of democratic ideas.

> *The principal argument which I have heard advanced against a system of national education in England is, that the common people would be put in a capacity to read such words as those of Paine, and that the consequences would probably be fatal to government. But on this subject I agree most cordially with Adam Smith in thinking, that an instructed and well-informed people would be much less likely to be led away by inflammatory writings, and much better able to detect the false declamation of interested and ambitious demagogues, than an ignorant people. One or two readers in a parish are sufficient to circulate any quantity of sedition; and if these be gained to the democratic side, they will probably have the power of doing much more mischief, by selecting the passages best suited to their hearers, and choosing the moments when their oratory is likely to have the most effect, than if each individual in the parish had been in a capacity to read and judge of the whole work himself; and at the same time to read and judge of the opposing arguments, which we may suppose would also reach him.*

> *But in addition to this, a double weight would undoubtedly be added to the observation of Adam Smith, if these schools were made the means of instructing the people in the real nature of their situation; if they were taught, what is really true, that without an increase of their own industry and prudence no change of government could essentially better their condition; that, though they might get rid of some particular grievance, yet in the great point of supporting their families they would be but little, or perhaps not at all benefited; that a revolution would not alter in their favour the proportion of the supply of labour to the demand, or the quantity of food to the number of the consumers; and that if the supply of labour were greater than the demand, and the demand for food greater than the supply, they might suffer the utmost severity of want, under the freest, the most perfect, and the best executed government, that the human imagination could conceive.*

> *A knowledge of these truths so obviously tends to promote peace and quiteness, to weaken the effect of inflammatory writings and to prevent all unreasonable and ill-directed opposition to the constituted authorities, that those who would still object to the instruction of the*

people may be fairly suspected of a wish to encourage their ignorance, as a pretext for tyranny, and an opportunity of increasing the power and influence of the executive government.[1]

One hundred and thirty-five years after Malthus wrote this statement, an American Schoolman warned his fellow citizens:

In its fundamental purpose, it is only too manifest that the public school system has not succeeded. Nor has it utterly failed. The production of a sound and intelligent citizen involves something more than teaching him to read. Indeed, unless something more than that is done, it is probably safer for people not to learn to read at all, for it only places a new and immensely powerful weapon in the hands of the demagogues and the literary psychopaths. But, until a very recent period, the schools have not been able to get and keep most pupils long enough to teach them much more than reading. Actually a formidable proportion of the whole voting strength of the nation cannot yet, in any true sense, read. They pass as literate. They can read highway signs and newspaper headlines, but they balk even at subtitles in the moving pictures. They cannot read discourse, especially expository discourse. They were not in school long enough to learn.[2]

This was the great fear that haunted many leaders of European and American societies alike — that the common people might be educated too much, that they might learn to think wrong thoughts, and that they might thereby become discontented with things as they were..

In England, this fear delayed the establishment of a national system of free elementary education for at least a century. As late as 1916 in the debates on the Fisher Act, a member of the House of Commons could inquire bitterly, "What is it that the Honorable Gentlemen would do? Would they stuff Latin and Greek down the throats of agricultural laborers' children with one hand while taking away their bread and butter with the other?" In the United States it furnished the backbone of opposition to the nineteenth century battles for secular, free, compulsory, elementary education, and it is still observable in attacks on the public schools, in attacks on higher education, and in the hysterical activities of self-appointed textbook "purifiers."

The real argument against public schools and in favor of parochial school has been for more than a century that children would learn godless things in the former and would learn only godly things in the later. The main argument against free education has been that only the economically superior classes can safely be entrusted with schooling.

[1]Thomas Robert Malthus, *An Essay on the Principles of Population*, book IV, chap. IX (1798), as quoted in Ellwood P. Cubberley, *Readings in the History of Education* (Boston: Houghton Mifflin, 1920), p. 522.

[2]Henry C. Morrison, *The Evolving Common School* (Cambridge: Harvard University Press, 1933), pp. 57-58.

In spite of these fears and arguments, however, for more than a century and a half the American people as a whole have steadily implemented their belief that an effective democracy requires an effective education for all its members and that men who have the right and duty to order their own ways for their own benefit must also accept the obligation of changing their ways through education in the direction of their own ideas. The American people have carried out this belief by setting up the most extensive system of public elementary schools in the world, by establishing secondary schools at an unprecedented rate of increase over the past half century, and by higher education to millions of young people who, under other societies, would have no opportunity to achieve more than simple literacy.

In practice, the Americans know that they still have a long way to go to achieve their goal of a completely universal education for a completely democratic society. Even on the elementary level, the American child's chances for education are tied to such factors as the locality in which he lives, his parents' economic and social levels, his color, his race, and his religion. On the secondary level, these conditions have even greater weights in reducing the democratic character of the education offered. In higher education, the inequalities caused by wealth, race, and religion are particularly severe and constitute one of the most pressing and serious problems faced by the American public today.

The state is theoretically the supreme educational authority and agency in this country. In practice it delegates much of its responsibility to individuals and private agencies. The Supreme Court, furthermore, in interpreting the Fourteenth Amendment, has assumed the power to decide whether state educational legislation deprives any citizen of life, liberty, or property without due process of law. Thus the court declared unconstitutional an Oregon law of 1922 requiring attendance at public schools of all children eight to sixteen years of age, on the grounds that it abridged the liberty of parents to educate their children in specific faiths and that it deprived corporations (private schools) of their property, without due process of law. In other decisions the Supreme Court has further clarified the concept that although the state's authority is paramount in education, its requirements must be reasonable and must not without good cause restrict the liberty of parents in providing unusual types of education for their children.

The value of nonpublic schools in the total pattern of education in a democracy is probably best measured by this one main question: How well does the non-public school explore areas and develop instruments which public schools cannot or do not discover and utilize? Many of the features of our modern American educational system were first adopted and tested by private schools. Kindergartens, industrial arts courses, music programs, child health work, physical education, commercial training, and graphic arts were all pioneered by private schools before they were made parts of the public educational offering. Nursery schools are today being operated mainly by private agencies. After they are developed and evaluated sufficiently, they will be taken over in many cases by the public schools. Adult education is still largely a private enterprise in this country, although the greatest single system of education for adults is operated by the United States Department of Agriculture.

Democracy needs a continuous stream of cultivated idiosyncrasy, developed individuality, and tested variations from the norm if it is to be progressive and dynamic rather than crystallized and static. A wide variety of nonpublic education is necessary in achieving this objective.

A totalitarian state must have education of the masses for mass goals. The state itself is regarded as being an end in itself, something to be worshiped and served for its own sake. Schools for totalitarian purposes must therefore be very different institutions from those of democratic societies. The totalitarian school must have cut-and-dried programs set by the national leaders and followed by the teachers and pupils unquestioningly. This simple fact dooms any totalitarian system to steady intellectual and emotional deterioration. Its teachers become more and more obedient mechanics of word and action; its pupils become parrots and automatons.

A democratic society is composed of individuals, recognized and treated as such. It has no existence except in its people. It has no purpose except the welfare of its individual citizens. The democratic state is not regarded as a sacred, unchanging entity; it is merely an instrument whereby its citizens order and direct their individual ways in association with one another.

The school for a democratic society must therefore be one in which the learners change their individual ways in the direction of their own ideals. This is not to say that teachers and parents in a democracy have less educational influence than in an autocracy. They are, in fact, much more influential in the school for democracy. In every phase of the child's growth and development, in every learning activity, the educators for democracy must examine and re-examine, scrutinize and evaluate, review and revise, with never ceasing care and industry, the peculiar abilities and potentialities of every individual, the items of experience affecting the individual's development, and the various possible ways to be followed in making the democratic society a better and greater instrument of human welfare.

Teachers, parents, and citizens of a democracy in general have to understand modern educational purposes and procedures on the highest level of insight and performance. No other level is safe for democracy. The best educational practice possible is not too good for democracy.

In recent years the people of the United States have had to fight against totalitarian states with weapons of steel and flame. They are now engaged in an ideological struggle against another totalitarian regime, a struggle in which weapons of education, propaganda, political action, and economic pressure are used. Some of the people of the United States have been so frightened by these various conflicts that they have tended to do what timid, scared men often do — imitate their enemies.

Totalitarian regimes commonly have secret police which get much of their information from secret informers who are not compelled to confront in public those whom they accuse.

Totalitarian states are commonly very frightened by possible wrong thoughts on the part of public servants. They are especially concerned that teachers shall be politically "pure." They censor reading matter, particularly for schools, with nervous concern, lest an unapproved idea should infiltrate the official lines.

If the old rancher described at the beginning of this discourse were alive today, he could be given astonishing news. He could be told of certain fright reactions affecting American education which are imitation — unconscious, without doubt, but still fairly faithful copies — of totalitarian practices.

What might we report to the old man?

"We keep men from government service because they are said to have been seen with men of wrong and bad notions."

The old timer would laugh. "That would keep a lot of us out of office. Most of the men I've known have had wrong ideas some of the time. When you come down to it they've always had wrong ideas whenever they've thought different from me."

"A committee of the Congress has asked school systems and colleges throughout the country to submit lists of textbooks and supplementary readings in order to find out how much subersive literature is used in education," we could report further.

The old man's smile would fade. "The Federal Congress?" he would inquire with heavy emphasis. "What the hell has the Federal government got to do with the books used in our schools and colleges? Either you've got your wires crossed, young man, or some congressmen have got theirs crossed! If any from our state have, we'll do our best to uncross 'em in the next election."

"We are requiring special oaths of loyalty from public servants, including teachers," we report.

"Everybody ought to take an oath of office, swear to do his duty, support the Constitution, enforce the laws," comments the Old Rancher.

"These oaths are in addition," we explain.

"What for?" inquires the old man. "You've got an oath of office, haven't you? What more do you need? A man who would fudge on his oath of office wouldn't be worth a damn to you if you had him swear a dozen oaths. What's the matter with you folks? You sacred about something?"

"Well, we have to be careful," we explain. "There's so much subversive thinking going on. We don't want the privilege of government service, the privilege of teaching, or the privilege of education being given to people who have wrong ideas, disloyal attitudes, or subversive notions."

The old man chuckles. "You young folks kind of make me laugh. Privilege? I suppose you talk about duty to the government and loyalty to your school boards too. I suppose you talk about people's rights to education. Education isn't a right or a privilege either. It's just common sense. If you want people to be better and smarter for your town or your state or your nation, you've got to educate 'em up to it. Right? Privilege? It's a necessity. It's a job. It's work. It's for everybody. It's what gives our folks room according to their size and strength. Stop crying about how scared you are of wrong ideas and start working on education. Maybe if you work hard enough on it, you'll get some new ideas and find out after a while they are right ideas. You'll be surprised."

Education Faces the World Crisis

What is the job of American education in the present world situation? Before suggesting an answer or two to this question, it may be instructive to recall certain of the ways in which education has faced previous great crises. For, difficult as the present world problems are, it must be remembered that the human race has always faced severe problems, that mankind has often regarded itself as standing at the crossroads of destiny, and that the members of the current generation are children of a thousand generations, each of which generally survived its difficulties.

Perhaps one of the first tasks of education today is to remind our people, young and old, that they are not sons and daughters of ancestors who were commonly weak and timid. Their fathers and their fathers' fathers tended to be men who rode their horses straight up, carried their carbines loose in their scabbards, and backed their hands with their lives. Their mothers and their mothers' mothers were not often women afraid to drive wagons across frontiers, bear babies in the wilderness, or load rifles beside the cabin loopholes. The American legacy of ordinary, rugged courage may not perhaps be easily apparent at a time of hysterical peeping under every bed for Communist bogeymen, but it is, nevertheless, a reality which its inheritors might well more often recognize.

Americans have indeed usually faced the great crises of their history with somewhat greater stocks of courage than of certain other desirable qualities, including developed intelligence, but in this respect, of course, they are not unique. "Humanum est errare" may be translated freely to mean "It is human to have more guts than brains."

One hundred years ago the American people faced the greatest crisis in their history to date. The black clous of national division hung over them. They lived in a country which had had Harvard College for more than two centuries, Yale and William and Mary for a century and a half, Princeton, Columbia, and Pennsylvania for a century, and a substantial number of other higher educational institutions — a very substantial number, considering the populations involved. They lived in a country which had no national university, a surprising fact in view of the statesmen-like arguments, supported by a considerable bequest, from the most revered and undoubtedly the greatest of their founding fathers, President George Washington. They had a national Military Academy, it is true, which had been operating for about thirty years, and a national Naval Academy

An address to the 1950 annual meeting of the American Council on Education.

only five years old; but neither of those institutions was more than a trade school, with little national appeal, as the wholesale resignations of Military Academy graduates for service against the United States were to demonstrate eleven years later. In all fairness, it should be added, of course, that a number of very distinguished Southern graduates of the Military and Naval Academies fought for the United States in 1861-65.

In 1850 the United States of America faced dissolution. Many of its people generally recognized that it was moving rapidly to a crisis. Other countries in various parts of the world, some of them far less advanced than the United States, with markedly fewer educational facilities, had already abolished slavery peaceably or would do so within a few years. What were the best efforts the political leaders of the United States could make to face this crisis in 1850?

I suppose most of us would agree that the main efforts of that year were the Compromise of 1850 and the revival and strengthening of the Fugitive Slave Act of 1793. California was admitted to the Union as a free state, but Utah and New Mexico were made territories with no ban on slavery. All police and peace officers in free states were directly ordered, under threat of stringent federal penalties, to cooperate with pursuers of runaway slaves. Some of them refused, and certain types of lawbreaking became socially and patriotically correct in a dozen Northern states. When Daniel Webster of New Hampshire, Massachusetts, and Dartmouth College supported the Compromise of 1850, whose chief architect was Henry Clay of Virginia, Kentucky, and three years in a country school, the Yankee was denounced as a traitor by his Abolitionist constituents, and the Southerner was regarded as having put the final touch on a long career of fence-straddling.

The truth of the matter lay far deeper than political evasion or expediency. It is a truth we do not like to face even after a hundred years. Clay, Webster, their colleagues in political life, the people of the United States were too ignorant, too uneducated, to avoid the catastrophe toward which the country was moving at a steadily accelerated pace. They had to kill one-fifteenth of their number and set themselves back into barbarism, because they were not smart enough to buy the peaceful progress after which they vainly yearned. These people were conscious of the need for peace; they could state flatly, or in the rolling periods of neoclassical oratory, their willingness to pay a just and proper price for peace; but they lacked the necessary balance in their intellectual banks to cover that price.

The people of this country in 1850, as now, knew that there was one price they could always pay for peace, if forced by circumstances to do so. That price was the price of organized violence, the price of applied physical force, the price of warfare.

We know today the unsatisfactory nature of a peace bought by war, and our people knew it in 1850, in 1861. They knew that the price of war was too high for civilized men to pay, yet they met a situation where they had to have peace, and the old, uncivilized coin was all they had on hand to make the purchase. So they threw their money down on the blanket — their money and their guns — their rifles and their ships — their men and women. They were a proud people, and when they decided they had to pay the price of violence for peace, they shot the works.

In this description no hint or criticism of our people's thoroughness in war is implied. We are properly proud of our people in war. We are proud that they are the kind of people who are willing, if necessary, to shoot the works, who are willing to buy a required peace with any available currency.

We shall have cause to be even prouder of them, however, when they have higher resources in their national treasuries than the price of organized violence — the resources of greatly increased political efficiency, of stronger economic systems, and of heightened spiritual integrity. nations are not born with money in their pockets to pay these higher prices. They have to earn the political, the economic, and the spiritual currencies required for those payments. They have to earn these funds by their own efforts. They cannot get economic intelligence by a loan from another power. They cannot inherit political efficiency from an army of occupation. They cannot attain spiritual integrity except by their own efforts. They have to pay these higher prices in terms of their own developed intelligence, their own matured character, and their own creative imagination.

These things are precisely the objectives and the measures of the education that was needed but was too scarce in the year 1850, and that is needed and is still too scarce in the United States today, and that must extend over all the world if we are to avoid coming again and again face to face with situations where the only coin we have to pay for an absolutely required peace is war.

The development of the education we need in the United States and in our sister states throughout the world cannot be attained by exhortation or even by prayer alone, of course. There are many specific measures which we need to put into action by hard work in this particular year of crisis.

Specifically, in order to have a better educational basis for improved political intelligence, economic efficiency, and spiritual integrity for all our people, we need, in the United States, federal aid to education. A bill has already passed the Senate and is bottled up in the House of Representatives which would provide that federal aid and would leave to the states the decision as to the extent to which such services to the child as transportation, health services, and school lunches should be granted to parochial as well as to public school pupils. The members of the House of Representatives, and, more specifically, the members of the Rules Committee, do not have enough developed political intelligence to put that bill, or a necessarily amended version of it, through the legislative mill.

Is it money we lack for this measure? Of course not. Even the members of the Congress who shout most loudly about economy know that it is not chiefly money we are lacking. The United State's greatest economy spokesman, the senior senator from Virginia, recognized the abundance of available federal money when he voted for new veterans hospitals which the Veterans Administration declares it does not need, has no medical staff to operate, and for which it cannot get the medical staff because Congress has no money for such purposes. The cost of a few weeks of recovery aid to Europe, of one minor battle in World War II, or of an almost unnoticeable skirmish in World War III would cover much more than the proposed annual cost of federal aid to education. We have plenty of money for federal aid to education; we do not have enough developed intelligence for federal aid.

We will have to develop enough intelligence as Catholics for example, to recognize that the United States of America is a great Protestant country, not only in formal church membership, but also in some of the basic traditions of more than one hundred millions of its people, and that a clerical-religious approach to the question of public education which may be suitable to a fine, little, green, and very Catholic country of three million people, and to which many of our greatest clerics are tied by kinship, is not always appropriate in the United States.

We will have to develop enough intelligence as Protestants, for further example, to recognize that the United States of America is a great Catholic country, the greatest Roman Catholic country in the world, both in terms of the numbers of the church's communicants and in the political and economic power it wields. A blindness to the great liberal resources of Catholicism and a rigid and uncompromising adherence to doctrinaire notions of the "separation" of church and state which may have been suitable to American conditions in the days of Horace Mann are not always appropriate to the United States today.

We will have to develop enough intelligence as voters to become more keenly aware of the disgrace and the danger to which we can bring the United States by selecting our local, state, and national representatives without sufficient regard to the intellectual and spiritual burdens they will have to carry for us.

Such outcomes require not only that everybody be educated, but also that everybody be given a dynamic and purposeful schooling as far above the general run-of-the-mill education of today in quality as the present level of our studies of individuals and communities will permit. Moreover, such outcomes require of us, with even greater force than of a people not aspiring to give education to everybody, that we afford special education to specially selected individuals on a scale more extended and a level more elevated than are possible or acceptable in a system where less than universal education is attempted. The second of these requirements, when carried into effect, will have profound impacts on higher education in this country — impacts of such tidalwave proportions as to reduce to pondlike ripples the mere influx of veterans and expansion of physical facilities in the years immediately following the late war.

A program of federally financed scholarships and fellowships, along the lines recommended in 1947 by the President's Commission on Higher Education should be and eventually will be established. It will in time be financed by federal appropriations to an extent which would now be regarded generally as fantastic.

The people of the United States set up early in their history the goal of a universal elementary school and pressed toward that goal resolutely and steadily. They moved then, after a generation of hesitation, to the ideal of a universal secondary school to which they are coming closer every day in practice. They passed then with little hesitation to the notion of a post-secondary education of some kind for all their youth, and they are implementing that notion with extraordinary speed. That they will hesitate, in the long run, to use in general support of higher education the instrument of federal grants, which they have long employed in certain phases of higher education, is improbable. Authorities in higher education may argue about the advisability of such grants. The people of the United States have already made their decision. They will make those grants, in my opinion, within the next decade.

There is another phase of the national effort in higher education which has not been discussed very much in recent years and which is of the highest importance in our efforts to prepare ourselves more effectively to meet the present world crisis and the series of continuing crises of which the history of the second half of the twentieth century will likely be composed. I refer to the higher educational activities of various branches of the federal government.

The United States Department of Agruculture's so-called Graduate School, the three academies and the numerous higher professional schools of the armed forces, the two teachers colleges, and the one university operated by the federal government in the District of Columbia, the Library of Congress, the National Research Council, the Smithsonian Institution, the Bureau of Ethnology, the Bureau of Standards, the many government research organizations, ranging from the great naval and military laboratories to the plant industry station, and the numerous special training tasks carried on for various departments of the federal government by universities – all these are merely a few samples of a tremendous scope of federal activity in research, instruction, and service on a higher education level.

I do not pretend to know which of such activities would be improved by being associated with a University of the United States, but I suspect that many of them would benefit greatly by such an association. I am convinced that the university system of education offers an instrument for doing some of these jobs much better than they are now done.

I assume that such a university would be set up like an American university, that is, with an appointed policy-making board of laymen, an executive officer elected by the board, and faculty members designated by the board on recommendation of the executive. In addition to the usual executive officer, it might be well to establish the un-American custom of appointing annually a prestige officer who could be called the rector or chancellor, whose duties would be ornamental, and who would normally be a distinguished elder statesman, soldier, industrialist, or perhaps in time – about 1980 – a scholar.

The University of the United States might well give instruction only to advanced graduate and post-doctoral students. In this respect, particularly in fields where the federal government needs to train specialists for its own activities, it would extend the kinds of services now being performed in distinguished fashion by such agencies at the Princeton School of Advanced Studies and the Harvard advanced fellowships in journalism and education. In the field of advanced military studies alone such a university would be in a position to furnish instructional and research services of a value far exceeding the cost of the whole institution. It would seem, further, that there might profitably be established a system of institutional memberships in this university whereby higher educational institutions and learned societies, both in this country and abroad, eventually could be associated with the University of the United States for the exchange of professors, advanced students, and research services. Speculation on the details of organization of such an institution is, of course, an idle pastime. The jobs which such a university would have handed to it immediately would determine much of its organization.

I have spoken of three kinds of possible federal support of education: (1) general federal aid to the states for elementary and secondary education, (2) a program of federal scholarships and fellowships for selected college and university students, and (3) a national university on the highest levels of instruction and research in fields of particular interest to government agencies. These are merely examples of the kind of educational enterprises which, in my opinion, should be undertaken by the federal government. Other examples could well be given, not only in the federal area, but also in the fields of state-supported, state-aided, and private education.

Many people have spoken of research and instructional needs in the humanities, in the social studies, and the natural sciences which the present crisis has intensified. The American people know how or have the necessary skills for learning how to develop these programs of education on any level. Their lacks are not so much in their "know-how" as in their "want-what." In the increasing amount of governmental support, national, state, and local, that is coming for education in this country, there are certain dangers, certain "don't-want-whats" which the people of the United States will seek to avoid, if they recognize them for what they are.

One of these dangers arises from a long-held belief, current over much of the world, that a bookish education, a literary-verbal training, a scientific-technological preparation, or some other combination of schooling skills is in itself the end of education, and that such a collection of activities can be given in an academic corner under a strict system of thought control. This is a very old belief. It has been tested in practice many times. Again and again a dictator, a totalitarian regime, a ruling class, or some other papa-knows-best agency has attempted to set up an educational system to study only approved doctrines, to search only for approved truth, and to produce only conformers to an approved regime.

Any system of education which requires conformity to a prescribed dogma in any field of study is digging its own grave in that field. All great educational achievement is the result of an intelligent search for, and a skillful cultivation of, idiosyncrasy. Any system which penalizes idiosyncrasy and puts a premium on conformity in intellectual matters will produce more bureaucrats than statesmen, more mechanics than scientists, more bill posters than artists, and more soap-opera hacks than dramatists.

There are plenty of people in the world who will insist that any education supported, aided, or even tolerated by the state must submit to thought control by the state. They are the spiritual sons and daughters of hundreds of generations of men who have believed that educational systems should be totally subordinate to systems relying on force and threats of force. Their illusions have been shattered again and again from the plowed site of Carthage to the rubble heaps *Unter den Linden.* A Mussolini or a Stalin, a Franco or a Peron, can say in purple oratory that he wants first, to insure strict loyalty to his regime and second to build a great educational system. He cannot do it that way. When he tries, he sends the schools and universities of his country back more and more to such intellectual exercises as the construction of doggerel odes of devotion to the glorious leader, the elaboration of philospohical "proofs" of the party's greatness, and the meaningless repetition of ceremonies of "loyalty" to the fatherland.

To meet the world crisis today, tomorrow, and in the years to come, we Americans need vastly improved and expanded educational opportunities, supported more and more by all our people, which is to say, in large measure, by our governments. We need to develop these opportunities with a maximum of original thinking and a minimum of thought control.

Education: Maker and Breaker of Nations

The people who are in the middle of the great historical events are very often not aware of them, and I suspect that is the case with us in the United States and in the World today. Certainly the historians tell us that the Western Europeans who lived in the Dark Ages generally thought that everything was light enough. They saw no darkness around. An I suppose that the cavemen who came right at the beginning of an ice age or at the tail end of an ice age probably thought that about half the winters were warmer than they had been previously and the other half of the winters were cooler than they had been previously.

In similar fashion I think the school people of our Western World, and particularly the school people of the United States, are generally unaware of some of the most revolutionary changes in education in the last half century. One of the most important of these changes to people in comparative education and in the field of philosophy of education has been the change in our views of the nature of national systems of education.

I can remember, for example, very well when students of education — comparative education, for example — thought it was very necessary to distinguish carefully between education and propaganda, education and other behavior-changing processes that they didn't want to call education.

A customary test of education in those cases, of course, was that it included purposes with which the definer of education agreed, and only those consciously organized changes in human behavior for approved goals was something that we would call education. They had to be goals that agreed with the definers.

Today we have only some amateur students of education, who by profession work in other fields, who have that point of view.

That reminds me that I would like to make a speech some time on some amateur field. The other day I picked out the field of submarine building as a good field for me.

I have just got the first part of my book or my speech on that topic worked out. That is the argument that all submarines should be built under water. They are used under water, so why don't they build them under water? Any intelligent person can see that is where they should be built.

If the present builders can't hold their breath long enough, tell them about those divers off Korea who can hold their breath for tremendous lengths of time

Address before the 1960 annual meeting of the American Association of School Administrators, Atlantic City.

under water. Let these present builders of submarines go to Korea and learn how to hold their breath long enough to build these machines.

That is as far as I have got, but I think it's an amateur contribution and it ranks up exactly with the contributions of some of these people who know exactly what American education is and exactly what European education is or used to be.

But in these descriptions, we used to say propaganda wasn't education, advertising wasn't education, preaching wasn't education, any method of modifying the ways of people that other countries used that we disagreed with — that wasn't education either.

But the events of the twenties, the thirties, the forties, of the present century have tended to jar many of us loose from these sorts of comfortable beliefs. Americans, particularly, have been forced into situations where they have had to deal with systems of education that have been built on ideologies which they regard as false. And yet they saw powerful, comprehensive systems in action. They saw the Fascist, the Nazi, the Communist states developing over-all behavior-changing systems for all their people from the cradle to the grave, and they saw them putting powerful educational agencies to work in getting comprehensive, sweeping educational results.

Since World War II Americans have served on educational missions and consultative projects in the countries of their recent enemies and in many other countries of the world on a scale hitherto unparalleled in history. They have been forced into the role of international educational statesmen. Whether they wanted that role or not, they have had to try to serve in it. They have had to study the educational needs, wants, desires, achievements, and attmepts of countries with cultural traditions and national aims very different from their own. In these circumstances they have had to measure the quality of national systems of education by reference to broader standards than those furnished by the goals of their own culture.

It seems to me in doing that there are four measures at least which I apply when I have to do some of these jobs and which I would recommend to my associates in this field, four measures which can be used to judge the greatness or the mediocrity or the smallness of a society and of its system of education — because these two go together.

The first of these measures is the measure of the single, ruling idea. No society, it seems to me, ever became great or even failed in the grand manner that had a host of warring ideas to live by — important warring ideas to live by. This has been pointed out by some thinkers in the past much better than I could point it out.

They have often referred, for example, to the great virtue of Christianity in this respect when it first appeared among the hoplelessly warring ideologies of the Mediterranean world. The Roman Empire at that period was getting more and more brilliant in its material achievements year by year, decade by decade, and at the same time was getting more hopeless in its intellectual and spiritual outlook.

The Jewish world was getting more and more enmeshed in the subtleties of the law and the ritual.

The Greek world was dissolving into philosophical whirlpools.

And into these hopeless worlds came the Christians with their single, simple ruling faith, a faith that could perform seeming miracles in changing human attitudes and behavior rapidly and effectively and permanently.

This first measure of a great society, the single ruling idea, is also the necessary and infallible mark of a great educational system. Students of comparative education often cite nineteenth-century Scotland as an example of a single ruling idea. The Scots' doctrine of giving the maximum intellectual and spiritual training to every boy of high ability who could be discovered in their poverty-stricken land − giving him that training without regard to any other factor whatever except his high ability − made Scotland one of the wealthiest countries in the world, and the only factor that actually produces wealth in the country is the distinction of its people throughout all of the English-speaking world and much of the non-English-speaking world today.

The Scots' ideas that a man has to do the very best he can with the abilities that God has given him and then has to work harder than his competitors has geared the schools of that country in such a way that the national achievements in education have brought international prestige to the Scotsman all over the world − Scot administrators, Scot engineers, philosophers, educators.

The same thing, the single growing idea, of course, can be found in many other educational systems. It was never more dramatically shown than in the Danish social, political, agricultural revolution in the last third of the nineteenth century, when Bishop Grundtvig and his followers served the simple ruling notion that a man's religious beliefs, religious attitudes, were the controlling elements in the life of the country.

Other countries had the same idea but couldn't make it work. The Danes made it work miracles for the simple reason they believed it with no if's, and's, but's, and maybe's. They put it into action in a single type of educational system, and they put it into successful action because they has great faith in its power.

The second mark of a great society and the educational system which must serve such a society is a clearly defined field or territory of operation. The borders of the territory and the ruling idea need to be nearly the same. When the territory is a French community, for example, all of the French quality and French concern in education must cover the territory. It must not stop at the walls of Paris or at the borders of metropolitan France. The ruling idea must go to all the territory.

The third mark of a great society and of its educational system is the unified program. An by that I mean more than the educational program. Take the example of the classical Athenian democracy in its brief hour of glory. You had at that time everything in the government organized around the assembly of citizens, and in education everything was organized around the preparation of the youth.

In every other golden age I know anything about, the same fact stands out clearly if you look at it carefully. No society ever gets out of the mud of ordinary existence that does not have a total program of living and learning so that all hangs together in one integrated whole.

Let's imagine a country — I am talking about a political country, and imaginary country, since I don't wish to slight any real country. This is a country which for 50 years to my personal knowledge has alternated between dictatorships and so-called democratic regimes. These democratic regimes operate in the dark even more than the United States of America does ordinarily.

But the army leaders of this country are willing at any time to turn the guns of their tanks on the parliament or on the presidential palace. At a moment's notice they are glad to do it. And they do it in the name of constitutional democratic processes, just so it will be generally recognized that the generals in the country have the final control.

The labor unions in that country are equally willing for organized labor to call a strike.

The secondary schools and elementary schools of that country are worlds apart. They are operated by different units of government for the most part. Their teachers are educated in very different institutions and hardly regard themselves as following the same profession. They don't belong to the same fraternity, the same trade.

You don't have to be a prophet to predict the future of this society and its educational system. It has no future. Unless and until it develops an educational program, it will never have a social future or an educational future.

The fourth and final measure of a society and its school system is its dominant method of operation. If it is a great society, it never has two or three main methods. A great society cannot serve two masters in this respect. And a great educational program cannot serve successfully two separate main methodologies. It serves one with all its might.

If it is a society, for example, that relies primarily on the method of force, it has to put its main reliance on that method. That is the kind of society that would flog children in school.

If it is a society that uses some other powerful method of changing and directing human ways — the method of reason, for instance, the method of affectionate understanding, or some other such technique — it has to put its firm faith in that method and subordinate its auxiliary methods to the main method.

Up to this point I have spoken of a great society and not necessarily of a better one. I do this because there are and there have been societies and educational systems which are or have been very effective, which have been great in their accomplishments, but which we and our people regard as very bad.

We want our society and our school systems to be great and good. We want them to become greater and better. When are they better? Well, of course, that is a value judgement. They are better when they have a better ruling idea, a better territory, a better unified program, and a better dominant method — better in terms of our whole history, better in terms of our philosophy of existence, and better in terms of everything that we rank dearest.

And to answer these value questions means not only that we must search our own hearts and our own history but also that we must be in clear concord with our own people. If we attempt to be mealy-mouthed and ultra-cautious about these questions, we will never land on the level of greatness, either in our society or in our educational systems. We will probably land in that haven of mediocrity which is reserved for people who cannot fully speak their own minds because they have no minds to speak.

Starting with measure number one, what is the ruling idea of our society in the United States? Is it the ruling idea of our school systems?

The ruling idea of the Americans in 1918 or 1944, on that day when some of us went into Belleau Wood or some of us went on the beach at Anzio, was that of individual liberty, or the rights of the individual citizen. It was that for which those gentlemen in Philadelphia pledged their lives, their fortunes, and their sacred honor. It was that no matter what the Confederate lawyers may say, that sent the long Blue Columns southward in 1861. It was that which Baron von Steuben used to turn awkward, timid farm boys and apprentices, with amateur officers over them, into that unit that took Stony Point with a bayonet against a vastly superior professional force.

Here was a people who had a ruling idea in their society, who, in their stronger elements at least, were willing to support it to the death. To such people it did not seem corny either to speak of freedom or to die for it.

What is the ruling idea of this people now? I believe it is the same one, but its edges are occasionally blurred by other ideas that crowd in on it. The international tensions, foreign trade, the health of the stock market, the length of the products of Detroit — these are all important but they are not in the same catagory with the ruling category of the free man's rights. Or are they?

That blurring we see is increased by and comes largely from the circumstance that the school of this people and their society does not have a clear, ruling idea. It has a number of ideas, some of them clearly dominant, some of them antagonistic to the others.

There are persons in the United States today, for example, who seriously believe the way to improve our schools is to copy the purposes and practices of other countries, particularly, of course, European countries — not the European schools of today, actually, but of the supposed European schools of yesterday.

The present American society undoubtedly wavers at times in its support of the ruling American idea, but in the main it sticks to that idea, as its actions in emergencies will indicate. The American school, however, has drifted away from that idea. On measure number one, the American school systems lack the mark of greatness their society deserves.

On the second measure, the American school and the American society both show uncertainty. In war, in international relations, in the coinage of money, and in other activities which we regard as having great importance, we Americans tend to consider the United States or even the United Nations as our territory. But in education we attempt to stick to a rigid pattern of localism, impressive in its achievements, but now seriously outmoded in some aspects by modern developments in communication, transportation, and current governmental procedures.

We say that local pride and the dangers of bureaucratic control from state or federal authorities keep us in our localized routines. Why does not a similar type of pride and fear keep our banks from accepting United States government insurance of their deposits? Why does not local pride and the dangers of bureaucratic control prevent the states and localities from not only accepting but also earnestly seeking federal aid and supervision of highways? Is it because we believe that education is more important than national defense, the financial system, or six-lane highways with cloverleaf approaches, or is it perhaps because we believe that education is less important?

The third mark of a great society and its educational system is the measure of the unified program. Here the American society and the American school have drifted far apart. In certain aspects of the society's achievements, as in finance, in industry, and above all in warfare, the country has taken giant strides forward in developing a unified program. In education we have not moved far in that direction.

This is a curious departure from the original American tendencies in education. We started with the notion of a single-track school system for all citizens, and then we departed from that notion here and there in various ways.

In teacher education, for example, we developed German-type normal schools for training elementary teachers, and we educated our secondary-school teachers in colleges and universities. We developed junior high schools to be like the middle schools in Germany and France, and we said they were part of our secondary-school program. But we operate them, very usually, as though they were extensions of the elementary school, as indeed they probably should be.

We admit that the general education purposes of at least half of our four-year college program is secondary in character but we still resist developing the thirteenth and fourteenth years of schooling as generally as our society needs and wants. Although adult education in every great society is at the heart of the educational program, we tend to regard it in this country as a superficial, remedial enterprise to be attended to after the important educational jobs have all been done.

In the fourth measure of a dominant method for our society and our school systems, we Americans are affected by a serious lag. We sometimes fight windmills, as when a hundred thousand people or more in this country were persuaded a few years ago that the schools were not teaching children to recognize the letters in reading the English language. We still talk about "progressive" methods when there never was a time in this country when even the people who called themselves educational progressives could agree on the simplest elements of method.

To develop a dominant method in education we need to discard the notion that everything a young person needs to know in modern society has to be taught to him by an instructor, preferably taught to him in a classroom with 25, 30, or 40 other boys and girls. We may well decide as a matter of dominant method to give general education on the secondary level by teaching a few things very thoroughly rather than by giving "survey" courses over wide areas of learning. We may discover that common learnings are not so much achieved by common subject matter as by common skills and common attitudes.

In speaking of attitudes, a dominant method in our schools could well be built around the proposition that moral education is the queen of the subjects and that a great educational system will find the method that teaches it well. The usual assumption that moral education is harder to attain than intellectual education is not borne out by the facts. Good systems and bad alike, powerful and lasting in their effects, have demonstrated the opposite. Grundtvig and his followers revolutionized Denmark with a strictly moral-education approach. Hitler changed the moral pattern of a great majority of the German people in six years, and although we do not like his purposes we must admit the efficiency of his method.

When a society does not know what it regards as moral, however, when it has a shifting and flexible code of morality with different standards for adults than for children, and when it speaks for one standard and practices another, it finds moral education difficult if not impossible to achieve.

These are the general levels we Americans attain on the four measures of greatness in a society and in the schools, as I see them.

What can we Americans attain on these measures? I am not speaking here as a visionary, I think, but as a practical schoolman required by my job to look at national tates as they make or break themselves as educational systems. It is a practical and considered conclusion that I offer here when I say that we Americans have, right now, at this historical moment, an opportunity to obtain an education which serves the society that never so far has been extended in this sweeping fashion to any nation.

We have for our great single ruling idea one which all the world looks at today with deep respect no matter how many curtains they are behind. We have a revolutionary history, along with this idea, which makes every other revolution of the last 200 years look pallid by comparison. And yet we seem to be afraid of it. At least we don't mention it in certain countries that are having revolutions.

We have an unique opportunity to make the whole modern world a cooperative area of cooperating nations. Relations with Asia, Africa, and Europe can be improved by relatively small amounts of money, large amounts of common sense, and few administrative surgical operations on government-aid machinery.

In the area of the unified program we have the most skillful core of educational workers in this country.

In the area of the dominant method, we have developed an increasing number of skills, decade by decade, in the teachers and administrators who, far better than those in any other part of the world, know how to use a method dominated by the concept of the individual learner. The individual is guided to his utmost potential for himself and his people.

Can we Americans capture this opportunity? We administrators, we teachers, we school board members cannot do so by our own efforts alone. We have to be involved in the necessary changes, of course, but the drive, the motive power, for these changes must come from the great body of our people, not from just a few of them, but from a massive representation of them. We school people can sound clear calls to arouse and inform our people; we can plant banners around which they will rally; we can serve them as technicians and executives. In our kind of society, however, the basic reforms must be understood, accepted, and carried out by the people themselves.

When and if this is done in the United States, I am sure that the rest of the world will regard it as a miracle in the general area of school-community relations and adult education.

Only in our kind of society can such a miracle occur. But our kind of people will know very well that it will not be really a miracle, but merely the results of hard and devoted labor inspired by an ambition for greatness in our society and in the schools which circle it.

Foreword to TRUE FAITH AND ALLEGIANCE

To you teachers of America, we sound this call.

It is a call to action, dangerous action, action which must be taken speedily and against great obstacles. It is a call to action in which a single misstep on the part of any of you may bring personal disaster. It is not an action for weak or timid men and women.

We will not talk of danger to you, however, for you are more commonly moved into action by the spur of courage than by the whip of fear. You come from fighting ancestry. Indian, Negro, Scotch, Irish, English, Welsh, French, German, Spanish, Slav, Scandinavian, and Magyar; these are samples of your many racial origins, all of them rich in the history of herosim. By blood and by tradition, you are sons and daughters of all those Americans, from Crispus Attucks and Colonel Warren to Joe Martinez and Simon Bolivar Buckner, who died in gallant action that the United States might become and remain a democracy.

There are those among you today who fought at St. Lo and the Bulge, at Anzio or in the Coral Sea, on the beaches of Guadalcanal or the Slopes of Attu, deep under the surface of enemy waters or high over the flak-carpeted skies of Germany and Japan. Many of you have lost a friend, a sweetheart, a brother, a husband, or a son in one of these or other great land, sea, or air battles of the late war.

To you, therefore, we will not speak of fear for the future but of courage for the future.

You are, most of you, Catholics, Jews, or Protestants. Some of the toughest road blocks in the action to which we are calling you will arise from prejudices for and against various religious groups. We know that you are pledged to fight these prejudices as a matter of principle. Those who founded and developed your systems of worship were agreed on the doctrine of the brother-hood of all men and the religious requirement that all men should serve all men. Loyalty to the highest concepts of the Jewish-Christian beliefs demands support of this doctrine in every classroom and in every community in this land.

The Foreword and the sections by the Ex-Sergeant of Infantry, the Elementary Teacher, and the Superintendent of the North Central City Schools have all been taken from *True Faith and Allegiance,* which Dr. Benjamin wrote as chairman of the National Education Association's Commission for the Defense of Democracy Through Education, in 1950. Permission from the National Education Association to quote from this publication is gratefully acknowledged.

This is the foundation of the democratic society to which you and your people have long borne flaming allegiance. This is the heart of the religions to which you and your people have given steadfast devotion. This is the soul of your greatest national documents.

We hold these truths to be self-evident, that all men are created equal and that they are endowed by their Creator with certain inalienable rights . . . in order to form a more perfect union.

Thou knowest, O Man, what is good, and what doth the Lord require of thee but to do justly and love mercy and walk humbly with they God.

That government of the people, by the people, and for the people shall not perish from the earth.

Freedom from want, freedom from fear, freedom of speech, freedom of religion . . .

Thou shalt love thy neighbor as thyself.

We call these words noble, but in our hearts we know that their true worth must be measured by the extent to which they are carried out in action. It is not nobility but a contemptible hypocrisy to mouth these words while operating a society which fails to support them or at certain times and in certain places is even flatly opposed to them.

What is the mission of education in helping to close the gap between these noble words and our daily practices? Let us examine the ways in which some Americans view this mission.

An Ex-Sergeant of Infantry, Now a Senior in The College of Education of a Middle-Western University, Makes This Statement

My ideas about education have been changed since I finished my junior year here in the spring of 1941.

When I was a junior I was told that all states had compulsory school laws, most of them requiring attendance to 16 years and some even to 18 years of age. When I got into the Army I saw a few boys from all parts of the country but particularly from the deep South, who could barely sign their names, and I heard of many more who were not accepted for military service because they couldn't read or write. This started me questioning a lot of things I had learned. The professors had told me that this country spent about two billion dollars a year on education, that good citizenship and character were primary objectives of the schools, and that every child in the land was entitled to as much education as his needs and abilities warranted. In the Army I found out that while this was true it added up to eye-wash, relatively speaking. I noted, for example, that we spent more money in a few hours for one little battle than the total annual grant to help equalize educational opportunities among the states, which educators have tried vainly for years to get from the federal government. I saw further that a number of the best schooled members of my battalion were the most vicious, prejudiced, and untrustworthy. I realized that the educational rights of millions of men in the Army had been abridged in their childhood on account of race, color, poverty, or geographical location. I realized that the prejudices that millions of other men displayed came from the education their communities had given them even though the schools of their communities may have been trying to educate them otherwise. It was such discoveries that made me question many other things I had learned here in this university before Pearl Harbor.

While I was still in the Army in Japan, after VJ-Day, I read about the Silver-Star and Purple-Heart wearing American soldiers of Japanese descent who had been thrown out of barber shops and restaurants by "patriotic" white men. I came home to be discharged and I heard of all the veterans in one state who could not vote because they could not "explain" the state constitution, and who could not explain the constitution, even though some of them were high-school and college graduates, because their skins were black.

Yes, I have some ribbons myself, including a couple that I can wear because I was lucky enough to stay alive while the really brave men died. Sure, I'm proud of those ribbons. They are special souvenirs from my people, the people of the United States, the people I have always thought of as being "them" whenever I took or gave the soldier's oath, "I do solemnly swear that I will bear true faith and allegiance to the United States of America, defending them against all their enemies whomsoever; so help me, God!"

I know what "them" refers to grammatically, but I know also that you will never understand what I mean by "American" until you can see all the people who come trooping through my mind whenever I hear or think of "them" in that old military promise.

They are not just my home-town and home-state people, people like my father and mother, my young sisters, the big logging-truck drivers, and the country girls picking wild blackberries along the fence rows, the finest black-berries and the prettiest girls in the world, bar none. They are also the disease-ridden Aleuts away out on Attu; the hungry Navajos on their overgrazed desert ranges; the share croppers and field hands — black, white, and brown — from the San Joaquin Valley to the beet fields of Colorado, from El Paso to Memphis and Mobile, from Atlanta to the sea; and the people with pallid faces forever herded in the big cities from tenements to subways, from offices and factories to movies and parks, from birth to death.

Sometimes I think these herded people, the ones I see when I go to New York, speaking all the foreign languages I have ever heard and some more besides, including an English which is often harder for me to interpret than Spanish, French, or the Chippewa which I learned as a boy on the banks of Red Lake — sometimes I think these big city people are the hardest of all for me to put into "them."

But there is something in that soldier's oath which says words to me very directly, which sings to me like a clear, high note on the E-string of a violin, which calls sharply for my attention like the staccato cough of a machine gun, "These people are even more your people, mister, just because they seem so strange to you."

I used to be a specialist in weapons. I was sergeant of a heavy weapons platoon in seven major engagements. I have heard about the A-bomb and the H-bomb, too. I have concluded, however, that the weapon most dangerous to the United States and to the world is not one of steel or flame or nuclear fission. It is rather the weapon of hatred and misunderstanding. The one defense against it is a dynamic education of information and attitudes and action.

The greatest enemies "they" have, the enemies hardest to defend "them" against, are not enemies against whose bodies you can draw steel and strike. They are shifty, evasive, sometimes disembodied, often shadowy, and always vicious and dangerous enemies. Provincialism, intolerance, prejudice, hatred, and ill-will are some of their names. They thrive on suspicion and ignorance. They magnify differences of color and curl of hair. They can take minor variations in modes of worship and erect thereon a mountain of bigotry. They can make wise men foolish. They can turn brave men into whimpering cowards. They can transform good men into monsters of cruelty.

Provincialism, intolerance, prejudice, hatred, and ill-will are active agents; they attack; they hunt for the weak spots in our line. We cannot plug all the gaps at once, but we can counter-attack and that is what I plan to do personally. More than 90 percent of the children of this country are in school until they are at least 16 years old. They are under the guidance of teachers. I realize that everybody in the community has some part in developing the attitudes of these children, but nevertheless, the teachers have the key job in this situation. On this mission, everybody in the community will have to help, but the teachers must go forward in the advance party.

Of course, casualties are likely to be heavy in advance parties, and no man wants to be a casualty. By training, by covering fire, and by taking advantage of the terrain, he wants to cut risks to a minimum but above all he wants to win. That is why I have been studying this mission, trying to see what will make it as safe as a dangerous job can be and at the same time to see what will make it work. I have studied this mission as carefully as I ever studied a mission for my platoon when I knew my own life as well as the lives of my men depended on getting the right answer.

First of all, I would like to be given some very careful preparation for effective action in the field of teaching human brotherhood and understanding. I have heard a great deal about such things as formal discipline, drill methods, and the recitation – all supposed to be rather bad, it seems – and also a great deal about activity schools, core curriculums, and sharing experiences – all apparently quite good. I would like to learn something more specific about how to teach young people and children to work together effectively, to respect one another's rights, and to defend the dignity of every member of the community.

If, when I get my first job, I can serve under a principal and a superintendent who actively wants me to teach better social attitudes and who will support me in that teaching, I shall be very lucky. The greatest break a man can have in attempting any mission is to get intelligent commanders.

If the school system already provides a curriculum for work in intergroup education, if experienced teachers are already developing such a curriculum in the system, I can get good preparation on the ground.

I know that I may not have these advantages, however; I may have to start on my own. I have been told that more than 75 percent of the school systems of this country have no organized work or activities in this field. If I hit one of these systems, I will have to help convince my colleagues of the need for such work. I will have to help organize and carry out a new program with my fellow teachers.

No matter how tough the situation may be, there are some things I can do at once. I can start by checking my own attitudes and beliefs about all groups and classes of my fellow men. I must do this in a detailed way. I am a white American of Scandinavian descent, a Lutheran, a member of a college fraternity, the son of a lawyer, and a product of a small town school system. I have got to examine myself specifically, therefore, on such attitudes as I hold towards Indians, Negroes, Jews, Catholics, and people of Japanese, German, Italian, Spanish, and other descents. I must analyze my feeling toward "barbs," children of farmer and laborers, Southerners, conscientious objectors, and people from big Eastern cities.

This sounds like a lot of work, but it must be done. A teacher is his own chief instrument of instruction. What he believes and does about the rights of other members of a democracy will show in his teaching and especially in that most powerful teaching which is done by example in action.

A second thing for me to do, one which can be carried out in my school system, will be to make sure that every pupil with whom I come in contact in the classroom, on the athletic field, or outside of school, is treated with respect and consideration, no matter who his father is, how he looks, what he wears, or what religion he follows. I shall treat him in this fashion myself, and I must see to it that his fellow pupils treat him in the same way.

This may be as far as I can go in some situations. If conditions permit – by that I mean if the community, the school board, and my superintendent and supervisors permit – I will organize or enroll with a group of teachers in which the problems of teaching tolerance and intercultural understanding can be discussed. I will also try to help educate the community through parent associations, the Church, and civic organizations to a better understanding of this problem.

Finally, in my classes in the social studies, I will work on the more formal and detailed phases of education in this field. By giving the pupils freedom to examine the facts, freedom to discuss the facts, and freedom to hold and act on beliefs according with the facts, I shall hope that all of them may have their levels of tolerance and understanding raised.

I do not intend to become a casualty on this mission, but I do intend to go into action. I will take only calculated risks. If my calculations are wrong, it will be bad, but not too bad.

Even an unsuccessful attack may weaken the enemy for the next punch.

An Elementary Teacher in a Large
Eastern City Gives Her Views

I was born a subject of the Russian Czar in the Jewish quarter of a Polish city. My father, a rabbi of our faith, died in 1911 when I was four years old. My mother was killed by rifle fire during the Polish-Russian war of 1919. How I lived the next three years I cannot say, but in 1922 my father's brother, a tailor in New York brought me to the United States where I learned to speak English and run a sewing machine on piece work. Later I became a waitress and after attending night school for five years, a stenographer. Beginning at the age of 25, I worked by way through teachers college as a part-time secretary for professors, as a part-time bookkeeper for merchants, and when I could not get those good jobs, again as a waitress.

I was graduated from the teachers college when I was 30. I got a place in this school where I have taught the fourth grade more than 10 years.

In the last war, I worked on rationing, donated blood to the Red Cross, and tried to teach my children the principles of being good Americans.

I was going to be married in 1941 but my friend was drafted. He was killed in action, May 11, 1943, on the beach of Massacre Bay, Attu. He was a private in the infantry.

So now I look forward mainly just to being a better teacher in the fourth grade.

At times, somehow, I think about the fourth grade quite differently from the way I used to think about it a few years ago. Some mornings I go into the fourth grade and it seems to me I have never seen it before.

Most people, most teachers perhaps, when they think of schools and schooling, think of desks screwed down in straight rows or a few chairs still kept in straight rows, no child talking legally to another child in the classroom, textbooks with the next lesson or the next ten pages assigned for study, reciting in class what had thus been set out to be learned, good marks for success in giving it back, bad marks for failure, monthly report cards, and papa and mama bawling the child out for a bad report.

So I think some mornings when I come into the fourth grade, and then I ask myself, "Can the memorizing of assigned lessons change a child's habits and attitudes? Will the child from a home where Jews are hated change his attitude toward Jews because his textbook, his lesson, or his teacher tells him to accept Jews as friends? Will memorizing affect the attitudes of a Ku Klux parent's child toward Negroes or people of foreign birth? Does reciting the pledge of allegiance to the flag make a child more patriotic. What kind of memorizing will make a citizen willing and able to carry through the promise in that pledge of giving liberty and justice to all his fellow citizens? Does learning the words of a catechism make a man a faithful follower of the religion which the catechism represents?

It took me a long time to find out that memorizing words from a book was not enough to change the real attitudes of people. I remember that when I read Hartshorne and May's *Studies of Deceit* I was told that belonging to the right kind of family will help change attitudes and habits but that going to Sunday school does not have much effect on the child's cheating in day school.

I have watched and studied my fourth graders. I have looked long and hard at the people in my apartment house. I have tried to observe and understand the citizens of this great city. I have seen plays and movies. I have even attempted to analyze novels, short stories, and poems. Always I have been looking for simple answers to simple questions.

Why is a Jew not so good as a Christian, provided he is good, relatively speaking? Why is he noisey even when he is quiet? Why is he rich though poor, a money-grabber though contemptuous of gain, and a boor though he exhibits the soul of courtesy? Why is it that a public-school teacher, a teetotaler, reasonably clean and modest in dress and appearance, cannot possibly, because of her religion, get a reservation at a vacation resort which will welcome a loudmouthed, drunken prostitute, wearing heavy layers of cosmetics to cover the dirt of her body and filling the air with perfume to disguise her stench, provided she does not carry the hated badge of Jewess.

I should add, of course, provided also she is "white."

This question is not based on imaginary situations. I was the Jewess in some of these dramas.

Now, naturally, I feel the weight of the anti-Jewish attitude, but in my heart I know that the burden of being nonwhite is immeasurably greater.

What is this thing? I stare at it. I am a teacher. I must know the workings of this phenomenon. I must learn its inner springs, its secret mechanism, its reason for being, that I may help my people, Jew and Gentile, white and nonwhite, schooled and unschooled, to escape from it.

But I cannot see it very clearly. It seems to be a thing of labels. I am a vacation-resort innkeeper, let us say. I want good guests, ones who will pay and not be too noisey, ones who will not get drunk and break furniture, ones who will not drive other guests away. I must screen my guests. Why not select them for those approved traits of cleanliness, sobriety, and courtesy? Why not require references? Or — but no! This is too hard. It would take too much pains, intelligence, and time. So I use the simple test — no Jews allowed and no colored trade wanted. That is easy.

At once, because every man is affected by every social event in all his society, the guests who are admitted are likely to feel at least a little superior. At the same time, the rejected ones are likely to feel a little inferior. The widening circles of waves, from every pebble of prejedice that hits the social surface of the pool, in time reach every minute part of the shore. Every label gets bigger and sharper outlines, has more credible features, and seems more reliable, with its every use as a substitute for free reason and intelligent choice.

The ephebic youth, when they came to adult life in their society, stood on the hill by the temple of that goddess of wisdom from whom their city-state took its name, holding their newly received weapons in firm hands, proud of their new dress and their freshly shorn locks of full citizenship, looking down at the white walls of their homes, repeating in a thousand voices made one, "I will never disgrace these sacred arms or desert my comrades in the ranks . . . I will pass on this city to those who come after me not only less and not poorer but greater and more beautiful than it was given to me . . . I will obey the present laws and those which the people may hereafter make, and if any man seek to set them at naught, I will do my best to prevent him both alone and with many."

If those beautiful words meant something in social action for ancient Athens, they must have symbolized a great comradeship among the free men who took it. For foreigners, for slaves, there were convenient labels which short-cut questions of individual virtue and worth. For each of the free citizens, there must have been a promise of unique dignity and significance in this concept.

The Athenians kept their system for a while. Did they know how to teach it, or were its origin and its obliteration both largely cultural accidents? Anyway, for a short time, fleeting as a breath of air against the backdrop of thousands of years, the Athenians seemed to tear the labels from their own people.

Sometimes I dream of a golden age in America, in the world, when bias and prejudice will not be automatically attached to labels. Perhaps I dream this dream in defense against the bias and prejudice I feel.

For I have felt bias and prejudice against myself and against my people. I have seen bias and prejudice displayed against other people in this country. I have tried to teach my children the right ideas about such matters. Now I am certain of only a few things in this connection. One thing I am certain of is this: that learning *about* bias and prejudice is not enough to make people *give up* bias and prejudice. We have to find some other ways of teaching and of learning this great thing.

If someone will help me find that way of teaching and learning, I promise that I will try with all my heart to put it into effect in my school.

It seems to me that nowadays this is one of the highest promises a teacher can make. I do not need to stand by a Temple of Athene for this obligation. For my fourth grade, for my country, and for the world, I can take this vow upon the altar of God.

The Superintendent of the North Central City Schools Is in Reminiscent Mood

I started teaching in this state when I was 17 years old. I began in a one-room rural school, District Number 42, Talking Lake County, at $35 a month. I believe I was worth that much, almost. I did my own janitor work.

Board, room, and washing cost me $10 a month, and I saved money. I played the guitar and fiddle for country dances. I sang in the church choir and in a male quartet at funerals, weddings, and parties. I worked one summer on a railroad construction gang and another summer I struck drill in a stone quarry. I ran a winter trap line for mink and muskrat.

I taught the children in my school as best I could, too, played with them at recess time, and went skating with them on clear, cold nights. I bought a good saddle horse for $10, gentled and sharp-shod him myself, and used him to haul the children's sleds up hill. Sometimes I would get a whole train of sleds at the end of a rope, with older boys and girls aboard, gallop my horse out on the heavily frozen lake, and crack the whip by suddenly halting and swinging the sleds in a wide circle to the accompaniment of hearty screams and laughter.

This was an old-fashioned school, back in the days of the three R's, but we had something more than drill inside the schoolhouse. There were ciphering matches, spell-downs, dialogues and speaking of pieces on Friday afternoons, songs twice a day, big children help the little ones, and not much trouble that I remember. The teacher was none too skillful, but he had attended a country school like that himself, and the pupils were among the best he has seen in 40 years of experience.

Those children and the teacher all "belonged" to that community. They were all of the same social class and the same religious group. Their parents were all farmers trappers, horsemen, and stock raisers. The community was homogeneous in blood, tradition, language, and political beliefs. Only teaching of extremely poor quality could have made that school an inferior educational institution.

When I was 20, I sold my horse and saddle for $40, gave my traps to my pupils, and started for college on a freight train. By tending furnaces, shoveling snow, mowing lawns, playing football, (I had a cot in the attic of the gymnasium for that service), and studying at odd times, (mostly from four to seven in the morning), I got a bachelor's degree in three years.

Then I became a high-school teacher and went to university summer sessions until I had a master's degree. Thereafter I served as a principal, first in elementary and then in secondary schools. About 20 years ago I was elected superintendent of schools in this city.

This recital may sound as though I have been going to school steadily, either as a pupil or a teacher, since that morning over half century ago when I entered the first grade. (They called it the "chart class" in those days.) That was in 1899.

I wish I could claim so long and constant an association with schools as that date would indicate, but unfortunately I cannot have that distinction. I spent eight years of my adult life in another occupation than teaching.

It was like education in some respects. It had the same general aim — to change men's ways. Beyond that, however, it was a decidedly different process.

I was a soldier from 1916 to 1920 and again from 1942 to 1946.

I will not pretend that I am ashamed of this circumstance, or even that I am modest about it. I am proud of the great military outfits with which I was lucky enough to serve. I remember with warm heart many of the gallant and able officers under whose commands I fought. Most of all, I am awed when I recall those magnificent young men, walking coolly behind their barrages at Vaux, charging from the forest of Villers-Cotterets on the first day of Soissons, going down the landing nets at Leyte, or following Martinez with a rush up Buffalo Head.

Historians can describe how Cannae or Gettysburg could have been avoided, statesmen can try to steer a skillful course through troubled international waters, the people of most of the world can work and pray for continued peace, and I will listen, follow, approve, applaud, and support them to the best of my ability. But these things are all unreal compared with my memory of those men, forever young in my heart, who stumbled in the advance, coughed a little, and then fell forward.

I have helped my people build their roads and houses. I have sung their songs and played for them to dance. I have laughed with them and I have grieved when they mourned. I have ridden with them to war, and I will be proud to ride with them again whenever they beckon me.

But always I have tried to teach them and their children the ways of peace and the high meanings of a good life. Lately I have felt increasingly impelled to tell them of a black danger to their peace and a menace to the goodness of their lives which I see rising like a cloud on the horizon of our times.

Let me go back to the boys I knew in 1916-1920 and 1942-1946. Because I happened to be born in a certain year, I had the opportunity, shared by many others of my generation, to observe thousands of my fellow Americans in what is one of the most character-and-ability-revealing situations in which men ever find themselves.

I saw them famished; I saw them satiated. I saw them drunk with fatigue as with alcohol. I saw them drugged with pain and terror. I saw them pushed to the limits of endurance and courage. I saw them live at top pitch, and too many times I saw them die.

I saw one generation of men under those circumstances, and then I saw their sons and nephews and younger brothers 25 years later under similar pressures. The differences between the two groups were illuminating.

In most ways the men who fought in 1942-1945 were incomparably better educated than those of 1916-1918. They had been in school longer. They knew more history, geography, science, and mathematics. They had read more. They could write and speak with greater effectiveness. And then, in addition, they had been schooled to a certain flexibility and independence of action and thinking above the average level of their fathers.

I do not know what part of this educational superiority should be credited to improvements in the schools themselves — some of it certainly and probably a substantial part of it. But there must have been much of it that arose from the differences between the 1920-1940 world in which the younger men had grown up and the 1895-1915 world in which their fathers had been boys. The younger men were born into a culture of automobiles, airplanes, radios, and movies. Many of them, for example, could not remember when they had first learned the principles of electricity and internal-combustion engines. To many of their fathers, such matters remained vague mysteries even after they had joined the Army.

Examples of such differences could be multiplied in many areas of learning. Whether it was acquiring a new language, an improved method of computing firing data, or a better scheme for navigation, the men of 1942 had tremendous intellectual advantages of those of 1917.

I said "intellectual advantages." There were also differences in attitudes and behavior.

I think there were more cases of drunkeness and quarreling in the average military unit in 1916 than in 1942, for example, but these matters are hard to judge. One's memory is unreliable and so are the statistics of courts-martial.

On the other hand, the discipline of the American Army in Rhineland in 1919-1920 seemed to me superior to that of the American occupation forces in Germany in 1946. But this difference, if actual, could have been caused primarily by differences in commanders.

In one important set of attitudes, I am sure that pronounced differences existed between these two generations of Americans. I refer to what may be called divisive attitudes, those which are directly opposed to that aim in the Preamble of the United States Constitution which reads, "....in order to form a more perfect union...."

When the Constitution was being drafted, the most dangerous divisive forces were those that operated between state and state. It ook three-quarters of a century and finally the most tragic and exhausting war in our history even to begin solving many of the problems raised by those forces.

By 1916 the sons and grandsons of the men who had fought so savagely against each other at Gettysburg and Antietam, Shiloh and Brice's Crossroads, were hardly conscious of the divisive forces which had produced the war of 1861-1865. Sectional and state loyalties were matters for tolerant respect and occasional joking reference. The divisive effects of the color barrier were, of course, present in 1916. Those of religious differences and those arising from tensions among Americans of various immigrant strains were also noticeable.

In general, however, it seems to me that the men of 1942-1946 showed evidences of much more serious divisiveness that did their fathers' generation. This was true in the fields of religion, race, and what, for lack of a better name, I will call political and social ideology.

In the old Army which I knew as a boy, for example, it was customary to have one chaplain for each regiment. Since the regiment operated pretty much as a unit in religious matters, furthermore, we answered the church call of our own regimental chaplain without regard to his or our denominational brand. In a certain limited sense, we were inclined to be more loyal to the regiment than to the denomination. In 1916-1920, for instance I was first in a regiment whose chaplain was a Presbyterian, and then I served in another regiment whose chaplain was a Roman Catholic. In those four years, I attended church calls and funeral formations many times. I do not remember ever missing any such calls except for necessary military duties. Shortly after the bugle sounded church call, if I was not on guard or patrol, in a trench or gun-pit firing at the enemy, or on some other detail that satisfied my captain and my first sergeant as being an effective bar to church attendance, I was standing at parade rest, listening to a mass or a sermon.

I do not remember attending any military religious services in those four years except with my own regiment. I do not remember that any of us in those regiments, Catholics, Jews, or Protestants, were particularly worried because the chaplain was not always of our "own" faith. Perhaps we were not religious in the current sense of that term. Perhaps I do not remember the things I should remember.

I do remember over these many years the most impressive religious exercise I have ever seen. I know now that I will never again be so impressed by a church service. I will never again be young and come from battle to stand by the side of the road just beyond the zone of enemy fire, watch the chaplain in the mud, as he moves precisely to set up his altar against a back drop of black clouds lightened by artillery flashes, and listen to the mass for the regiments' newest dead.

I remember, too, the day I regained consciousness in a field hospital and watched the doctor lifting a crucifix from my breast as he examined me. One of my men had hung it around my neck to help me pull through until the stretcher-bearers picked me up.

I am a Protestant. That boy and his gesture still mean somewhat more to me than my particular denomination of religion.

In 1942-1946, we had chaplains for most of the faiths. The men went to their "own" services, if at all. They seemed to me more divided religiously than their fathers had been.

In 1916-1920, we were conscious of race barriers, but not so much as in 1942-1946. In World War II we carried our "white" doctrines over five continents. We had Americans of Japanese descent in our Army camps and their families in concentration camps. We had Negroes as officers (for Negroes only), but we showed more divisiveness with respect to color than in World War I.

In the ideological realm, the Americans of the decade 1941-1950 showed perhaps their greatest divisive increase over the decade 1911-1920. The rise of fascism and communism in Europe and Asia in the intervening 20 years, the economic falterings of the 30's and the growing tendencies of Americans to copy European solutions and concerns worked a change in our attitudes toward those who differed from us on social and political questions. The doctrine of guilt by association, the assumption that to agree with one tenet of a disapproved faith implies agreement with its entire creed, and a pattern of secret-police dossiers for "official" interpretation only are some of the many signposts along a new, yet very old road. It is a road that leads back to Robespierre and the days when to have been associated with aristocrats was hardly more disastrous than it is today to have contributed in 1936 to the defense of the Spanish Republic.

These divisive forces are the greatest present dangers to our country. We have to fight them with education, and education of attitudes, an education for all our people and particularly for the adults of our communities.

You can teach a child to multiply fractions a great deal better than his father can multiply them; you cannot teach a child to have a much better attitude than his father has toward people of other races, colors, religious beliefs, or political views.

An education of great scope and power for the adults of this country is the nations's most pressing defense requirement. In our proper concern for school education, we must remember that children and young people do not control and direct these great divisive forces. Adults operate peonage systems, display race prejudices, vote to retain poll taxes, and send men to the United States Congress who, under the cloak of Congressional privilege, smear with impunity anyone with whom they disagree on political questions.

One day in May long ago, I saw American riflemen, their heavy weapons not yet in action, stop a well-armed and resolutely advancing enemy in his tracks. They stopped him with their Springfields. That division – my division – was a professional outfit. Sixty percent of the men in some of its companies were rated as sharpshooters or expert riflemen. The enemy had machine guns and artillery, but the riflemen stopped him cold. How?

They aimed at definite targets. They took ranges from their sergeants and set their sights precisely. They tossed sand in the air, estimated its slant in falling, and adjusted their windage knobs. They fired coolly and deliberately, tightening their gun slings and squeezing their triggers as though they were firing for records at Camp Perry.

The enemy stopped where that fire hit him. The helmets of his soldiers, with neat .30 caliber holes in their fore centers, piled up along the ridge to which his advance lines came and upon which they crumpled as they put their heads in sight.

I want my people to fight their present great and dangerous enemy of divisiveness as my outfit fought that old and simple enemy on the ridge along the road from Paris to Chateau Thierry.

What do I mean?

I mean that I want my people to see exactly what the targets are, to know how to adjust their weapons in each battle, and to direct their fire coolly and precisely.

I do not want them to attack blindly and indiscriminately like amateurs. I want them to call their shots like professionals.

This is going to take a lot of practice, a lot of instruction on the ranges, a lot of good coaches on the firing line.

The schools must show our people why this training against divisiveness is needed. The schools must help with the long and careful period of instruction. They must do this job specifically, with attention to particular conditions, laws, and persons.

It is not enough merely to have respect for the National Colors, if one at the same time has a color-based contempt for races of fellow Americans and fellow men. Education must pin-point the targets here, one by one.

How specifically, are Negroes, Jews, Catholics, Protestants, Democrats, Republicans, conservatives, radicals, industrialists, laborers, tenant farmers, or any other group discriminated against at particular times and places in this country?

This pin-pointing of targets is a very hard job. That is why it has not yet been well and extensively done.

Our people and our educational institutions can do this job. They will do it. By accurate and hard-hitting education they will stop this great enemy of our nation, this thing I have called divisiveness. They will one day drop him in his tracks.

And when they have done this thing, they will need no battle streamers on their Colors to proclaim to all the world the power and glory of their victory.

IV | DANGERS TO AMERICAN EDUCATION

As has neen mentioned previously Harold Benjamin's work in Central and Latin America covers more than two score years. His interest in the educational systems of this area has been matched only by his enthusiasm for the history of the southern portion of the western hemisphere. In his study of South American history he came across the following quotation from the great Venezuelan general and statesman Simon Bolivar:

> *"Para juzgar el valor de los revoluciones y los revolucionistos, preciso es observarlos muy de cerca y observarlos muy de lejos."*

To the best of my knowledge this may be translated, "In Order to judge the worth of revolutions and of revoltuionaries, it is better to observe the former closely and to observe the latter from afar." In his study of American education Dr. Benjamin has used a paraphrasing of this dictum as his guideline, "In order to judge the worth of educational systems and of educators, it is better to observe the former closely and the latter from a considerable distance." From his experiences and research he has defined two major areas which constitute a primary threat to American education. These are:

1. *The educational encroachments of non-school agencies (the so-called pressure groups).*
2. *The pressure for uniformity.*

The enfringement upon the schools by non-school organizations is inevitable – not always desirable but inevitable. Most of these agencies have commendable motives and are sincerely interested in children and youth. Unfortunately, their chief concern is not the education of the children, it might better be described as the indoctrination of youth. They have an axe to grind, a product to push; their major concern may be health, the inculcation of a certain religious belief, emotional security, or the dissemination of news. The worse kind of pressure is that which espouses an extreme political persuasion and in reality has no genuine concern for the children. Professor Kenneth H. Hansen, in his book PUBLIC EDUCATION IN AMERICAN SOCIETY, most aptly describes this situation when he says, "The school remains in our society as the one agency which has as its chief (and only) aim the education of children and youth, but in this task it has many partners – and some competitors."

155

In 1949 Dr. Benjamin was invited to serve as Inglis Lecturer at Harvard University. The Inglis Lectureship had been established in 1926 by friends and colleagues of the late Professor Alexander Inglis of the Harvard Graduate School of Education and intended as a memorial to him. It has become tradition for the Inglis Lecturer to make suggestions for the solution of problems in the field of secondary education. The list of luminaries who have served in this capacity includes, in addition to Dr. Benjamin, Abraham Flexner, C. H. Judd, E. L. Thorndike, Mark Starr, Ordway Tead, and Margaret Mead.

After a great deal of study Benjamin chose to title his contribution to the lecture series, "The Cultivation of Idiosyncrasy." In this work he introduces his readers to two of his favorite characters, "Old Man Coyote," and "Tom Gunn's Mule." For these two personalities Benjamin is indebted to his father who, in addition to being a successful rancher, was also a fine story teller.

Old Man Coyote may well be described as an educational mountaineer. He wants the best education possible for every child regardless of his I. Q., creative ability, or what-have-you. He has the twin concerns for American public education and American military education and the two are skillfully interwoven. In order to build an enlightened society, a safe country, and a peaceful world it is first necessary to identify, study, and develop every intellectual, social, and physical idiosyncrasy in our children and youth. The educational mountaineer firmly believes, as Benjamin states in his lecture, that "that society which comes closest to developing every socially useful idiosyncrasy in every one of its members will make the greatest progress toward its goals."

If Old Man Coyote is the educational mountaineer, Tom Gunn's Mule exemplifies the educational plainsman. To present a clearer picture of Tom Gunn's Mule it is necessary to relate a story which was told to me by Dr. Benjamin and which he has used on several occasions.

Tom Gunn's Mule was an enormous animal, he stood sixteen hands high and weighed over eleven hundred pounds. His mother had been half German coach horse and half Eastern Oregon bronco; his father was a registered Andalusian jack. In spite of this impressive pedigree Tom Gunn's Mule was peculiarly liable to confusion of his goals; hence the common expression around Umatilla County, Oregon, "No more sense than Tom Gunn's Mule."

One summer when ranch work was slack, Tom Gunn's Mule was grazing with the other animals in the Horse Heaven country of Washington, just across the Columbia River from Umatilla. One hot, July day it suddenly occurred to the mule that he must be thirsty for he had not been to water that day nor the day before. So he started at a steady trot for the river some five miles away.

If you had asked this mule what his purpose was, no doubt he would have replied, "To get a drink." Actually he had another and more dominant objective that overrode his attention to immediate goals. This objective was to keep other creatures from ridiculing his ears. He was abnormally sensitive about those ears. On this day he came plunging down the bank toward the little sandy beach where he had often drunk before, his eyes fixed on the water, his nostrils dilating in anticipation. Just as he moved through the last clumps of sagebrush, however, a startled jackrabbit sat up and stared at him, its ears moving in alternate fore and aft stances. The mule forgot his thirst in a quick flash of anger.

"What in tarnation are you looking at?" he snarled.

The rabbit conscious only of a snorting, lathered mule who seemed hostile, dropped his ears back over his shoulders and took off. The mule seeing primarily those ears, every movement of which seemed to be insulting, charged after the rabbit, his front hooves flying for the kill. "I'll learn you not to make fun of me," he yelled.

The rabbit ducked, took off again, and finally hid in a clump of sagebrush at the water's edge. The mule plunged headlong into the river and headed for the Oregon shore. Occasionally he raised his head in an effort to spot his tormentor who, he thought, was swimming ahead of him. When he reached the opposite side he promptly flushed an Oregon jackrabbit who looked exactly like the Washinton one and moved its ears in the same insulting manner. Why did not the mule note at once that this new rabbit's fur was dry and that it could not have just emerged from the river? Ah, this is a crucial question, and its answer is equally crucial. The mule could not, would not, look at any evidence that clashed with his view of his mission. His ear-sensitivity had taken care of that.

So the mule followed the Oregon rabbit's evasive flight, lost it at the water's edge, and swam back to Washington to overtake it. The poor mule was very tired now, but when the original rabbit or its twin jumped up, wiggled its ears, and began its circling tactics, he started after it once more. Again he lost it in the sage at the river's edge and again he swam the stream, this time quite slowly for even his great strength was waning. At last he staggered up on the Oregon bank, still trying to locate that elusive rabbit. At the high-water line he tripped over a piece of driftwood and fell heavily. There he lay, too exhausted to rise, and there he might have died of thirst had not Tom Gunn himself happened along.

The rancher, riding along the river road, had seen the animal stagger out of the water and fall. "That sure looks like my crazy dun mule," he said, and as he rode nearer he saw that sure enough it was. He brought a hatful of water from the river to revive the animal and then noted that the mule seemed to be very thirsty. He brought another hatful and let the mule drink. Next he put a rope around the patient's neck, snubbed the rope to his saddle horn, and pulled the mule to its feet.

"Talk about a feller that don't know enough to come in outa the rain," mused Tom Gunn. "Here is a mule so dumb he can swim the Columbia and not know enought to take a drink."

Old Man Coyote and Tom Gunn's Mule disagree at every turn and on every issue. Through the use of these provocative characters in "The Cultivation of

Idiosyncrasy," Harold Benjamin draws dead aim on threat number two, "the pressure for uniformity." And this lecture is considered by most people to be Benjamin's most important work.

The Cultivation of Idiosyncrasy

In a tale given to American educators by George H. Reavis, the wild creatures once had a school in the woods. All the animals had to take all the subjects. Swimming, running, jumping, climbing, and flying made up the required curriculum.

This was a school of no nonsense. It was a good, liberal education institution. It gave broad training — and instruction — and education too.

Some animals, of course, were better students than others. The squirrel, for example, got straight A's from the first in running, jumping, and climbing. He got a good passing grade, moreover, in swimming. It looked as though he would make Phi Beta Kappa in his junior year, but he had trouble with flying. Not that he was unable to fly. He could fly. He climbed to the top of tree after tree and sailed through the air to neighboring trees with ease. As he modestly observed, he was a flying squirrel by race. The teacher of flying pointed out, however, that the squirrel was always losing altitude in his gliding and insisted that he should take off in the approved fashion from the ground. Indeed, the teacher decided, that the taking-off-from-the-ground unit had to be mastered first, as was logical, and so he drilled the squirrel day after day on the take-off.

The flying teacher's practice in this case was in strict accord with the educational philosophy of the school. The teachers recognized that students would necessarily display great variations in their abilities. In the Woods Normal School, as a matter of fact, the teachers had learned a great deal about individual differences and the consequent tremendous ranges in human capacities. They set themselves doggedly, therefore, to the task of reducing these differences as best they might, that sane likenesses, safe unities, and nobel conformities might prevail in the woods.

The squirrel tried hard. He tried so hard he got severe Charley horses in both hind legs, and thus crippled he became incapable even of running, jumping, or climbing. He left school a failure, and died soon thereafter of starvation, being unable to gather and store nuts. He was cheerful to the last and was much beloved by his teachers and fellow pupils. He had the highest regard for his alma mater, regretting only the peculiar incapacity which had kept him from passing the course in flying.

The 1949 Inglis Lecture delivered at Harvard University. Permission from the Harvard University Press to quote this lecture is gratefully acknowledged.

The snake was a promising student also. Being a combination tree-and-water snake, he was excellent in both climbing and swimming. He was also a superior runner and passed the tests in that subject with ease. But he began to show antisocial tendencies in arguments with the instructor in jumping. When he had been given the basic instruction in that subject and it came time for him to make his first jump, he coiled up and threw himself almost his full length. This was not jumping, said the teacher. It was merely striking — a snake skill — and not at all the general-education jumping which all cultivated creatures had to know.

"What kind of jumping is of any use to a snake," demanded the student, "except this kind?" Then he coiled up and struck again, or jumped, as he called it, with the beginning of a bitter sneer on his face.

The teacher of jumping remonstrated with him, tried to get him to jump properly, and used the very best methods taught in the more advanced demonstration schools, but the snake became more and more uncooperative. The school counselors and the principal were called in and decided to attempt to vary the snake's education by teaching him flying, but to their distress he flatly refused even to attend the preliminary classes in that subject. He did not say he was unable to fly — he merely scoffed at the notion of flying for a snake and said that he had no intention of ever bothering with the subject. The more the teachers argued with him the more he coiled and struck and sneered, and the more he sneered and coiled and struck, the more bitter and introverted he became. He left school and made his living briefly as a highwayman, murdering other animals along the woods paths, until he struck at a wildcat one evening and was clawed to death for his lack of judgement. He died detested by all and mourned by none.

The eagle was a truly brilliant student. His flying was superb, his running and jumping were of the best, and he even passed the swimming test, although the teacher tried to keep him from using his wings too much. By employing his talons and beak, moreover, he could climb after a fashion, and no doubt he would have been able to pass that course, too, except that he always flew to the top of the problem tree or cliff when the teacher's back was turned and sat there lazily in the sun, preening his feathers and staring arrogantly down at his fellow students climbing up the hard way. The teachers reasoned with him to no avail. He would not study climbing seriously. At first he turned aside the faculty's importunities with relatively mild wisecracks and innuendoes, but as the teachers put more pressure upon him he reacted with more and more feeling. He became very aggressive, stating harshly and boldly that he knew more about climbing than did the professor of that subject. He became very successful when he left school and he attained high position in the woods society. He was dogmatic and dictatorial, respected by all and feared by many. He became a great supporter of general education. He wanted the curriculum of his alma mater to remain just as it was, except that he believed climbing had no general cultural value and should be replaced by some more liberal subject, like dive-bombing, which in his view, gave the student a certain general polish superior even to that given by the study of flying.

The gopher parents thought that the school was very good in most matters and that all the subjects gave excellent results if properly taught, but they wanted their children to learn digging in addition to the general education. The teachers regarded digging as a manual skill, not elevated enough for general culture. Besides, they did not know how to dig and they resisted learning such a subject.

So the gophers withdrew their children from this institution and hired a practical prairie dog to set up a private school in which an extensive course was given in digging. The prairie dog schoolmaster also taught a course in running, jumping, swimming, and climbing. He did not teach flying. He said it was an outmoded subject. Digging, a more practical subject, took its place in the curriculum. So the ducks and geese and wild turkeys and prairie chickens all scoffed at the prairie dog's school. They set up schools of their own, very much like the other schools except that the ducks gave advanced courses in evasive air tactics.

At this juncture, Old Man Coyote, who had been studying the development of education in the woods, shrewdly observed, "All these pedagogical characters are going at this business wrong end to. They look at what animals and birds — a lot of animals and birds — do and need to do. Then they put those needs and those doings into formal schoolings and try to make the little pups and cubs and fledglings fit the schoolings. It's haywire, wacky, and will never really work right."

Tom Gunn's Mule, a sour visaged individual, ready to criticize all theories, heard Old Man Coyote's remark and demanded harshly, "If you're so smart, how would you do it?"

"Why, I would turn the whole thing around," explained Old Man Coyote modestly.

"Turn it around?" scoffed Tom Gunn's Mule. "What d'ye mean, Turn it around?"

"These school people start with things that birds and animals do — or even more often what they did some time ago," explained Old Man Coyote. "Then the teachers hammer these doings — or as much of them as they can handle and as they think high-toned enought — into schoolings, courses, curriculums, and subjects. Then they hammer the pups into the schoolings. It's a rough and dopey process, and the teachers have had to invent good explanations to defend it. Discipline, culture, systematic training — things like that — are what the teachers use for this purpose. I don't know what they mean and I think the teachers don't know what they mean, but I do know they make a lot of cubs and pups and fledglings mean and rough and dopey when they could and should make them good and slick and smart."

"Sure, sure," snorted Tom Gunn's Mule, "but you still haven't told me how you would do it."

"Turn it around," snorted Old Man Coyote. "Start with the pups. See what the pups can do. Then see what the school can do for the pups. Then see what the pups and school together can do for all the creatures in the woods. Simple — forwards instead of backwards — right end to instead of wrong end to."

Old Man Coyote turned triumphantly and started to trot away.

"Hey!" shouted Tom Gunn's Mule. "Wait! These teachers have schools now. They have to run those schools. They are practical people. Just how, specifically, and precisely, would you tell them to change their schools so as to get their education right end to, as you call it?"

Old Man Coyote patted a yawn with the back of his forepaw. "I lay down general principles," he said. "These schoolteachers have got to figure out some of the minor details themselves."

This is the end of the story, but I am a schoolteacher myself, and so I have been trying to figure out a few of the details upon which Old Man Coyote touched.

I may be accused of having manufactured Old Man Coyote out of whole cloth. His real birth, or at least the origin of his main ideas, occurred long ago under more scholarly auspices than I can provide.

It has been almost a quarter century since Truman Lee Kelley presented evidence to show how nurture operates upon children to reduce certain of their most socially useful idiosyncrasies. He observed parenthetically in this connection that school men appeared to resent oddity in their pupils, that too often they were pedagogical plainsmen, lovers of the dead level and organizers of mediocrity, and that under an egalitarian banner they flouted democratic equality by plying a Procrustean trade of forcing the weak and stunting the strong. Hugging their precious averages and norms, said Kelley, they spent their professional lives in a process of weary shoveling to fill valleys and steady erosion to remove mountains of human capacity. He asked that the policies and practices which produced this kind of education should be rigorously examined and drastically modified.[1]

This lecture is in the nature of a report, therefore, to Old Man Coyote, to Truman Lee Kelley, and to others holding their views. It is a report on the class of questions raised by these critics. It is a report on a matter which I regard as being of sufficiently great moment to warrant its consideration in this lecture, for I believe that the central question of this class is one which a democratic society may ignore only at its deadly peril.

The question is double-barrelled:

    1. How much uniformity does this society need for safety?
    2. How much deviation does this society require for progress?

[1]T. L. Kelley, *The Influence of Nurture upon Native Differences* (New York: The Macmillan Company, 1926).

The insight with which the line of safety is drawn and the skill with which the conditions or progress are embodied in an educational program determine in large measure whether a particular society will be a great society or a mean society, whether it will be strong or weak, whether it will be enduring or evanescent, whether it will be a creator and bearer of high meanings or a purveyor of the insignificances of ignorance and brutality.

The first step in determining an educational program, whether for an entire national group, for a particular profession, or for a small number of students in a classroom, are the steps that are most commonly slighted. They are often assumed to have been taken when in fact they have been by-passed.

What are these first steps? Let us look at an example. Because the defenders of educational plainsmanship are often especially worried over a lack of the uniformities which they consider necessary for national security, let us take our first example from the area of military education.

We examine the present state of international affairs, let us say, and decide that the safety of our people and of our people's possible allies requires us to have the best-educated professional soldiers we can get. We decide further that among these professional soldiers we are going to need annually one thousand newly commissioned second lieutenants of infantry. We want to educate them or to have them educated so that they will contribute most effectively to the safety of our country and the peace of the world.

The simplest and most satisfying way to educate these officers is to find some overall magic touchstones, formulas, shibboleths, or charms which reveal the traits needs by all leaders of infantry and then to give them a schooling to broaden and intensify those traits. Thus, in an aristocratic society, where all noblemen are leaders and only noblemen are leaders, we can give every young man of noble rank a military commission and we can then seek to enhance noble traits by appropriate noble practices; for example, dueling to develop his courage and honor, gambling to develop his courage and honor, horse racing to develop his courage and honor, woman chasing to develop his courage and honor, fox hunting to develop his courage and honor, and of course, war itself to test his courage and honor.

For purposes of later identification, let us call this approach the noble-traits system of education.

Now the trouble with this simple system is that it works only when opposed to an equally simple system. Suppose that courage-and-honor officers with approximately equal forces are opposed to courage-honor-and-discipline officers, or that the latter are opposed to courage-honor-discipline-and-concentration-of-force officers. In such circumstances the simpler system is liable to go down in defeat. A noble-traits system of education tends to become more complex whenever it meets the test of fire, and conversely it tends to become less complex when protected from strain and conflict.

In the noble-traits system of education, the aim is to turn out one thousand accurate copies of a model second lieutenant. Courage, honor, discipline, loyalty, devotion to duty, and any other magic traits we regard as standard matters. We want every second lieutenant to possess each of these traits completely. We want one thousand faithful reproductions of the perfect second lieutenant of infantry. We want all these copies to think and act alike. We want them to be interchangeable parts of a machine. Any differences they may display after we educate them are merely indications of our failure to produce accurate copies of the model second lieutenant.

This system often looks good. The only trouble with it is that we find that we lost battles and even wars with such second lieutenants. So we reject the noble-traits method of selecting and training these men. We reject it because it fails to give us safety. Of course, we may continue to feel that we must talk to the prospective second lieutenants about courage and honor and discipline and principles of war, but actually we believe that an infantry officer's effectiveness is composed of many specific skills, rather than noble-traits. We note that he must be able to walk, run, jump, climb, craw, and creep with a technical efficiency beyond that of a non-infantryman. He must know how to shoot pistols, rifles, machine guns, mortars, rocket launchers, and infantry cannon. He must have skill in patrolling and reconnaissance. He must know how to teach his men these skills. He must be able to organize and lead his men in attack and defense situations of various kinds. As he grows older and advances to the higher grades, furthermore, he must know how to meet larger responsibilities. He must know how to adapt his skills to new situations, all of them very specific. He may have to write a speech on universal military training for his commanding officer to read at the annual convention of the National Association of Woolgathers, for example. He should be able without undue stumbling, to read aloud such a speech which has been written for him by one of his staff officers. He may have to administer a conquered village, province, nation, or continent.

Then we hunt for learning activities to produce these skills. For some activities, the search is easy. Obviously, to teach the young officer to shoot a pistol, the best thing to do is to have him shoot a pistol. Of course, we can first lecture to him about the pistol, have him memorize the names of all the parts of the weapon, teach him to take it apart and put it together again, show him how to load it, aim it, and squeeze the trigger without firing it. But after a while we take him out to the pistol range, have him load the weapon with ball cartridges, and then actually have him shoot real bullets into the target or into the ground near the target.

Let us call this approach the specific-skills system of education. It comes into full flower when the real bullets hit the real target. This is the moment of triumph for the specific-skills system.

Now we apply the specific-skills system assiduously to the prospective one thousand second lieutenants of infantry in an attempt to make them all alike in their skills. We are again trying to produce one thousand copies of an approved model. Of course we may specialize some of these young men, but even the specialization is standardized. We may take one hundred of them, for example, and give them special training to make them leaders of heavy-weapons platoons. We want them to be faithful copies of an ideal heavy-weapons platoon leader with respect to the use of heavy weapons, and in all other respects we want them to be faithful copies of the model second lieutenant of infantry, regardless of specialization in a particular class of weapons.

We Americans often put these young officers into battle after we have so trained them on a thorough plainsman's level and are lucky enough to have stout old human nature — tough, resilient, and resistant of uniformity — come to our rescue. Many times in our history it has been this triumph of native difference over a dead level of training which has enabled us to win our battles. Individual idiosyncrasy, brilliant nonconformity, and daring disregard of the tenets of military plainsmanship have consistently dragged victory from defeat which had been prepared by faithful copying of standard models.

"Whenever I met one of them generals who fit by note," said Nathan Bedford Forrest accurately and without false modesty, "I always whipped him before he could pitch the tune." If Forrest could have been sent to West Point in his youth and trained into being a more faithful copy of Braxton Bragg or Samuel D. Sturgis, if General George Washington had been commissioned in the British Regulars at an early age and made much more like Lord Howe or Charles Lee, if Chief Joseph of the Nez Perces and Crazy Horse of the Ogala Sioux could only have had the advantages of a military education to model them after Captain Fetterman and Colonel Custer, the history of the United States' wars would be considerably less marked by peaks.

It is an ironic testimonial to the power of the educational plainsman's philosophy that in the very field of human endeavor where cultivated idiosyncrasy pays off most spectacularly and in clearest-cut physical terms, the doctrine of the approved doctrine, the uniformity of the uniform practice, and the massing of mediocrity should have held such undisputed sway. Here if anywhere it might perhaps seem that educators would revolt against the practices of pedagogical plainsmanship and become educational mountaineers. Here was where mountaineering would give results which nations commonly assess at high value. But the strength of the conformity-enforcing agencies was too great. The shadow of Frederick of Prussia with his stiffly aligned peasants-in-arms moving in unison was too much even for men who saw demonstrated almost every year the battle superiority in American woods of non-alignment and non-unison. No matter; the principle of the pedagogical plainsman still triumphed. It was never more brilliantly expressed in action than on that memorable day on the Monongahela when Major General Sir Edward Braddock lined up his exhausted men as they staggered from the woods and gave them a stiff dose of manual-of-arms and close-order drill in preparation for the coming attack of the French and Indian

Skirmishers. Almost two centuries later, his spiritual and professional descendants still keep his memory green by an improved manual-of-arms and an improved close-order drill which are just as effective today as their predecessors were in the middle of the eighteenth century.

We still educate second lieutenants by a combination of the concepts of noble-traits and uniform specific-skills. How else can we train them? Is not war a demander of standardized routines, of interchangeable parts? We dress soldiers alike; why should we not educate them alike?

There are Old Man Coyotes even at West Point and Fort Benning nowadays, however. They say that there is another way, a better way, an opposite way of educating second lieutenants. They say that in many ways war has been getting less and less uniform in its demands upon men since the days of Frederick the Great. They say that war calls for unique abilities here and differently unique abilities there and that, of all the situations which men face, war as much as any requires highly developed strong points of ability on the part of those who engage in it.

Let us begin, therefore, say the military Old Man Coyotes, with men instead of noble traits and specific skills. Let us start with individual boys who have intellectual, social, and physical idiosyncrasies which we study carefully, looking for the possible foundations upon which to build mountain peaks of traits and capacities.

If we find a boy with a sure grasp of the meanings of terrain and a strong interest in maps, let us give him terrain studies and maps, geographical and tactical exercises, aerial photographs, and area defense probelms; not to give him noble traits of any kind, not to give him the skills of a model soldier, but to develop that particular boy's personal capacities so that in all the ways he is going to be unique he will be uniquely great in his understanding and use of geographical factors in war.

If a prospective second lieutenant has strong interests and abilities in mathematics and in guns, let us give him the automatic weapons, the grenade launchers, the infantry cannon; not to make him a standardized leader of a heavy-weapons platoon but to make him a unique officer in whose total pattern of skills those relating to heavy weapons are outstanding.

If another boy has high lingusitic interests and abilities, if he is trying to learn Russian by himself, let us give him Russian, and Turkish and Mongolian and Tibetan too. Let us give him area studies in the history, government, geography, and culture of the Russian, Turkish, Mongolian, and Tibetan peoples. Let us do all this with no notion of meeting a standard of noble linguistic traits or of specific linguistic abilities but rather with the object of making this boy such an officer as no other army in the world can duplicate. Thus we shall not be afraid of building his ability peaks too high. In the possible demand which the future may make upon our Army, we may well find that this officer's strongly developed idiosyncrasy is worth more to us than a division of ordinary trained soldiers.

Would you then not have a standard education for infantry officers? Would there be no minimum essentials for second lieutenants? Gad, Sir! I can see the veins turn purple in the colonel's neck. I can hear his fist hammer the desk.

But not all colonels would so respond — not nearly so many as you might think; not even so many colonels, perhaps, as presidents and chancellors, deans and professors, superintendents and principals, teachers and headmasters, regents and trustees, parents and clergymen, legislators and those men-in-the-street who sometimes retire to their homes and write letters to the editor.

All of us tend to echo these doubting cries. All of us are prisoners of our schooling — a schooling based on some combination of the concepts of the uniform and level noble-traits or specific-skills. The first article in our pedagogical faith is the *credo* of minimum standards. That *credo* lies flatly athwart the law and the gospel of Old Man Coyote's theory of education.

Old Man Coyote insists that the boy whose mathematical, linguistic, geographical, or other peaks of ability are built to great heights will have his valleys of ability in other areas pulled up towards his peaks until the sum of his achievements will be far above the minimum essentials ever set by plodding plainsmen. Old Man Coyote insists further that the learner must go above his present peaks and valleys as a free, daring, and enterprising individual and never as one herded under the lash of a minimum standard.

This is a hard doctrine for us to accept. It is hard for us because we have confused our minimum standards with our objectives.

Our objective, in the case of military education, for example, is to keep the peace as long as possible and, when wars break out, to stop them as quickly and as efficiently as we can. The minimum essential is a lazy plainsman's device for short-cutting the objective. The sturdy mountaineer looks keenly across the land at the goal as he ascends every peak.

The observed facts of human development support Old Man Coyote's doctrine. Few if any men ever became great historians or great citizens by studying the outlines of history required in the freshman year. Few if any men ever became great infantry leaders by concentrating on the dead level of infantry fundamentals.

Few if any great jurists, painters, industrialists, or musicians ever attained their heights of uniqueness by drill on the minimum essentials.

"But, Gad, Sir!" repeats my hypothetical colonel or professor or Tom Gunn's Mule, "We are not educating great generals, unusual soldiers, geniuses — we are just aiming modestly and in a common-sense way to train ordinary, dead-level, good infantry officers — interchangeable-standard-uniform. You'd have them at least speak English, wouldn't you? You'd have them know how to load and fire an M-1, wouldn't you?"

"Ah!" says Old Man Coyote, "I would have no ordinary, dead-level officers — they would all be great officers in terms of their abilities — because that's a better way to win wars — and certainly some of them might not speak English or know how to load and fire an M-1 rifle. Some of them might speak only Spanish, for instance, in the San Martin Corps of the United States Foreign Legion, and some of them might command only mortar platoon."

"A likely situation," snorts Tom Gunn's Mule.

"It would be a lot more likely in the American Army," softly observes Old Man Coyote, "if the present brass had been educated forwards instead of backwards."

I have used these second lieutenants as examples in part because the objective of their education is relatively easy to see. Let us now consider examples of a kind of education which perhaps does not have such easily seen objectives.

Suppose it is teachers rather than infantry officers whom we are educating. Suppose we need one thousand new teachers in Massachusetts or Maryland next fall. Shall we seek in the teachers' colleges of these states to turn out a thousand more or less faithful copies of a model teacher? Shall we give marks of A to those most nearly approaching the approved pattern and marks of C or D to those furtherest away from the pattern but still not so far away as to deserve being failed? Do we really want them all to act, look, talk, teach, and think alike? Are the deviations from the model which they display merely the measures of our inefficiency in teaching them, in bringing them up to the straight-A standards of near perfection?

"Ah! No, no!" we say hastily. "We who educate teachers have studied individual differences. Most of us who are old enough to affect the policies of teacher-training institutions studied individual differences in Volume III of Edward L. Thorndike's Educational Psychology, first published in 1914. We have known about individual differences for a long, long time. We try to develop the individual differences, the idiosyncrasies, of these teachers. We want to develop their idiosyncrasies in groups. We want blocs of idiosyncrasy. We need fifty different kinds of teachers next year, English and Social Studies teachers for small high scholls, boys physical education teachers who can also take a section in geology, mathematics and physics teachers, girls' counselors who can teach French, vocational agriculture teachers, home economics teachers, and so on. Certainly we want idiosyncrasies — in standard groups, that is."

The Old Man Coyotes murmur that we want developed useful idiosyncrasies. Useful for what? Useful for our objectives?

Are those objectives standard, minimum-essential objectives? They should not be. They should be as varied as the children whose learning these teachers are to aid. We want one thousand uniquely educated teachers. We want teachers whose idiosyncrasies have been nurtured for unique learnings in schools.

Here is a prospective teacher whose interests and abilities in the nature and processes of child growth and development are exceptional. We shall not try to hold him back in this idiosyncrasy in order to flatten his ability peaks. We shall work with him to build up those peaks.

Shall we then ignore this prospective teacher's valleys of ability in written communication, in science, or in mathematics? Not at all, but we shall try to haul them up only by tying them to his rising peaks of ability. If we build his peak of understanding and skill in child growth and development high enough, his lower abilities in speaking, writing, computing, and biology can be brought far above the modest levels set by a plainsman's minimum essentials.

Suppose it is a citizen of the United States that we are educating in the secondary school, for example. Is not this situation fundamentally different from one in which we are trying to produce Army officers or schoolteachers? Can we not make a better case here for the plainsman's education? Do not all citizens have to vote intelligently; read newspapers and listen to radio commentators critically; write letters to friends; make a living by applications of science, mathematics, economics, and manual skills; be an amiable member of a family; and perhaps even create and enjoy beauty in line, form color, tone, melody, and rhythm?

Do we not have in these activities of the good citizen the bases of the general standards which education must meet? Are not these the doings we must use to construct schoolings through which all good citizens must pass? Is not this, the secondary school, the real yoke of general education to which all proper citizens must learn to bow? Must not all educated men and women pass under that yoke in true subjugation of spirit and intellect to make a society strong?

Sub jugum mittere was merely symbolic of military surrender to Julius Caesar, but to his big-jawed successor two thousand years later it became a complete statement of a completely general education in "Believe, obey, fight." Probably it reached its highest expression and fullest significance of the present historical period in the disciplined chant above the hobnailed boots hitting the cobblestones in unison for the "Reich of a Thousand Years."

> *Leader, we belong to thee;*
> *Thy comrades we will ever be.*
> *Our flag is waving in the van;*
> *We march to the future man by man;*
> *We march for Hitler through night and dread*
> *With the flag of youth, for freedom and bread.*
> *That flag will lead us to the fray;*
> *That flag is the flag of a brand-new day.*
> *We'll follow that flag to our last, last breath.*
> *That flag is more than Death. Yes, Death!*

These references to the educational plainsmanship of the teachers in the regimes of Mussolini and Hitler are not made in any attempt to belittle the plainsman's doctrines by coupling them with unpopular causes and characters. They are made simply because they exhibit the outcomes of educational plainsmanship in logical completeness. If the teachers in the Soviet schools should succeed as completely in educating their pupils to the civic standard of being like Stalin, if the teachers of Georgia should work as effectively to give the minimum essentials of a Talmadge concept of white superiority, if the teachers of New Jersey should teach as completely a level of patriotism set by J. Parnell Thomas, or if the teachers of Maryland, Minnesota, or Missouri should labor as successfully to put all the children of all the people on a conforming, obedient, uniform level even though it be dictated by a Caesar of the purest motives — and what true Caesar ever has any other kind? — then they would furnish as good examples of real pedagogical plainsmanship as ever did Baldur von Shirach's cheering, marching ranks of *Hitlerjugend.*

If, instead of the Hitler Youth Song or the Communist Manifesto, the minimum essentials were Lincoln's Gettysburg Address, the Declaration of Independence, or the Ten Commandments, would the fundamentals be changed? Do we have in such materials truly sacred subjects which are good in themselves and which must be part of the general learning of all our people? Should *Hamlet* and *Paradise Lost* be studied by every English-speaking person, *Don Quixote* by every inheritor of the Western European culture, and The *Republic* by every citizen of a democracy? Do all children everywhere need to learn that seven times nine are sixty-three?

Questions like these provide the real test of adherence to a theory of education as the cultivation of idiosyncrasy. The educational mountaineer replies to them by saying that no subject is pedagogically sacred, no matter what its patriotic, religious, or utilitarian status may be; that only the individual personality is an end in itself, and that education must therefore be a process of developing individuals by means of schoolings rather than a process of bringing learners up to a standard of schoolings.

The plainsman does not often say just the opposite of this, but he has to act thus or betray his plainsmanship. He is forced into a series of acts which constitute much of the business of many modern systems of education.

There is first and always the business of curriculum construction. In general education, it is a process not only of determining what is a sacred subject but also of assessing degrees of sacredness and indicating where in a child's life the subjects should be learned. Thus the Gettysburg Address is obviously sacred and must be memorized by all sixth graders. What is the verdict on Washington's Farwell Address? It is not quite so sacred perhaps and does not need to be memorized. Let it be studied by all ninth graders carefully and respectfully. What of Franklin's Autobiography? Of Hamilton's and Madison's essays? Of Grant's memoirs? Of Franklin D. Rossevelt's speeches?

If Cervantes is to be studied by everyone in high school, where are Goethe, Dante, and Racine to be met? If the multiplication tables to twelve times twelve are needed by everybody fourteen years of age, twelve times thirteen, fifteen times nineteen, and many other combinations as far as twenty times twenty must be good general education for many if not all persons who are eighteen years of age.

This is the first mark of the pedagogical plainsman, therefore; that he is continually constructing curricula, sorting subjects, fussing over facts, determining the significance of dates, tampering with time allotments, and computing percentages of sacredness.

He can be seen most clearly when he is working on very simple materials. "Ah, 1492," he mutters, "there's a must for Americans; and 1776 − no doubt about that one − it goes in the *all-100 per cent* compartment; so do 1812, 1861, 1898, 1917, and 1941. Those are easy, but some of these others are difficult; 1789, 1848, 1912, and 1933, for example; 1789 can't be quite so sacred − it is French and hence foreign − put it in high school European history where it is not required; and 1933 is college stuff and not really a foundation of Americanism − it is New Dealish besides."

The most popular exemplification of the pedagogical plainsman's curriculum theory is found in the radio quiz program; its most high-toned manifestation is in current lists of great books. It was never more dramatically displayed in action on this continent than when the Ghost Dance craze swept over the Western country in the eighties of the last century. Here was a sacred schooling for a defeated, staring people. The Indians must dance, the ghostly teachers said, and Tanka Wakan would then wipe out the white men and bring back the buffalo. There was just one subject − the sacred dance. It made its graduates immune to white man's weapons. It was the greatest single educational short cut ever offered to Americans but its vogue ended abruptly on December 24, 1889, as a battery of four Hotchkiss guns poured explosive shells into a huddled group of Indian men, women, and children.

The quiz-program masters are just playing at education for a sheltered people's escapism, and thus they have need for only play counters in their game. The great-books professors have a closed game, very serious, and, since they pay all bets in great-book chips, they can operate happily so long as they stay inside the charmed circle. The unfortunate Sioux ghost-dancers at Wounded Knee Creek were forced to count their scores with their lives; their subject was not sacred enough for Hotchkiss guns.

A corollary activity for the pedagogical plainsman is the drawing of curricular distinctions. He traces the boundaries between general education and special education, between liberal studies and vocational training, between pure science and applied science, between the arts and the humanities, between philosophy and religion, between psychology and sociology, between history and anthropology, and so on and on into the academic night.

The more boundaries he surveys, the more new ones he discovers. He finds subjects within subjects, heaps classifications upon dichotomies, and uncovers new fields for education in never-ending labor.

In the plainsman's practice, the duty of the individual learner is clear. He must acquire, adjust, and conform. He must acquire subjects, knowledge, skills, in proper blocs and sequences and at the proper time. He must adjust to the teacher, to the class, and to the community in terms of his knowledge and skills. He must conform in those adjustments to the dictates of society, vocation, government, religion, and other ruling systems of behavior and thought.

The acquire-adjust-conform combination has seldom been so well exemplified as in the pre-1945 Japanese system of education and culture which began with bowing to the Emperor's portrait and ended with thought police. It is a matter for sober reflection that a very similar education could be initiated with flag idolatry and developed, through avoidance of disloyal acts, to a complete rejection of any ideas which might be held by subversive groups.

I say *could be*, since it is hard for us Americans to conceive of a situation in which our thoughts would be policed. Unconsciously we rely upon a type of mountaineering in our education to protect us in the free exercise of idiosyncrasy in thought, at least. We should ask ourselves, however, whether the official thought-control process is not already at work when a committee of the Congress through the newspapers accuses a government scientist of disloyalty, and then refuses for months to give him a hearing. How much freedom of thought, under such conditions, remains to government workers or to young men and women aspiring to be employed by the government?

Not long ago almost any student of American education would have said that thought policing by applying the doctrine of guilt through thought association would be impossible in the United States of America. Today he could not be so sure. The year 1949 marked the issuance of a document by the headquarters of the Supreme Commander of the Allied Powers in Japan in which American citizens were solemnly told that the history of a Soviet spy ring in Japan prior to World War II shows us that we cannot trust the loyalty of our closest friends or even relatives, and that persons who have sympathized with Communist causes, even though not themselves Communists, must be prevented from occupying security positions.

Upon this basis, of course, the Commander-in-Chief of the United States Armed Forces would be called by any Dixiecrat a very poor national security risk. He should not be given access even to restricted and much less to confidential or secret materials. He has proposed a civil-rights program for Negores which the Communist Party supports. Every public-school man in he United States who beleives in free and compulsory education is a poor security risk. Every Communist government in the world preaches the same doctrine. The president of the University of Maryland has been assailed by a local news sheet on the chief grounds that he is trying to give higher education to young men and women whose parents cannot afford to pay private college tuition fees. According to the guilt-by-association theory, the paper has an open-and-shut case against the president. Every Communist in Maryland agrees with him. So do many of the clergymen of the Roman Catholic Church, and the president might well be accused, therefore, of subservience to a foreign power, the Holy See.

There are not merely straws in the wind — they are more like haystacks in the cyclone. The loug-mouthed declaimer of the correct thought, the patrioteer who screams most passionately of loyalty while stealing from the tax payers, the defender of the United States who often never bore arms for the United States but is quick to protect his country by accusing a dead man of treason with no grounds for the accusation except a love of headlines — these are signs of a culture passing in some parts under the tutelage of pedagogical plainsmen.

The defense against this drift towards pedagogical plainsmanship cannot be bought by arms, by law, or even by exhortation. It can be purchased only at the price of a mountaineering education of democratic power and scope.

The creed of the educational mountaineer provides that force to do democracy's work. it contains two main articles of faith. The first is that of equality of opportunity; the second is that of equality of efficiency.

To give equality of opportunity, the mountaineering educator starts with a maximum of understanding for every child. That means that every child will be studied as precisely and extensively as present techniques allow. The crippled, six-year-old colored girl of modest intellectual ability will get just as much understanding as research and practice can provide. The physcially perfect six-year-old white boy of highest intellectual capacity will also get just as much understanding as research and practice can provide.

Why not give more understanding to the child with the higher ability?

It cannot be done. There is no more understanding available than the educational mountaineer gives to every one of his learners.

To give equality of efficiency, the educational mountaineer develops the crippled six-year-old's personality, let us say, by teaching her tap-dancing. She can move her right foot only by dragging it on the floor, but she can lift her left foot off the floor and move the toe and heel. She learns to tap-dance with her left foot.

"Tap-dancing a first-grade subject?" screams the plainsman. "If it's good for one child, it's good for all of them. Democracy demands that they all learn the multiplication tables. If democracy demands tap-dancing at all, it demands it for all."

The mountaineer says, "I am not teaching tap-dancing. I am teaching a shy child to be more confident. I am taking a tiny peak of ability and trying to make it a tower of idiosyncrasy by which one who may be some day a great woman in her own right can get her first secure moorings."

The educational mountaineer develops the six-year-old of high intellectual capacity by encouraging him to study osmosis.

"Osmosis in the first grade?" cries the plainsman. "Osmosis is a high school subject. That's where we teach it for everybody in good democratic fashion."

But the mountaineer says again, "I am not teaching osmosis. I am teaching one who is a great genius to be in truth the great genius that he is."

Here I pause to point out the inescapable fact that the mountaineer must know how to teach tap-dancing and osmosis if he is going to use them as means of developing personalities and characters. In a reasonably long lifetime of observation of educational plainsmen and educational mountaineers in many kinds of schools and in many parts of the globe, I have seen no slightest evidence that those teachers who believe that education starts, proceeds and ends with a developing individual have as a group any less erudition and command of subject matter than have those teachers who believe that education starts with a required curriculum and ends with mastery of a minimum essential. I have indeed seen evidence to indicate that a truly profound command of a field of knowledge inclines men toward the pedagogical peaks. How else can we account for the prevalence of mountaineers in the great graduate schools?

Whether the mountaineer is in the graduate school or in the first grade, whether he is educating citizens in the high school or officers in the Army, his answers to the double-barrelled question raised earlier in this lecture are clear, concise, and unequivocal.

How much uniformity does this society need for safety?

It needs only that uniformity which the achievements of its greatest goals require. It demands security of life and health for its people. It demands wide opportunities for its people in work and play, in song and prayer. It must provide each individual with maximum aids to the development of his powers to contribute in every way possible to the great goals of his people.

Are their necessary restrictions on the individual's development? Of course there are. Should there be guidance, direction, in the building of his abilities? Of course there should be. The child with an idiosyncrasy of aggression cannot be permitted to develop it into an idiosyncrasy for brutality, mayhem, or murder. He must instead be helped to develop it into an idiosyncrasy for fighting disease through the practice of medicine, battling hunger by farming, breaking down isolation by blasting highways through mountains, or doing some other aggressive job commensurate with his pattern of abilities.

How much deviation does this society require for progress?

It requires just as much deviation, just as many uniquely developed peaks of ability, just as much idiosyncrasy as the attainment of its goals will allow and need. All societies are wasteful of the capacities of their people. That society which comes closest to developing every socially useful idiosyncrasy in every one of its members will make the greatest progress toward its goals.

The key decision on both the matter of minimum safety and the matter of maximum progress is this decision concerning the amount of caution needed to protect the society's goals and the amount of daring required to advance the society toward those goals.

Who makes that decision?

In a democracy, the people make it.

In this democracy, I have heart and faith that our people will not make the decision very wrong. This is because I believe they are a great people and a strong people, not just in population or in number of tons of steel they can produce annually, but in those measures of meaning which God Himself uses to gauge the tides of history. I think they will make educational room for themselves in the future according to their size and strength.

America Must Be Strong –
And Smart, Too, If Possible

Since I received your kindly invitation to speak, a good deal of water has gone over the dams of the Susquehanna River. What I thought of when I received your invitation and heard that the theme of the Convention was to be "America Must Be Strong," was "America Must Be Strong – In Case." I now think of it as "America Must Be Strong – Or Else!"

There is a lot of difference in the two concepts. It is like the contrast in the story of the two Swedes who were picked up for fighting by the police patrol and taken to the magistrate. The magistrate looked at them with pitying eyes for they were so badly battered up they seemed to have been punished terribly already. He said to one of them, "What's your name?" "Olie Veburg, Your Honor," he was answered. "What's the origin of this difficulty?" he asked. Olie said, "Can't say, Your Honor."

So the police magistrate turned to the other and said, "What's your name?" He answered, "My name's Sven Larson, Your Honor." "What's the origin of the difficulty down there?" he was asked. "I don't understand what you mean 'difficulty,' " Sven replied. "How did the fight develop?" Sven answered, "I don't know what you mean 'develop.' " "Well, how did the fight start or begin?"

"Oh, you mean how it began. I can tell you that," said Sven. "I was walking along in front of Nels Johnson's livery stable. Olie, he shoved me off the sidewalk. So I shoved him. Then he hit me in the nose and gave me a bloody nose, so I hauled off and hit him in the jaw. Then he hit me along side the head, and I hauled off and hit him along side of the head and knocked him into the street. Then he knocks me down, and I get up and knock him down and kick him in the slats. Olie goes behind the livery stable and gets a neck yoke and hits me over the head with it. So I get an axe and I hit him on the head with it. Well then, we both got kind of mad and then we started to fight."

That was the situation when I was asked to speak at this banquet. The United States was trying to engage in a war without fighting. Now we're kind of mad and we've started to fight. The United States is ready to fight now, no matter how many wars are involved, and none of us have any doubt that the

---

This address was delivered before the December 30, 1941 meeting of the Pennsylvania State Education Association, and is obviously dated. I have included it, however, because I feel the basic thought is as appropriate to the "cold war" of the 1960's as it was to the "hot war" of the 1940's. RMB.

United States is strong. We have no doubt but that her eventual strength in respect to the war will be tremendous, that she will display much greater strength than the people of Europe, Asia, and Africa ever dreamed of, greater strength than the people of the United States ever dreamed of. Some of the bad things that will come out of this war will be due to the fact that the United States will have to display great strength in this war and she will probably display more strength than she really needs because that is the nature of the people of the United States.

But unmodified strength is not enough. I do not mean to muddle terms or split hairs. But unmodified strength in the sense of weight of materials and men and planes and bombs and tanks and guns, submarines and destroyers – all those things of material strength – all that phase of national strength – will not be enough. That kind of being strong will not be enough. Germany is strong that way, but she has not been smart along with the strength. That is the real reason Germany is going to lose the war. To be strong enough to carry on a war without being smart enough to finish the war is to be ineffective.

Therefore, because I want my people, as you do, to be intelligent in order to be powerful I speak on the subject, "America Must Be Strong – And Smart, Too, If Possible." I do not mean that in a joking sense. Perhaps if I has spoken some months ago on this topic I might have been able to put more jokes into it but that last – "And Smart, Too, If Possible" – is the most important part.

It is hard to suggest the educational efforts we need in order to be "smart too, if possible," without seeming to criticize the material war efforts of the country, and if you sense that I am criticizing I hope you will not judge me harshly. One of the reasons we are willing to fight for the United States is because the United States is the place where we can make criticisms, where we still try to collect all the judgements from the mass of citizens. If you think any of my suggestions are wrong, I want you to remember there are two million fellow teachers and one hundred and thirty million fellow citizens who can say they are wrong. That is one of the great reasons why the United States is a country for which we are proud to fight.

It is impossible, furthermore, to consider some of the educational jobs brought about by a condition of war without considering the military objectives of war. I do not claim to be a military expert. I do not claim to be a military commentator – although when I read some of them it appears to me that one does not require much technical knowledge of war to be a military commentator.

At one time I had first-hand experience with war and like all of you, I followed what appears to me to be the second phase. The 1919-1939 phase as well as the present phase all seems a part of the Great War that started in 1914 and of which the 1914-1919 phase was only the first, the beginning of things.

In my opinion, that war which began in 1914 will end not when our people are merely strong enough to end it, but when our people are smart enough to end it. Hard as it is to think it, the people who eventually will have to be smart enough actually and finally to end this war will include not only Pennsylvanians and Marylanders, and Americans of the United States and Americans of the other countries in the western hemisphere, and the British Commonwealth of Nations, and Scandinavians and the Dutch and the Czechs and the Yugoslavs and the Poles and the Greeks and the Russians, but those people — our people — who will eventually have to end this war finally and properly will also include the brown rice growers of Japan and the wheat farmers of Italy and the factory workers of Germany. If we do not believe that those people will be included, then I think we will not have been actually smart enough to end this war and end it properly.

Parenthetically, I would like to mention that I have noticed as one of the first war educational efforts of the federal government, a poster in the post office which depicts four German soldiers in a poisonous fashion. These must be a special group of German soldiers, like none I ever saw in battle and I met all kinds on the field of battle — a special kind of German that exists only in the propaganda imagination of someone in Washington. If that poster which I see in the post office represents the type of education for war which someone in authority in the federal government believes to be necessary to make people smart and motivated enough for war, then somebody who authorized that poster knows very little about education and very little about the processes necessary to get people like the Americans of the United States ready for war.

Battles are not won by such posters. Battles are won by speed and concentrated power, and wars are won by the weight of men and weapons at the proper point and the proper places. Peace is won — real peace is won — only by making available every possible ounce of intelligence and good will you can find and develop among all the peoples in the world.

That is the job for good teachers, teachers who are the engineers of intelligence and good will. Teachers who are not first and foremost engineers of intelligence and good will are pedagogic mechanics such as those who fill the Third Reich today.

At the outset let's look at the simple but astonishing fact that thousands upon thousands of young men in this country are being rejected for military service because they cannot meet the fourth-grade educational requirement of the United States army. To date we have rejected these men for no other reason. But most of these men can be educated and equipped rapidly by intensive instruction. There are officers in the United States army, and we see some of them in this room tonight, who are trained schoolmen, professional schoolmen. These officers, with the help of the enlisted men with the same training, can educate these men. They can be taught military construction for work in the labor battalion, they can be taught to use a rifle, a hand grenade, they can be taught to read and write. They can be taught the few simple arithmetical principles they need, the principles of hygiene and sanitation. They can acquire a knowledge of geography and history and government of their country and thus be added to the reservoir of our military manpower. When the war ends they will have acquired fundamental education that will add to the weight and quality of our national life. Here is one chance to be smarter than we are at present and eventually be stronger if we operate in terms of strength alone.

Of these rejectees for educational deficiencies twenty per cent, I am informed, in some states are negroes. I don't know all the reasons why this rejection should be so high among the negroes. You all know some of the reasons but no one of us knows all the reasons. We do know, however, that one of the reasons is founded in the fact that the states of this country that have the greatest educational burden have the least wealth and also have the largest negro populations.

Federal grants for special vocational education and agricultural vocational purposes through the WPA, the CCC, the NYA, for general adult education have aimed to advance vast sums of money, but we still shy away from federal grants to the school systems of the United States.

And so in times of war we find that twenty per cent of young men in certain areas of our country are not literate to the fourth-grade level. It is important to me that an Alabama negro boy, willing, eager, and able to serve his country, a boy like many of the negro troopers who made so enviable records for themselves during the Great War in the New York 15th Infantry Division should be rejected because Alabama did not offer educational opportunities to him and did not enforce the compulsory education laws in his favor? Is that important to me, a Marylander and a white man? Perhaps not, as a Marylander and a white man, but as a citizen of the United States it is important to me. As a citizen of a country engaged in a war when every last ounce of mental and physical ability will perhaps be needed, as the father of a college boy who has lately been not in college but working with a pick and shovel in a far-off island of the Pacific to build a military outpost for the United States and who may at this moment be facing the bombers of the Axis, I am rather keenly conscious that we citizens of the United States should not only long ago have repaired that Alabama disability but should make the necessary trifling grant to Alabama to make it possible for her to reduce this educational disability in the immediate future.

It is the old cry that federal grants to education mean federal control of the system. But that doesn't make my heart miss a single beat any more. It used to but it doesn't any more. The federal government is only our government, isn't it? It will interfere as much or as little as we want it to, won't it? It will be just as bureaucratic and dictatorial as we want it to be, won't it? Or is it our government? I cannot understand this argument any more. It is ridiculous to think, in my opinion, that we have any more bureaucracy than we want, that our government is any more dictatorial than we want. When this war is finished, I predict that we will see more clearly than today that the tough question, the really hard question is not so much how bad our federal government might be as how intelligent are the voters who select our representatives in the federal government.

. . . .

We have in the armed forces of the United States approximately two million men and we are putting in a great deal more general education along with the technical training than was ever given before. This is very important to the people of the United States. I know the officers are conscious of its importance. A type of education is being given these boys which is very different from the instruction which once characterized ninety per cent of the military education of this country, and I speak as one who was under the influence of this instruction for four years. Today I know from what the army officers tell me and from what I have seen myself that the program of technical training and military education is much better carried out than ever before.

However in this period of war effort we must not overlook the greater army of many more millions of boys and girls, men and women, adults in the schools of this country extending all the way from the elementary schools to the universities and night classes. The education given to this army throughout the United States is inadequate. You may truthfully say it is a tremendous enterprise that overshadows the education given in any other part of the world, but it is still inadequate. It is not enough for the highest efforts we want in winning the war and not enough for the highest efforts we must have for a peace-time when we shall invoke the energies of the people to peaceful purposes, in the same clear-cut way those energies are now being devoted to wartime purposes. We must improve and extend the educational opportunities open to the people of the United States so that those opportunities will be much more equal for all peoples, higher and finer than are current today.

One night nineteen hundred and thirty-two years ago Augustus Caesar, ruler of what was then most of the civilized world, paced his quarters in sleeplessness and anguish. As he walked back and forth he cried, "Quintilius Varus, give me back my legions!" But his legions were never returned to him for far to the north Quintilius Varus had led these legions to overwhelming disaster. To the Roman officials and to Augustus Caesar this was cause for great anxiety. They were worried for to their minds the outcome of the war being fought on the boundaries of the then Roman world boiled down to the necessity that the legions would be strong. So by one means or another they secured more legions and these legions defended the boundaries of the Roman empire. After the year 9, for two centuries after the Christian era, they maintained relative peace long after losing the Roman legions at Teutoberger Wald, but the real cause for worry about the Roman empire was one which neither the ruler nor the people of Rome recognized. It was the simple but crucial question of what the skills, attitudes, and knowledges of each individual Roman citizen should be. The Roman rulers and masters worried about their legions for defense, their weapons and military transports and equipment, the money for defense, but they did not know about the problem of how people can change their ways and organize their methods more effectively in order to achieve the greatest results. They did not recognize that their first worry should have been national education and for that reason the Roman world was doomed in the year 9.

They were strong, but they weren't smart, too, and they were doomed, not because the barbarians to the north wiped out the legions of Quintilius Varus but because the people of Rome did not see the greatest war problem and so Roman society developed within itself the seeds of its own decay. The Roman people forgot that a nation, no matter how much wisdom is attributed to its rulers, cannot be wiser than the developed intelligence of its individual citizens all put together, that a nation, no matter how clever its chiefs or how great their skills, is no greater than the sum of the skills of each citizen. A nation no matter how great the character and sweeping the vision of the leaders cannot carry out purposes greater and higher than the combined purposes of each individual man, woman, and child within the boundaries of that nation.

So Roman society entered upon its peaceful autumn. The quality of citizenship and its skills and attitudes declined. While the frontiers were guarded, while the Romans thought their defense system was working well, suddenly their way of life crumbled of its own accord.

I suppose we might consider, if it were not a matter you have already considered, what things we fight for in time of war, whether we fight for territory or for material resources, or just what we fight for. Think — what are the things we actually fight for? What are the eventualities back there, clear back behind all the obvious things, that we fight for? When you look at those things, no matter what disguise you see them in you will see an educational problem, something produced by the engineers of intelligence and good will, not pedagogic mechanics. It is easy to say the kind of education you need costs money and we need the money for guns, but in the modern world as in the days of Augustus Caesar money is symbolic of the organized efforts of the people. Education costs effort. Guns cost effort. Planes cost effort. Good government costs effort, and the more efficient and well organized and intelligent the effort the lower the eventual cost.

Education of a purposeful kind is the greatest cost reducer in organized society. If we want a powerful people for a strong war defense effort we cannot afford to be legion wise and school foolish.

The Poverty of Nations

Adam Smith published his celebrated economic treatise, *The Wealth of Nations,* in 1776. By practicing some of the main principals that he enunciated, the country born to independence on July 4 of that year has become the most prosperous in the world.

A central thesis of Smith's argument was that labor is the true source of wealth. He included in the concept all work which added to the exchange value of a commodity. He measured the prices of goods in terms of what it took to produce them. In Smith's view, labor was the yardstick of economic value.

It followed, therefore, that division of labor was a chief means of increasing a nation's wealth and that specialization of productive skills was of crucial importance to a country that sought riches.

Smith's predecessors in economic science had directed their thought mainly toward problems of production. He went an important step further by insisting that the sole end and purpose of production was consumption.

In the eighteen decades since the publication of Smith's work, the United States of America has amply demonstrated her mastery of the processes which he described. She has developed and trained great labor forces with highly specialized skills. She has invented, set up, and operated industrial assembly lines and their counterparts in commerce and agriculture. She has poured vast amounts of her earnings into research and techanical training in a hunt for new and better methods of production. She has piled up steel and fuel, cotton and corn, tobacco and motor vehicles, and bombs and butter on a scale hitherto unparalleled in the world's history. Although she has taught her people by advertising and by schooling to consume these products of her hands even when they are basically so hard to sell as beverages that make men truly distinguished, creams that carry beauty in their price tags, and nausea-pink and dejected-lavender automobiles, as over-powered, over-gadgeted, and over-priced as they are over-colored. On these and the great flood of more or less valuable and significant articles that roll from her factories and processing plants and are prized by her people for uses good or bad, the United States of America is today unquestionably Exhibit A for the kind of free, competitive, sophisticated economy, hampered by a minimum of state controls, that Adam Smith envisioned.

The keynote address at the annual convention of the American Personnel and Guidance Association in Washington, D.C., March 26, 1956.

Why, then, in opening a convention assembled to consider the theme, "Guidance and National Policy," should I presume to call for a look at the reverse of Smith's title? Why study "The Poverty of Nations" in a country which has so much wealth?

The question is pertinent, but the answer is obvious to men and women who have our professional concerns. An American economist, Richard T. Ely, suggested the answer only a generation ago in unforgettable language when he said that we must not forget that "there are two kinds of poverty — one a lack of goods for the higher wants, the other a lack of wants for the higher goods. . . .," and that the poverty of wants is by far the more terrible.[1]

It is my theme here that the wealthiest nation in the world is facing some of the direst poverty in the world, that as she tallies her material achievements, as she counts her silks and nylons, her jewels and furs, her machines and weapons, and her rich piles of wheat and eggs, the cold breath of a Poverty of Wants is on her neck. This is a specter that will not be exercised by power brakes and power steering, by two television sets where only one flickered and blared before, or even by clover-leaf approaches to unlimited freeways from every hamlet in the land. It has to be fought more skillfully. It has to be driven back by concerted, intelligent effort. The campaign against it needs to become a dominant feature of our national policy.

In warfare, the prudent commander studies the military situation before him in all its negative as well as its positive aspects. He examines the possible routes by which he may be attacked. He seizes the high points on which hostile guns may be emplaced. He sends patrols to woods from which ambushes can be launched against him. He fires exploratory bursts along the hedgerows. He orders his reconnaissance aircraft aloft to scout the enemy's disposition and numbers. He is cautious, suspicious, and pessimistic.

Let us first, in similar fashion, therefore, look cautiously at this potential national enemy, a poverty of wants. Let us consider the ways in which it may attack us. How can a people, as wealthy as we Americans are, ever become poor From what ambushes can poverty spring upon us?

Let us look once more at the main idea in Adam Smith's classic exposition. Labor was what made wealth in his scheme. Suppose that we wished to make a wealthy nation poor (a strictly academic supposition, of course, since no one would consciously support such a diabolical objective in any country). But just suppose we would start chipping away at the main block in the foundation of the country's wealth, the skills of its people. If the country was the technologically most advanced in the world, if it had moved rapidly through the first and was just entering upon the second industrial revolution and this required a

---

[1]Ely, Richard T. *Outlines of Economics.* New York: Macmillan, 1926.

greater quantity and a higher quality of scientific and technical education than ever before, if its minimum defenses against potential enemies also called for more and better special and general education, the teachers in these areas should be reduced in numbers, fewer of them should be trained, they should be underpaid, they should be overloaded, they should be given inadequate equipment and they should be required to spend much of their energies in clerical work. When the representatives of the national government would be asked to consider this grave threat to the nation's prosperity and safety, they should start looking intently at the need for longer, broader, and faster highways, they should search for ways to renew old wars, they should spar for political position, but they should never permit the formulation of a national policy of national support for the education of their countrymen.

Suppose, moreover, that in this hypothetical country the changing birth rates of the past forty years have been such that there are now relatively limited numbers of men and women in the twenty-to-forty-year age groups but that the numbers in the groups aged less than twenty are tremendous both in fact and in implication.

Looking at this imaginary situation, our vision untroubled by the pressure of reality, we can see at once that here is a chance for a double ambush on the country's prosperity. On one flank the attack can be launched by dissipating the scant manpower resources of the twenty-to-forty-year-olds. On the other flank the quality and scope of education can be reduced for the younger groups as their numbers increase.

Let us suppose, further, that this County X, because of steadily lengthening life spans, has a growing number of older people each year. Here is another soft spot in the battle line against poverty. Retire the older people at sixty or sixty-five. Refuse to employ them at even earlier ages. Support them with the labor of twenty-, thirty-, and forty-year olds. Impress upon them the joys of uselessness. Teach them to be happy with their symptoms of approaching senility. Let them hit the highways on the quest for climate, their play things stowed in the baggage compartments.

This is enough speculation concerning hypothetical attempts to make an imaginary country poor. We have looked at several main routes of possible attack on such a country's basic source of wealth, abilities of its people. There are really just two of those routes:

1. *The first is by way of frontal assault. The ability-discovering and ability-developing services are reduced. Education and guidance programs are lowered in quality and narrowed in scope. It is as though the enemy fire were decimating company after company in the attack and smashing battery after battery of its supporting guns.*

2. *The second is a route comparable to military envelopment. The abilities which the people have are not fully used. They are scattered and*

misdirected. Whole blocks of them are kept out of action. It is as though the enemy cavalry were harrying them on flank and rear, cutting them into aimless refugee parties, until they throw their weapons away and cry for quarter.

A little while ago I mentioned the prudent commander who studies the situation before him in all its negative aspects. I spoke of his caution, his suspicion, and his pessimism and how he displays these qualities in his search for possible road blocks and ambushes against his advance.

Let me speak now of the truly great commander. He is prudent, too, and at times he cannot be distinguished from an ordinary commander who is merely careful. But there always comes a time when the great commander turns to positive action. He backs away across New Jersey with superior British forces slamming his green militia roughly at every step. He ponders his many weaknesses and details them to the Continental Congress. He lacks almost everything; men, money, clothing, equipment, arms, ammunition, food, and transport. He notes them all; systematically, gloomily, and forbodingly. Then, one bitter night he moves with dazzling decision. He crosses the river, he marches, and he strikes. Christmas day, 1776, and the guns at Trenton salute the first and, some us think, still the greatest captain who ever wore the American uniform.

We too must move from the negative to the positive campaign. We must not only look at the weaknesses of our present practices relating to the abilities of our people but also envision and seek to put into force a sound national policy for discovering, developing, directing, and distributing those abilities to maximum effect. A piecemeal and timid policy is not enough; we should have a comprehensive policy; daringly conceived and executed.

Our guidance and personnel tasks today are first of all affected profoundly by the population figures familiar to all of us. In the schools our buildings and professional personnel are being overwhelmed with burgeoning numbers. Within five years that flood will have hit the colleges with stunning force. In state after state, and in the country as a whole, the output of training programs for teachers and other educational personnel, including guidance counselors, is steadily falling behind in a race against mounting enrollments. This situation is desparate; it will generally be so recognized tomorrow; and tomorrow always seems to arrive before we expect it.

I have earlier referred to the second industrial revolution. The mechanization of muscle labor which brought the first industrial revolution has been going on for a very long time. It started, no doubt, when the first savage picked up a rock to use as a pounding or cutting instrument. It was advanced a long way by the time he put a handle on the rock to make a hammer or an axe.

The mechanization of brain work which is introducing the second industrial revolution has also been going on for a long time. The invention of written records as an aid to memory is an ancient example, and the thermostat connected with the furnace is a recent example that is certainly not very new.

The advance of automatic control is just getting under way, however, and it is undoubtedly going to cause a revolution of some kind, no matter what we call it. If it does not bring considerable changes in education, it will be because education is missing the tide.

There are many white-collar workers in this country. The labor in the offices of government agencies, banks, commercial establishments, and research agencies of all kinds is largely paper work, and we have already found that macines can do paper work that men cannot do because human nervous systems are not built to handle so many items of certain sorts at such high speeds.

As a result of this development, there will be technological unemployment on a scale proportional to the lag in our educational and guidance programs. For every job that is replaced by automation, however, a number of new jobs will be developed. We will find, as usual, an oversupply of people who can do only the old job and a shortage of people so educated that they can learn readily to do the new jobs.

The best insurance against a future national poverty is therefore a flexible and imaginatively planned program of education and training for all our people. In war or peace, we will need to tap every source of manpower. Our married women, as soon as their children are in school; our handicapped citizens; our people in all age groups above forty; our younger citizens, whether in school or out; all these people should be taken into account in formulating our national policy in guidance.

Let me give an example from my own field of education. This country is tragically short of teachers. So far as the lack of financial attractiveness in the profession is concerned, it is not so much the lowness of the initial salary in teaching that keeps young people from entering it as the relative lack of spread between the initial salary and that to be expected after ten, fifteen, or twenty years of service. Consider the possible better utilization of the services of a single, well-trained teacher of high school science, for example if, after ten years' service, he received twice his initial salary, had a seventeen-year old laboratory assistant, who might still be in school part time, and an associate teacher from among the ranks of the married women or the "retired" citizens of the community who had a baccalaureate degree in a scientific field but was not a professionally trained teacher. A sum equal to the cost of one jet bomber, if granted to a state of average population in this country, would permit a careful tryout of such a scheme. I use this comparison not for a moment to imply that we should neglect the manufacture and manning of jet bombers, but rather to emphasize the belief that we can afford both the bombers and an intelligent national attack on the dark cloud of rising numbers of pupils and weakening educational facilities and personnel.

A president of the United States recently asked for about $5 billion to be spent on foreign aid. I know that the Congress has many members of both our political parties who are highly competent to examine this request carefully in the light of sound policy and to decide on the manner and the extent to which the request should be met. I look forward to the time, in the near future, when our executive and legislative leaders will be at least equally interested in carrying out a sound policy for the identification, guidance, and training of all our people for all our people's work.

I have spoken of only a few of the danger spots in our line of defense against a possible national poverty. There are others of great importance. How much do we lose in manpower on the most crucial levels every year by neglecting to discover, guide, and educate our most highly gifted children? How much of the mounting toll of juvenile delinquency is related to fragmented and inadequate guidance, personnel, and educational policies? What are our national aims and how shall we put them into action in these and other areas affecting the one source of the nation's wealth, the developed abilities of its people?

We can continue to neglect these crucial matters, regarding them as of less import than some of the symptoms of our neglect of them. Juvenile delinquency, for example, is a symptom of poor or non-existent guidance, education, and employment in home, school, and community. A shortage of science teachers is a symptom of poor guidance, poor education, and poor distribution of manpower. Someone might add, "And poor pay," but I would think that is also largely a symptom, a symptom of poor guidance and poor education of the citizens of the community with respect to the teacher's tasks and responsibilities.

The peril at which we neglect these crucial matters was picturesquely phrased by King Solomon long ago: "So shall they poverty come as one that travelleth and thy want as an armed man."

The Challenge to Public Education

. . . The great challenge to American education is this century, in this decade, at this very moment, no matter how disguised in varied masks, is directed squarely toward our concept of the individual and what we propose educatioally to do about that concept.

The United States was not founded on material resources. We have a lot of land, certainly, and on some of that land we have raised a lot of corn, rye, wheat, rice, oranges, and tobacco, but this country was not founded on cereals, on bourbon or rye beverages, or even on cigarettes, hard as the two latter exceptions may be to permit when some of the presumably greatest athletes, actors, travellers, and singers insist on the merits of smoking; and those distinguished gentlemen about town and country, who are pictured so expensively by one great thirst-slaking agency, assure us not too subtly that culture prosperity, and prestige are no further away than the tips of the fingers clasping a properly filled tall glass. This country was not founded, furthermore, on other much more widely approved products of our soil and our skills. It does not rest upon a base of iron, coal, timber, petroleum, or water power, valuable as these gifts of nature are. It does not come from cotton, wool, nylon, mink, or any other material for physical protection or ornamentation. Its spirit is not derived from automobiles, airplanes, telephones, radios, television sets, or even plumbing fixtures.

The United States of America was founded squarely on a great faith. It was a faith in the individual. The greatest challenge to American education at this time is also the greatest challenge to our whole concept of American life. That challenge is associated with various attempts to weaken and even to destroy that faith.

The belief on which the United States was founded was an old belief long before 1775, but it was given a new application to national life by the American revolutionists.

We Americans are now in the middle of what seems to us a very rough current over rocky rapids in the stream of our national existence. At such a time we need to look, however hurriedly, at some of the figures upstream who set our original course. They were very gallant and engaging figures, from the Boston hot-heads of driving energy to the great Philadelphia printer of suave genius,

An address before the 38th convention of the American Association of Collegiate Registrars and Admissions Officers, Washington, D.C., April, 1952.

from the Monticello planter of prophetic wisdom to the incomparably daring and steadfast master of Mount Vernon whose heart was equal to his sword. They and their countrymen established this nation on the rock of a belief in the unique worth of the individual.

We Americans set up our government, our religious systems, our schools, public and private, our economic activities, and our channels of artistic expression on that general foundation. We put solemn guarantees in our Federal and State constitutions that the individual citizen would have freedom of pray in his own fashion, to his own God or gods, or not to pray at all if it suited him; that he could speak his mind freely either orally or in writing, in peaceable assembly or in petition, standing on a soap box or working over a printing press; that his personal dignity would not be endangered by unwarranted arrest or invasion of his privacy; and that his property would not be seized or searched without process of law due his individual worth as a citizen of the United States.

No government could take these rights away from the individual according to these guarantees. The government was the creature of the individual citizen and so could not be their master.

The education the Americans set up and operated was the kind they felt they had to have to make such a system of popular government work. They invented lay and local boards of control to keep the schools responsive to the wishes of individual citizens. They developed elementary schools that were increasingly designed for the education of children in terms of their individual needs and capacities. They established and multiplied in the most dramatic fashion the American comprehensive high school devoted to the individual guidance and personal development of each boy and girl of secondary school age in the country. They set up colleges and universities on a scale and, I believe, on a level of total productive and cultural accomplishment not closely paralleled in any other quarter of the globe.

Of course this view of government and of education as being servants of individual citizens has always been opposed by some groups in this country. Once, for a long generation, a century and more ago, one section of this nation was under almost complete control of men who believed sincerely that the guarantees of individual worth and personal dignity did not apply to members of one race. Teachers were forced from their classrooms, clergymen were driven from their churches, editors were taken from their desks, and members of the general public were otherwise punished for attempting to exercise freedom of speech, freedom of the press, freedom of assembly, freedom of petition, and freedom of teaching on this subject that state and local governments did not want discussed. The greatest tragedy this country has ever faced in its brief history was the direct result of this policy.

The United States still has people who do not believe in education for individual development any more than they believe in government as a servant of free individuals. They have always fought public education in this country. They were against taxation for elementary schools just as they were against universal suffrage. They were against publicly supported secondary education as they were against graduated income taxes. They were against the establishment of state colleges and universities as they were against public health and welfare programs. They have fought every important measure in the country's history to serve the individual citizen better. They furnish the bulk of the opposition in our communities, in our states, and in the nation against any proposal to improve our elementary, secondary, or higher educational services and facilities.

It is my opinion that most of these people are basically actuated in opposition to educational improvements by the old motive of money. They try to disguise their positions in various ways. They cry that colleges promote godlessness, that high schools teach the use of narcotics, and that elementary schools train delinquents. They are particularly concerned about patriotism, not so much the kind that is demonstrated in action for the country and its people, but rather the kind that can be attested by oath and by protestations of orthodoxy.

This country was not founded on oaths and orthodoxy. It was founded on service to free individual citizens; that particular man — and what if he does belong to a small, dissident, religious sect? — that specific woman yonder — and what *of* her color? — and this child right here — and what do I care about his parents' political views?

Right now, right in this year, right in this month, . . . is a time for us who play active roles in higher education to stiffen our resolution to keep education free, to direct our renewed effort to the strengthening of our services to individuals, and to resist the ever-present pressure which has been heightened in the last few years for purse control disguised largely as mind control.

Mr. Justice Holmes once remarked that when a battle is joined the only thing to do is to form your battalions and fight. In the schools and colleges of the United States we have certainly got a battle on our hands to get sufficient financial support for the educational services our people need and expect us to give them.

The battle has started. We cannot fight very well without forming our battalions. Those battalions are out there, some of them in bivouac and many of them already on the march. They are our people, our alumni, our parents' organizations, our civic and service clubs, our fraternal and religious groups, our patriotic and professional associations, our chambers of commerce and our labor unions. They believe, most of them, in our great American cause. They will form themselves in defense and development of American education if we give them a chance to the extent of our professional vision and courage.

The one greatest job before us in all the schools and colleges is to put our institutions into new and better relationships with our supporting communities. They can and probably will form their own battalions and if necessary win this engagement without us, but then we shall have been guilty of skulking in the face of the enemy.

Effect of Community Forces Upon the School

The most impressive thing about man is his ability to change his ways; the most depressing thing about him is the poor use he makes of that ability.

Man has many forms of explanations for his failure to use his tough and complex nervous system more wisely . . . . He claims he cannot avoid his difficulties because he is plunged into them by social forms beyond his control. . . . But no matter whether he speaks of the will of the gods, the decree of fate, the fortunes of war, national honor, stern economic necessity, or the manifest destiny of a people, he is always presenting the same argument — the argument that he cannot order his own ways properly just because he is blocked by his own peculiar behavior.

Mysterious, complex, uncontrollable, unpredictable, dangerous, these social forces are merely men in action together for the attainment of goals which they set up in action. In dealing with social forces in a community, therefore, the first step is to discard all the traditional claptrap which makes social forces out to be mysterious and dangerous. The task of directing social forces is merely a task of modifying human behavior — a hard task surely, but not a particularly mysterious or impossible one. . . . Much of our difficulty in making any community educational system effective arises from the fact that our little formal educational system has its efforts nullified by other behavior-changing systems in the community which are very much under the control of men.

There are three main lines of attack on any attempt to make the public school a more effective behavior-changing instrument. . . . First, the attackers shake their heads solemnly and say, "Human nature is always the same. You can't change human nature." Second, they maintain that public education cannot possibly be as effective an instrument for changing human ways as are other instruments over which the public has little if any control. Third, they claim that it is financially impossible to support a public education system complete enough to change the ways of a community against opposing social forces. . . .

Against the notion that human nature cannot be changed there is opposed the evidence of the tremendous diversity of cultures which has been almost endlessly documented by the anthropologists. A particular type of human

Address before the February 28, 1939, convention of the American Association of School Administrators, Cleveland, Ohio.

behavior is found to be nonexistent in one society; in another society it is so dominant that practically every social situation is organized and comprehended only in terms of that behavior. . . . Men can change their ways in literally thousands of opposed directions. . . .

In face of the claim that public education cannot possibly be as effective an instrument for community change as are other instruments hidden under the convenient disguise of mysterious social forces, we must reply that the force of education is dependent upon the clearness of its goals and the effectiveness of its procedures, and that opponents of public education have worked indefatigably to keep its goals clouded and its procedures restricted. . . .

The most dangerous question which can be repeated in the face of any autocratic system of human living is this question of who should have the right to tell how the ways of the people are to be changed. There are in every community groups of persons, often very important and powerful persons, who do not want the masses of the people to consider such a question at all. They want to set behavior-changing goals for the people, not for the people's benefit, but for the benefit of particularly privileged groups. . . .

These powerful special groups have taken part in every battle for the development of a democratic school system in America, and they have always been on the wrong side. . . . As the masses of the people — the farmers, the working men, the professional men, the small merchants and tradesmen — came to realize the true motives and character of this opposition, they rose up and smacked the opposition down.

One of the chief defenses of the opposition in recent as well as in earlier times has been associated with the claim that it is financially impossible to support a system of public education on a truly democratic basis. . . . Since the property tax and the sales tax are most carefully designed to lay a disproportionate share of tax burden on the less-than-wealthy members of the community, this economy argument has been most effective of all. It seems difficult for the people to recognize the absurdity of this argument in a country which still spends vastly more for a few luxury articles than for public education, in a country whose most vociferous objectors to the crushing burden of taxation often spend more money for hard liquor than they spend to help support public education. . . .

It may well be urged that the quality of the public education we now offer is not of so high an average as to warrant lasting faith in its power to direct community changes wisely even if it were given the opportunity. Yet I must confess to a strong optimism in this regard. When public education steps out and observes the people of its community carefully and sympathetically, when it forgets its subject matter superstitions and studies the needs and desires and longings and abilities of the masses of men, when it can take all its people up on the heights of self-analysis and self-understanding and show them their own hearts — then public education will be the most powerful social force in the community. Then the masses of men will come more and more to see that the direction of social forces in any community is a matter of changing all the ways of all the people, and they will insist that the direction of so important a process should be carried on by the people themselves through executives responsible to them. They will confide to their own public educational system their hopes for a better community in the future, and the public education system will use all its resources to educate them in the direction they indicate. "And if any man seek to set them at naught," the education system will fight him at any weight and in any ring. —

...And with the Other Hand ...a Weapon

When Nehemiah and his men were repairing the walls of Jerusalem, their enemies, the Arabians, the Ammonites, and the Ashdodites, were understandably disturbed and conspired to halt the work by force of arms. Nehamiah took security measures. "They which builded on the wall," he reports, "and they that bear burdens, with those that laded, every one with one of his hands wrought in the work, and with the other hand held a weapon."[1]

This was a tiny conquered nation of 2,500 years ago, a numerically insignificant people in the vast empire ruled over by Artaxerxes I. Their problem was simple, to get their defenses completed before they were attacked.

I will not speak further of this ancient people and their ancient problems of combined construction and security. I will speak instead not of a small nation of long ago but of a great nation of today, a nation in whose concerns the regions of the former empire of Artaxerxes figure as objects of relatively minor charity and intrigue, but a nation which still faces the problem of balancing the needs of construction against the demands of security.

The United States of America is the most powerful nation that has hitherto appeared in the world's history. Although she has only six per cent of the world's population and certainly no more than, probably not so much on the average as six per cent of the world's material resources, she has by far the greatest ability to build, to make, to do, to produce, to process, to transport, of any people in the world. She can manufacture half the world's goods with only half her maximum potential effort. She can produce mountains of surplus butter, eggs, wheat, cotton, tobacco, and steel with one economic hand tied behind her — and often does. She can build two automobiles tomorrow where only one today pursues it chrome-smiling way through burgeoning traffic jams — automobiles with 400 horsepower engines instead of those with only 250 or 300 horsepower, automobiles with wheelbases so long that all residential garages will be increasingly obsolete and parking lot real estate more valuable than bank sites, automobiles in four instead of only two tones of nausea pink, leering lavender, bilious mustard, opulent orange, passionate purple, and virulent violet — automobiles with vertical tail fins twice as elevated as those now in vogue and of proven aerodynamic worth at all speeds in excess of 200 miles per hour. She can build super highways from coast to coast and from border to border with

[1]Nehemiah 4:17.

The Frank Lee Wright Memorial Lecture given at Washington University, St. Louis, Missouri, April 30, 1957.

super service stations every ten miles selling super gasoling, super-super hot dogs, and super-super-super beverages, both those which rot only the teeth and those more potent ones which make men truly distinguished in social life as in traffic death. She can construct clover-leaf approaches to these highways from every hamlet in the land.

But the United States of America does not need to have hamlets any longer. She can expand those hamlets into towns, suburban areas, and cities. She can build, build, build streets, houses, refrigerators, television sets, automatic washing machines, authentic modern replicas of antique furniture, boats, golf courses, motels, swimming pools, and all the other appurtenances of a pround Madison Avenue and chamber-of-commerce civilization.

She can and she does and she most probably will.

And all the time, while the United States of America builds all these objects with one hand, with the other hand she holds and builds weapons, tremendous weapons, powerful weapons, weapons with which she can, if she should come to deem it necessary, obliterate her enemies. At least she can wipe out those enemies against whose bodies she can draw steel and strike, against whose cities she can press a button releasing flights of intercontinental ballistic missiles with atomic warheads.

Not all her foes are of that particular vulnerable nature, however. Like other nations, the United States of America must face an enemy who is already within her gates, an enemy protected by the walls of defense she erects, an enemy hidden within her own nature and institutions. Against that enemy she cannot strike with weapons of steel, fire, or atomic fission and fusion.

That homegrown enemy is ignorance in all its manifestations from the merely ridiculous to the deeply tragic. It is a force that can be successfully attacked only with weapons of developed intelligence and sensitive spirit. It retreats only before the power of education.

No people honor education with their lips more than do the Americans, and none has a firmer foundation in educational history to support that devotion. Here is a nation that early in her life decided to educate all the children of all the people. She developed free compulsory systems of schooling to carry out that objective. Before she had completely reached the goal of universal elementary education, moreover, she decided to give secondary education to all of her young people who could profit by such schooling, and she modified the conventional notions of secondary education again and again to make it possible for greater and greater numbers to achieve that profit. Of late, furthermore, she has extended this doctrine of universal education upward into the higher schools. As before in secondary education, she has stated the theoretical proviso that the young man or woman shall have sufficient ability to pursue college and university studies effectively, but in practice she has modified many higher educational programs and standards to admit larger and larger numbers of students of moderate if not low ability.

Some of the results of this American extension of educational opportunities are readily apparent. One of them has undoubtedly been at the source of the great capacity of American industry, agriculture, commerce, and transportation. Another has been the steadily increasing demands for consumer goods. A related effect has been the development of the world's largest body of customers for advertising.

As the American program of schooling has been built, as it is being built today, however, those who are working on its construction and those for whom it is being developed have been subjected to increasing dangers. The most serious of these dangers come from three main sources.

The first great danger to the American school arises from agencies outside the realm of education that seek to usurp the educational functions of the school. A very simple but significant example of this process may be cited. Not long ago I noted in a chain grocery store alongside the shelves exhibiting cigarettes certain packages bearing familiar brand names, pictures, and symbols indicating that they too contained cigarettes. In fact some of them were marked "cigarettes." But they were also marked "bubble gum" in a modest, discreet lettering that would not distract juvenile attention too much from the dominant information that here were cigarettes in the same size, shape, and style of container that mother and daddy used for their smokes.

I am not a specialist on the gum-chewing aspects of American culture, but I assume that the use of bubble-gum is not widespread in the secondary school. It is largely a three-to-thirteen-year-old phenomenon, let us say. I believe also, and I think that 99 per cent of my fellow citizens agree in this view, that no sane parent wants his child to be trained to smoke cigarettes of a particular brand or of any brand before he reaches at least the age of well-developed adolescent discretion when he can decide for himself whether to begin cultivating lung cancer.

Why, then, in a society proud of its educational institutions is this sly, huckster encroachment on the educational domain permitted? The answer is clear. The Americans tell how much they believe in the school, but they pay little attention to its character. They increase its responsibility and restrict its authority.

In a myriad of ways, the non-school agencies of modern American life repeat this pattern. The warm heart, the rough exterior, and the hairy chest are made to triumph over the polished mind even in the most difficult situations that the radio, television, and cinema experts can devise. The Cult of Ignorance has its own idiom and its own gods. "Most of the people in our country are ignorant," the cultists seem to say, "and therefore I must at least act ignorant because I cannot be different."

This brings our attention to the second main danger to our American schools, the steadily mounting pressure to uniformity. It has been said that the two greatest fears in the United States today are the fear of failure and the fear of being different. Both these fears boil down to the single fear of being unlike the masses. The good citizen is successful in his business, goes to church except on good fishing or golfing Sundays, donates one day's pay to the United Fund and thereafter throughout the year supports the Red Cross, the Polio Fund, the Heart Fund, the Cancer Fund, Christmas seals for tuberculosis victims, Easter seals for crippled children, May Day seals for sick labor leaders — wait a minute, no!

"Are you trying to joke about the American way of life, Mister? There is no uniform regard for labor leaders, sick or well."

"Those other matters are uniform?"

"Right. Don't wander away from your people."

These excellent activities have been aided by the American pattern of uniformity, but many equally valuable ones have been neglected because they have not yet struck the proper uniformity producing chord. Many useless or even dangerous activities are also supported by the doctrine and practice of not being different. It is no accident that a country with a national safety council, bodies of similar intent in many states and cities, and armies of traffic police should systematically kill its people with motor vehicles in impressive numbers day after day and year after year. To be like his fellows, the American motorist must deplore this situation, organize to remedy it, and drive fast.

The power of the uniformity-imposing agencies is in many important aspects of our lives incomparably superior to the power of formal schooling. We teach citizenship, problems of a democracy, social studies, and American history to all our children and young people from the time they enter kindergarten or nursery school to their graduation from secondary schools or colleges. One principle of civic action is taught and re-taught until it must be verbally automatic with most Americans — the *good* citizen votes — and when voting time comes the Americans stay away from the polls in droves. Some studies have indeed indicated that college graduates are less likely to vote than those whose schooling ended at the eighth grade level or earlier.

Why? Because our "friends" don't vote.

The schools and colleges teach their learners to appreciate the works of the great poets, dramatists, novelists, and essayists. What do these learners commonly read after their period of schooling ends?

Time, Life, Reader's Digest, and any "whodunit" with a lurid cover.

Why? Because these are the things "everybody" reads. "Nobody" reads Chaucer, Shakespeare, Cervantes, or Keats — except in school.

Do you want to be a nobody?

No, I want to be a somebody, and therefore I must be like everybody.

This danger to American education can be illustrated almost endlessly. The need for uniformity is overpowering in housing, clothings, food, recreation, communication, transportation, occupation, and religion.

The third main danger to American education is closely related to the two already mentioned and indeed derives in part from them. The pressure of agencies outside the school and the imposition of uniformity on school and non-school people alike, together with the rapid technological changes affecting society, have combined more and more to isolate the school and school population from the rest of the community.

This phenomenon can be observed in many seemingly small but often startling ways. The give-away programs originally developed modestly on the radio and later expanded to gigantic proportions on television furnishing one of the most arresting examples of the widening gulf between the school and its society. For generations the school has been emphasizing in theory and in practice that the memorization of facts unrelated to problems calling for action is always useless and often intellectually and emotionally dangerous. The give-away hucksters, concerned only with the sale of their sponsors' products, have systematically cultivated precisely that outworn notion with their millions of listeners and viewers.

When I was a student at a certain great university a third of a century ago, we had a local character, a cobbler by trade, who gave occasional "lectures" from the steps of one of the main buildings on the campus. He could prepare his lecture by studying encyclopedias, and at the end of his remarks he would graciously answer our questions; "When was Sir Walter Raleigh born? What color was the hair of Mary Queen of Scots? Where was William of Occam buried?"

It was all a joke to us students and, I suspect, to the cobbler himself. He answered our questions, and as a reward we always gave a new honorary degree.

If that man were living in this generation and made the right contacts to appear on the right program, it would be no joke. It would be deadly serious. It would be just as serious as the cigarette that tastes "like a cigareet should" or the dentifrice that makes one "wonder where the yellow went." The erudite answers would be paid for, moreover, not in the supurious currency of student-granted degrees but in coin of the realm.

We modern American teachers study the nature of our learners. Child growth and development can properly be called the foundation of our professional training. Understanding the child is our first goal in teaching. We have long known, as our predecessors did before us, that pre-adolescent children do not commonly have romantic attachments to children of the opposite sex. Observe a small child being interviewed in public and see what the non-school element of society thinks of this professional belief. Almost any newspaper, cinema, radio, or television presentation involving little children will furnish nauseating examples. I will not give examples. They abound in sufficient number to show clearly how far away the American public is in many of its stereotypes from the spirit and the practice of the best American schools.

The school tries to teach a child to make reasoned decisions after careful scrutiny of the facts; non-school agencies teach him to make snap-judgements on the basis of slogans, snob-appeal, and sloppy sentimentalism. The school seeks to ground him in a profound respect for each individual; non-school agencies brush the individual to one side in scrambles for money, status, and power. The school teaches him courtesy based on sensitivity to the canons of good taste; the newspaper proudly shows him the grief-contorted face of a mother who has just been informed (by a reporter, of course, with a photographer at his elbow), that her only child has been killed by a truck.

These are the main dangers to American education: (1) the educational encroachments of non-school agencies, (2) the pressures for uniformity, and (3) the isolation of the school from its society. How may they be combatted? As we build and operate our school programs with one hand, what weapon shall we hold with the other hand?

I believe the weapon lies ready to our hand. It is an educational weapon, but we professional educators have generally neglected it. It is the weapon of an expanded, vitalized, and goal-conscious education for adults.

The nature of a society is determined by its adults and not by its children. We Americans have long gone on the assumption that if we educated the children, the adults would direct their own activities effectively. In our review of the three dangers already mentioned, we have seen where that view gets us. We have taught the children of the United States for generations to say "I am not." We have drilled them on the evil effects of alcohol and tobacco. We have inculcated in them the precept that the courteous driver is the safe driver. We have taught these and a thousand other truths and virtuous acts to the children. They have learned well. Everything in this picture is good except for the one little circumstance that when these children grow up, many of them become the most striking collection of ain't-sayers, liquor-guzzlers, chain-smokers, and careless drivers in adult history.

The obvious fact is that an adult speaker, drinker, driver, parent, voter, worker, or citizen in general has to learn his job in each category as an adult. His childhood and adolescent educational experience may and ideally will give him indispensable preparation for his adult learning, but he has to be schooled as an adult for every affair of adult life.

Most of these necessary learnings are and should be acquired on the job. In many cases, however, they need to be supplemented by adult schooling. The optimum time for a young woman to learn the skills of parenthood is when she is facing that status. The time for a young man to learn to vote intelligently and faithfully is when he reaches the voting age.

The United States is crowded with more and more adults, and more and more of them want to engage in education as adults. The adult population of the United States is increasing at a rate of about 1.8 per cent per year. Enrollments in public-school adult education courses are increasing annually at a rate of 13 per cent, in college correspondence courses at 12 per cent, in the cooperative Extension Service at 11 per cent, in university correspondence courses in high school subjects at 8 per cent, in junior college adult classes at 5 per cent, in management training courses of the American Management Association at 87 per cent, in university extension classes at 42 per cent, and in university and college short courses and institutes at 36 per cent.[2]

The desire of American adults for education is present. The volume of adult education in the United States is growing. To channel that desire and that growth is a professional educational job. It is a job that needs to be accepted wholeheartedly, studied carefully, and carried out enthusiastically by the schools, colleges, and universities of the country. It is a job that needs to be done with daring, with imagination, and on a hitherto unpredicted scale.

In view of the financial difficulties always confronting the administration of educational institutions and particularly pressing in some areas today, it is heartening to remember that American adults are generally willing and able to pay the costs of their own learning. The chief problems in organizing and operating the needed adult education enterprises are therefore not mainly money problems. They are rather those of personnel. With the right kind of teachers and administrators, the problems of program and organization become relatively simple.

This, then is the weapon ready to our hands. If we pick it up and use it intelligently, there will be no real battle. Our enemy's battalions will drift away and his guns will be silenced. We can then use the metal of our weapon to form the cornerstone of a newer and grander educational edifice, worthy of a newer and more glorious nation, and forerunner and architect of a newer and better world.

[2]Homer Kempfer et al., *Education Throughout Life,* Washington, D.C. President's Committee on Education beyond the High School, 1957, pp. 8-9.

Whom the Gods Destroy
They First Make Ludicrous

Being a lover of music, I listen to all singing commercials, since their musical quality is superior to that of the program they follow or precede. Thus I heard recently the announcement of the imminent unveiling of a new model of a popular automobile. Musically this performance was not up to the current standard for singing commercials. It did not feature a barber-shop quartet. It was a solo rendition of an air so modern as to be virtually tuneless. The soloist apparently had been selected not for her ability to sing so much as for her capacity to project through vocal undulation and innuendo the complex of stimuli commonly called sex appeal.

I pondered this phenomenon. I am a student of the institutions and methods whereby societies change their ways consciously in the direction of their drams. For comparative purposes I compelled also at times to observe the manner in which they sometimes have their ways changed for them in directions of which they have never dreamed.

So here we have a great motor-car manufacturer (I speak of him in the singular although he is now a dynasty), who makes very good, very well-engineered automobiles. He is one of the leaders in an industry demanding and commanding some of the finest manufacturing brains in the world today. It sells its products to one of the best-schooled people in the world, the citizens of the United States. To the proverbial visitor from another planet, therefore, it would surely seem inevitable that such a manufacturer in such a country should seek to interest such a people in such a product by using some approach to the intelligence, the reasoning ability, and the sophistication which he would naturally assume their schooling must have given them. If their schools are good at all, he would suppose they would at least be that good.

But of course, the hypothetical observer would be wrong. How wrong he would be cannot be comprehended without going back and listening to that leering bleat over the great mass medium of communication. "You're gonna love, love, LOVE that car! (I paraphrase rather than quote.) "You're gonna flip your lid when you see that new, new, NEW car!"

Address delivered before the thirty-seventh annual convention of the National Council for the Social Studies in Pittsburgh, November 1957.

I do not need further to document this lyric. It or one of its counterparts is familiar to you. The entire approach, intonations and all, could have been observed at its best on certain streets in Hong Kong, Port Said, Tangier, Panama, Marseilles, and the Barbary Coast of old San Francisco. One wonders dazedly whether these cars were designed to be sold only to drunken sailors, but that shot is obviously wide of the mark. The manufacturer made a deliberate choice in this sales appeal. He knew the nature of his product. He knew the educational background of his people. Yet he pitched the appeal on the lowest possible intellectual level because he believed that was the level that would secure the optimum results in sales. He may have been wrong, but I assume that he was right. In this field he is a professional operator of great competence. I always follow a professional judgement, in preference to an amateur one, unless I have substantial evidence that it lacks validity.

An engineering company sponsors a television drama in a campaign to enlist graduate engineers, mathematicians, and physicists in its enterprises. In its commercial statement it speaks with feeling, even eloquence, of its need for highly schooled men and of the great significance of the work it will have them do. It wants electrical engineers, men with masters' degrees preferred, and above all, if possible, holders of the doctorate of philosophy in mathematics or one of the physical sciences. This is the audience it seeks to persuade.

Then it presents the dramatic entertainment for this audience. In the play, the heroine is a young librarian. She lives among books and presumably reads many of them. She wears glasses. She is, if not a teetotaler, at least unaccustomed to regular rations of alcohol. She is shy, introverted, ill-at-ease, and untapped by the wand of Romance. All these hanicaps doom her to misery. She enters a bar, why and how are not important, and there she meets a young man. He admits that he read a book once, but says bravely that he has largely overcome this handicap. He persuades her to forget her books. She takes a drink and then another. She removes her glasses and thereupon becomes beautiful. Love blooms and Happiness gallops onstage in a glorious mist of alcohol and ignorance.[1]

It seems to me that if I were a doctor of philosophy in mathematics, a master of science in physics, or merely a bachelor of electrical engineering, I would be initially impressed by this company's invitation to join its scientific enterprises and then so repelled by the stupidity of its drams that I would decide instead to get a job with General Electric or even stay on the university faculty.

[1]Issac Asimov. "The By-Product of Science Fiction" in *Fantasy and Science Fiction,* Vol. 12, No. 4, April, 1957.

But I must be wrong. The engineering company must know what it is doing. In this field it is a professional operator, and I have to follow its professional judgement unless I have good evidence of its invalidity.

On the last minute selection shelves in the glittering chain-grocery store next to the attractively displayed cigarettes, are packages of bubble gum dressed in Old Gold, Camel, and Chesterfield clothing. There are the familiar brand designations, the pictures, the colors, all just like the smokes of Mommy, Daddy and Uncle George. I am not a specialist on the bubble gum phase of our culture, but I assume that it is largely a pre-adolescent practice. So here we have the great tobacco interest getting their educational licks in very early. When those infants reach the age of discretion and start developing lung cancer of their own free adult will, they will be fortified with the proper brand loyalties.

One wonders that soft drinks designed for elementary school tastes are not put in Old Crow or Smirnoff bottles. It could be done with the same skill and ethics as those with which the bubble gum is packaged. We could have Four Roses Kola and Ron Rico Pop. Whey don't we have the soft drinks so packaged? I'll tell you why. The American people are not yet quite that ignorant.

This theme can be documented endlessly. The bubble gum cigarettes appeal presumably to or at least do not insult the intelligence of parents who are literate enough to read the labels. The newspaper-inspired kissing between the little Arabian prince and the tiny American girl, both of pre-nursery school age, is arranged and reported for the delectation of readers who are at least sufficiently schooled to decipher the oh-so-cute captions under the oh-so-clever photographs (which show the directing hands of the adults who propelled these infants into incipient osculation for the betterment of international relations).

I must not elaborate these examples. You can supply them as well as I, ad nauseam. For they are not really important except as symbols of the rising tide or an old cult and the rising power of its gods.

That cult is the Cult of Ignorance, and its chief gods are three: Snob-Appeal, Sentimentalism, and Uniformity; and the greatest of these is Uniformity.

I say that the greatest of these gods is Uniformity because I suspect that the fear of being different from the crowd, which is Uniformity's main instrument, is also involved in the creeds of the other two deities of the day. Let us look at them one by one.

Keeping up with the superior Joneses, the principal aspect of Snob-Appeal in our society, undoubtedly has a considerable impact on our whole social pattern. An unknown but undoubtedly very large number of our people contribute to the Community Chest, buy opera tickets, send their sons to Podunk

College, drink dry martinis, or bloody Marys, smoke Stencho king-sized, triple-filtered cigarettes, vote for Politician X, buy a new 350-horsepower Mountain Fin with headlights set in V-formations, and indeed perform a large share of their public and domestic functions because they believe that the upper classes of their world operate in that fashion. They want to be like those upper classes.

As Snob-Appeal operates, however, its devotees are forever doomed to be questing, searching, moving on, because as soon as the inferior classes become sufficiently like their presumed superiors in any particular characteristic, everybody becomes dissatisfied with that characteristic. It is no longer a mark of the upper crust, and so that layer of society and all aspirants thereto look for another and more distictive symbol of status.

The effects on education of Snob-Appeal are generally recognized but probably under-estimated. Why, in a country where the individual state is the supreme authority in matters of schooling, and often delegates much of its authority to local units, does the United States of America have such a nearly standardized curriculum, requirements for teachers' licenses, and administrative procedure? Of course, we could answer by saying that it is because we all want good schools and we have all followed the same road toward that goal because it is the one right road.

Even our most devout members of the Snob-Appeal sect will wince at this analysis. We all know that copying the supposed good policies and techniques of the school system of another city, state, or nation is still the chief process of educational reform.

Why do we have so many junior high schools in this country, for example? First we got them because we thought we were imitating the upper-class schooling of France and Germany and because our own educational upper-class kept telling us that the organization was a must. Then, when certain cities adopted the organization, they became upper-class in this respect overnight and thus exercised pressure on other districts to do the same.

Some of the most raucous and ignorant criticisms of American secondary schools are obviously triggered by those who believe that upper-class in school procedures is best represented by European secondary schools that have long served the ruling elements of their countries. A young evanglist against the devils of educationism, who is determined to find nothing good in the high schools of his native country even if he has to manufacture statistics to support his case, is so awed by Eton and the Lycee Louis le Grand that he would not dream of attempting two plus two in their august atmosphere. He can only breathe deeply and bow his head.[2]

[2] I refer to the proposition widely quoted in the popular press, that the young people of high school age in 1900 were better educated than the young people of today. See Harold C. Hand's brilliant "Black Horses Eat More Than White Horses," Bulletin of the American Association of University Professors. Volume 43, No. 2. Summer 1957, p. 266-279.

It is the melancholy triumph of Snob-Appeal in education that it substitutes reputation for facts and that it determines reputation by reference to the views of a presumed upper clsss.

Sentimentalism is in many ways a more amiable god. It tries to protect its supporters by interposing a warm mist of feeling between them and the reality which strict attention to cold fact reveals. In schools it uses flag waving as a short-cut to the teaching of patriotism; the careful study of history, economics, and politics seems too long and rough a road to that goal. It substitutes slogans for reasoning and labels for analysis of abilities. It helps the public to equate school and college achievement with high-stepping drum majorettes and the athletic victories they celebrate. It keeps some teachers in service who might well be paid to stay out of the schools.

Sentimentalism, too, draws much of its strength from its wide-spread acceptance throughout the country. Failure to drop a tear or to join a cheer at the right moment is more dangerous to a teacher's career than intellectual lapses can be.

If the symbol of Snob-Appeal is the uplifted nose, that of Sentimentalism is the tom-tom. When the drum is beating steadily, it is easy to keep in step with both feet and heart. If an institution shows signs of failing to heed that rhythm, the power of Uniformity is quickly brought into play.

It is now perhaps clear why I have said that the greatest god of the Cult of Ignorance is Uniformity. It is the chief of the pantheon because of its pervasive and persistent power.

Where does Uniformity get that power?

It arises primarily from the fear of being different. Snob-Appeal usges us to be like the "People Who Matter." Sentimentalism wants us to be like our fellows because that is folksy, democratic, and non-high-hat. But Uniformity demands that we be like everybody because Uniformity abhors idiosyncrasy. It wants to see no heads rising above the level of mediocrity.

In education we have certainly followed this god too often and too far. As Truman Lee Kelley suggested long ago and as I developed the argument late, we have gloried the concept of educational plainsmanship by putting our children into standards molds, trying to fill up their valleys of ability while eroding their peaks of interest and capacity.[3] We have practiced educational plainsmanship by taking a child who is advanced in reading and music, for example, and slowed up his instruction in those subjects while we have laboriously tried to bring him to a standard performance in arithmetic. The doctrine of the approved doctrine, the standard of the minimum standard, and the effort to make one child like all the rest are hallmarks of educational plainsmen.

[3]Truman Lee Kelley, *The Influence of Nurture Upon Native Differences.* New York: Macmillan, 1926; Harold Benjamin, *The Cultivation of Idiosyncrasy.* Cambridge, Mass.: Harvard University Press, 1949.

The practice of educational plainsmanship is increasingly supported by some of the main currents of our society. I am informed by an editorial in a recent issue of *The Reporter* that the Canadian Broadcasting Corporation has issued a directive to its announcers, commentators, and other program people that hereafter the term "Yank" will not be used. It is one of those opprobrious terms like Dago, Mick, Greaser, and Frog, says the directive-maker, and it is now on the Index Expurgatarius of the CBS.

This is in line, of course, as *The Reporter* well observes, with the policies of motion- picture, television, and theater authorities who have decreed that in casting villains for their dramas they shall not reflect discredit upon a particular race, vocation, or religion. No more evil half-breeds can pursue the heroine, no more physicians can flount the tenets of the Hippocratic Oath on the screen, and no more can any other individual be evil except, of course, you can still have an unemployed, white Protestant, of clear Anglo-Saxon descent, be a villain. His people are not well organized on this matter yet.

So we have *Huckleberry Finn* removed from the reading list. We have the school glee club's male quartet crooning "Sandman am a-comin' to this little friend of mine" when they render "Sleep. Kentucky Babe." As one who used to sing that song in happier, less uniform days with my distinguished friend, the late Charles S. Johnson, I feel that every such bowdlerization is an insult to that great Negro educator's memory. When God and the South and all the other great factors that shaped Charles Spurgeon Johnson completed their task, the mold was broken. There was no other Charles Johnson for me, and when I sing "Sleep, Kentucky Babe," I will not sing it as the devotees of Uniformity tell me to sing it. I will sing it the way Johnson and I used to sing it.

That reminds me that *The Reporter* did not tell me what the Canadians are going to say instead of "Yank." It reminds me also of another country, or rather late country, where the term is very common in three syllables. I refer, of course, to the Confederate States of America. If the Federal authorities try to make the Southerners give up that term they will really start saving their Confederate money again.

The symbol of this chief god of the Cult of Ignorance is, naturally, the uniform. That is a device for making people look alike. It came from the armies where the soldiers were presumably taught to act alike. It was well fitted to Frederick the Great's peasants in close order. It is symbolic of a power that seeks to reduce people to a dead level of comfortable mediocrity, a gray mass of interchangeable parts, faceless weapons-carriers, anonymous voters, and loyal and indistinguishable sons of this and that.

I hope I have not given you the impression that I look with pessimism on the outcome of our campaign against the Cult of Ignorance. I am not pessimistic about it. I note with optimism that most American citizens, so far as their own child is concerned, do not want an education dominated by the uplifted Nose, the Tom-Tom, and the Uniform. They want that particular child, whom they know to be different from every other child, to be given an education that will help him become the unique person his unique capacities and interests make possible.

How good, then, should our schools be?

Henry Barnard, pioneer of American educational scholarship, answered that question long ago with a concise directness worthy of his Connecticut-Yankee accent and orientation, "What we want of the common schools," he said, "is enough education to educate ourselves."[4]

Does an educated man bow down before the gods of the Cult of Ignorance? Does he allow himself to be led by Snob-Appeal's uplifted nose, dragooned into step by Sentimentality's tom-tom, or hypnotized by Uniformity's epaulets and gold braid?? Well, hardly, Barnard would have said. A man who educates himself is bound to get a unique result; his teacher is peculiar. He is not likely to show himself how to know-tow to the whims of his supposed superiors, march to the beat of another's drum, or grind off his idiosyncrasies to make himself a more interchangeable part of a mass. Those ends are better served by training imposed on him from outside than by self-directed education.

Our schools should therefore be good enough, have enough education in them, to make it very difficult for the gods of the Cult of Ignorance to operate against their people. Our schools should give us enough education to educate ourselves.

In a society in which the rate of change is accelerating, does this mean that our schools have to be better now than yesterday?

It means they have to be different and if that involves being better, we will have to make the most of it.

---

[4]Quoted from manuscript by Richard K. Morris, "Parnasus on Wheels, a Biographical Sketch of Henry Barnard, 1811-1900" in *Trinity College Gazette* 2:8; February 1955.

Protecting Our Educational Ideals
Defense Is Not By Guns Alone

I have just returned from South America, where I have been received by presidents and cabinet ministers and educational authorities; I have talked with laborers and school teachers; I have looked at cultural institutions of all kinds; I have ridden weeks on ships, days on trains, hours on airplanes. The most important activity in which I have engaged, however, has been to ponder the topic assigned to me for this occasion. I will try to limit my presentation to a few pictures drawn in part from my travels, with a few suggestions concerning the ways those pictures fit into the great pattern of activity necessary for the protection of American educational ideals.

The border town of San Juan de la Frontera on the Argentine side of the frontier sprawls at the foot of the Andes as it has done these four hundred years. The HUASOS and GAUCHOS still ride with swinging BOLAS and ready knives. The men of Chile and Argentina still seek better ways for the ordering of their lives.

Yet many things are different in these lands from what they were in 1811, and some of the most important of these differences owe much of their origin to a boy born that year in the frontier town of San Juan. He became the man who labored with the schools and the press of his adopted country, Chile, to make of them instruments of a truly democratic education. He converted novels and essays and editorials into a battering ram of public opinion, continent-wide opinion, against dictatorship. He was the man who turned from his schools and his writing again and again and once again to ride with the rebel regiments across the mountains until the dictator was finally overthrown. But always he was the teacher — in classroom or in press, at home or in exile, in victory or in defeat, in Chile or in Argentine, in Europe or in South America, as a sweating laborer in the mines of northern Chile or as constitutional president of his native land, Domingo Sarmiento was the schoolmaster who never ceased teaching to the utmost limits of his strength and skill those facts and ideals and motives which he believed his people needed.

Today the marks of his teaching remain. San Juan is a better town than it was a century ago. Aconcagua and its foothills look today on scenes of intelligent labor done by men educated in schools which Domingo Sarmiento labored to establish. The fields and orchards of Los Andes and Mendoza are cultivated in more effective ways because the great schoolman, who more than once rode

An address before the 1941 convention of the American Association of University Women, Cincinnati, Ohio.

their trails with a gun on his saddle, also fought with ideas for an education of living for the masses in preference to one of ornament for the classes.

The man himself would have said that it was not he but education that did these things, and of course that is true. Education is a powerful force — when it is used by men who actually have faith in it rather than faith in its tools, its books, its degrees and rites and ceremonies, as ends in themselves.

No man in the Americas ever had more profound faith in the power of democratic education than had Domingo Sarmiento. Within the limits of his times and his own very human weaknesses, moreover, no man ever translated that faith into more stirring, colorful, and effective practice.

But the picture I set out to show you is of Sarmiento's childhood. An ugly little boy is weeping. He stands before the doorway of the poor adobe house and watches his father ride down the street. The salt water stings his eyes, but he stands erect and looks resolutely until the gaunt figure of the horseman dissolves in a mist of dust seen through tears.

The man who rides away is smiling. He is only a simple peon, but he is riding to join the partiot army of General San Martin. He rides with ready carbine; he rides to use force methods that his people may order their own ways for their own benefit. But he is not smiling at the thought of the battle to come or of those who will have to die to prove that brave men cannot live without the privilege of ordering their own ways for their own benefit. He is smiling that day for other reasons — because at last, established only that year, there is a school for all the children of all the people in San Juan de la Frontera, the first democratic school of the community. He is smiling because that school has just completed its first term with good success. Above all he is smiling because his little son, Domingo, for good scholarship, punctual attendance, and exemplary deportment is at the head of the class. He is smiling — that illiterate man riding into battle — because he is dreaming, not of battles, but rather of a day to come in one of the new universities which the great new fatherland will need and will build; a day when a distinguished professor will be lecturing to an audience; generals, priests, scientists, statemen will be there; and in the back row, the speaker's father and mother, unlettered themselves, but they had worked — they had even fought for these things — and now. . . .

The man rides on to battle and exile and poverty and death. He carries a carbine on his saddle, but in his heart he carries that which all the carbines or seventy-ton tanks and their fellow instruments of force can never overthrow.

I tell this story because it seems to me that our country and all the countries of the Americas are riding into a future fraught with increasing danger of the mass use of force instruments for changing the ways of men and of nations, but I think they are all riding with more than carbines on their saddles. I think the countries of the Americas carry with them as they did in the past a faith in education, education of the democratic schools, education of the free press, education of the freely exercised religion, education of the freely organized political parties and social groupings, education in all the channels whereby free men change their own ways in the direction of their own ideals. This is the heart of the American educational creed: that the men of a democracy should examine the possible outcomes of their national and individual behavior and take intelligent measures to modify that behavior in their own way and for their own benefit.

The men who founded the United States of America and the men who liberated the Latin American countries from the rule of Spain in that dramatic half century from 1775 to 1825 were agreed that "popular government without popular education was but the prelude to a farce or a tragedy, perhaps both." That is why the Washingtons and the Bolivars, the Franklins and the Sarmientos, preached the doctrine of an education of the people, directed by the people, for the benefit of the people.

The leaders of democracies with their backs to the wall seem often to have forgotten education. But the reverse is more likely to be correct; their backs are to the wall because they have forgotten too long the right kind of popular education.

There is a story of George Washington's response to the pleadings of a close friend and relative that he be allowed to take a certain easy, comfortable job, instead of the hard and disagreeable task that the general wanted him to do – simply because it was something the people of the United States needed to have done for them. When he had listened to the argument, the older man said with simple finality, "The other thing must be done – it must be DONE."

Washington knew what had to be done, and he had the cold, inflexible courage and the tough, unyielding devotion to his people to stand solidly and do every ounce he could, day after day and year after year, to see that what had to be done was done.

Democratic education is our ideal in America, in other countries of the Americas as well as in our own. Now what we have to do is to stand solidly in the path of events, resolve of that ideal that it must be done, and then ride out to get it done.

Let us get down to cases. The American educational ideal provides for equal educational opportunity, for all the children of all the people, at the expense of all the wealth of all the people. Does that ideal need protection now? Well, not the verbalization of the ideal. The words expressing that ideal are accepted throughout this hemisphere and certainly throughout these United States. But you and I know that it is a long way from being carried into effect in much of the Western Hemisphere, and that it is too far from realization in our own country.

The greatest natural resource of this country or any country lies in the developed intelligence and health and energy of its people. Without that primary resource the other resources of wind and water, coal and iron, soil and timber, are merely environment for savages. The greatest waste of natural resources in this country or in the Americas as a whole at the present time comes from a lack of proper education for millions of its people. Right in the United States I can show you one school district where a boy of ability can without money go through one of the best secondary schools in the nation, while three miles away in another school district a boy of equal or greater ability cannot go beyond the country school unless his parents can afford to pay tuition and send him to the neighboring district.

We are meeting this threat to our ideal of democratic education in many states of the country by improved legislation, by consolidation of schools, and by state grants to school districts, but among the states themselves we still have great inequalities in ability to support education as compared with the educational burden which must be assumed to give even a minimum schooling to the children. We have to face, moreover, a curious complacency on the part of our fellow citizens. They are accustomed to believe that, just as it is, the American school system is the most democratic in the world — why improve it? We have no more money that we can possibly spend on education, they say. We are doing all we are able to do to give equal educational opportunity to all the children.

And yet, as they say that, they spend their money in keeping up the inefficient system of thousands of local school districts in state after state; they keep up hundreds of county organizations that belong in the horse-and-buggy era; they have a multiplicity of state boards of education and trustees and regents and competing institutions where one state system of higher education would do the job much better and more democratically; they waste public money at every turn for political arrangements rather than for administrative results; and still they say they cannot give a democratic organization of public education to their people.

The first purpose of American education, so listed in all the official codes and statements of principles from 1893 to the present day, is to teach health to all the children of all the people. We all accept that ideal verbalistically, but what proportion of the school children of this country have even the simple minimum service of an annual health and dental examination? You would be surprised to find how many in your own state do not.

I have been in the country of this hemisphere which regards itself as just beginning to set up a system of democratic education — Brazil — and in school after school, simple, poor schools in many instances, the school physician and the school dentist were there at work in their little offices, with their cumulative health records for every child in the district, feeling that their efforts were inferior to what a rich nation like the United States could do, but resolving that school health was a thing which must be attended to and that they would come as close to carrying out the ideal as labor for long hours would take them.

How many of you live in districts where the school teachers are required to pass even an annual health examination? Is there any assurance that there are not teachers in your school who have active tuberculosis, for example? There are thousands of school districts in this country where neither teachers nor pupils ever have any health examinations except such as are given to them by private physicians in the case of illness so severe as to cause their collapse.

In the curriculum, furthermore, what is actually done about health education? Is it still kept in the subordinate realm of the fads and frills?

In the field of mental health, moreover, what is our record of actual accomplishment as compared with our ideal? How many teacher-education institutions in your state accept candidates for entrance in the teaching profession without regard to their mental health so long as they can pass required academic subjects with minimum grades? How many classes of elementary school children in the United States are subjected to daily mental strain because a teacher is thought to be entitled to his job long after he has become so maladjusted as to be a mental hazard to every child with whom he comes into contract?

We have the educational ideal in America that the quality of teaching is what makes a school, and that teachers must be among the best qualified leaders of community life. How near does your community come to seeing that this particular ideal is carried into practice? Do you still have high school teacher-training departments in your state where rural teachers are given about the same amount of scientific preparation for their profession as they were given thrity years ago? The successful practice of teaching in a truly modern school calls for skill and background inferior to those needed in no other profession. To what extent do your normal schools, teachers colleges, and other teacher-education institutions give such skills and background? Do you have ten, thirty, or fifty such institutions in your state when it is obvious that two, five, or ten could do the job better?

So we could ask similar questions about the quality of our efforts in support of the American educational ideals of education for good citizenship, for vocation, for happy family life, and for healthful and useful recreation.... We Americans have these ideals; we have now got to do more about carrying them into complete practice than we have done in the past.

As we talk of education for peaceful progress and civilized order, there may be those who would say to us, "Observe the impractical dreamers who talk of the ways of peace when there is no peace, of civilization in the deepening dusk of a new barbarism, or order in ever-mounting chaos, of education in a world whose final word is death and whose ultimate instrument of social control is the fear of death. Cannot these starry-eyed ones hear the distant rumble of the guns?"

And of course we can hear those guns. It may be, indeed, that they are hammering in our ears a little more loudly than they were yesterday, that they carry a more insistent threat to our lives, that they drum a little more ominously in our hearts. We know, too, that when they begin to drum, time begins to shorten. We remember how a day, an hour, a minute which seemed so innocently unimportant before the guns began to speak can grow more and more threatening and pressing, carrying more and more portent, until all the fate of our people, of our whole culture, of the world itself, seems bound up in that one unit of time, until no spending of strength or of blood is too great to save that day, that hour, that minute for the guns — our guns.

It seems so, but it is not so. The guns are not most important, no matter how insistently they call for our time and our lives. The most important thing is to set up intelligently and energetically a system of changing ways whereby our people can direct their own behavior into gracious and lovely channels. If we cannot work wholeheartedly towards that great goal even when the guns are drumming, we can never work for it.

Let us not in the present emergency or in any other that may arrive make the mistake of believing that when we use time for the guns we have no time available for the truly humane activities of which guns should be only guarantees. We waste time like water in any emergency. Consider, as a minor example, the amount of time wasted by women who knit by hand articles for military wear. Consider, as a major example, the deliberate waste of human intelligence and energy of which we are guilty in this country by our asinine refusal to employ married women — particularly, of all places, in schools.

In country after country I have asked ministers of education, school principals, business men, professional men, peons, gauchos, vaqueros, whether it is not unfair to single women that married women are employed as teachers, and I have always received the same general type of response. The educated men explain patiently and at length. The more unlettered men answer politely but briefly. But they all have the same implication, an implication well expressed by the farmer who said, "We are a poor people, Senor, and we cannot afford to run our schools for charity. We run them to give our children as good an education as possible."

Consider, as another example of time expenditure which might be made, our preparations for defense of the Western Hemisphere. The preparation for defense with guns is good, I am sure. We build up a navy with powerful guns, we sell guns to our Latin American neighbors, we loan them money to buy guns from us, we send them military and naval and air missions to show them how to use the guns. All the while other governments furnish those countries with professors for their universities, free of charge, professors working hard to teach those people upon what side to use their guns when the necessity arises.

One country in South America would like to have the help of an expert in elementary education from the United States for one year in organizing a new national system of primary schools. Another asks for a specialist in secondary education. Still another wants help in school administration. University after university wants professors from the United States. Why cannot they have them? A lack of money? The cost of ten or even fifty such men in Latin America would be infinitesimal in the expenditures for hemisphere defense. It is not lack of money; it is a reflection of the old battle psychosis which holds that war begins and ends with guns.

War begins and ends in a struggle for the control of men's minds, and if we do not recognize that defense of our hemisphere or our nation or the principles and practices of democratic living involves educational measures, intelligently and daringly conceived and executed, we might as well put on our breech cloths, paint our faces with our tribal colors, and take the war path for its own sake as the earlier savages of this continent were wont to do.

The war for the liberty of men's minds must be fought and won all the time — it must be fought and won every day by every good educator in every classroom, laboratory, newspaper office, broadcasting studio, club meeting, theatre, pulpit, or other spot from which men teach and learn. It must be fought and won incessantly if the human race hopes to write even the prologue to a true civilization. The little struggles of guns are never anything more than mere skirmishes for position in the one great war for the freedom of men's minds. The teacher or journalist, the writer or speaker, the civic leader or politician, the artist of ideas or the artisan of words, who retires from this great battle to fumble with his accustomed routines or to recite his beloved verbalisms while the shortsighted call for time and guns alone is a casualty more pathetic than one who drops before a swinging bayonet or the tearing crash of a bomb.

Time for guns? Yes. But time for life for my people too.

V | ON TEACHERS AND CURRICULA

It is for teachers that Benjamin feels a particular affinity. He has been working with and for teachers for almost fifty years so this affection should not be surprising. His work with teachers and in behalf of teachers has carried him literally to the four corners of the earth. He served on the Teacher Education Commission, 1937-1942; the Carnegie Mission to South America, 1941; the United States Delegation to the Constitutional Convention of UNESCO, 1945; the United States Army Education Mission to Japan, 1946; the UNESCO Mission to Afghanistan, 1949; and the United States Army Follow-up Mission to Japan, 1950. He was also chairman of the National Commission for the Defense of Democracy Through Education, 1947-1950.

There has been a hue and cry for decades in this country for greater prestige for the teacher. Cries to dispel the stereotyped image of teachers as they were described by Washington Irving, Mark Twain, and Charles Dickens, and as they are frequently portrayed in movies and on television programs. It is indeed paradoxical that in this country society has always held education in the highest regard and, at the same time, has looked down at teachers with a patronizing eye. Teaching is looked upon as the highest service one can offer while the teachers are often regarded as persons who couldn't make a living in some other field.

Benjamin is, of course, concerned about the relatively low status of teachers but he casts the problem in a new light. While agreeing that society unjustly looks down on teachers the teachers must realize that prestige does not come with the conferring of an academic degree and the receipt of a license to teach. The prestige must be earned and the earning might not be easy. Teachers must work and sometimes fight for this prestige and they will never achieve it except by their own efforts. In his eloquent convocation address entitled, "Riders to Set Upon Them," which he delivered at the Glassboro State College, Benjamin describes the elements of manners, style, and drive which teachers must develop.

Manners are based on an understanding of the wants, needs, and motivations of others. *Style* includes the teacher's ability to communicate with students, his teaching methods, his degree of professional activity, and his

involvement in the life of the community. *Drive,* simply stated, is the courage of
your convictions. Teachers should have the courage to attempt what they feel is
best for the students and for society. Only then will society afford to them the
status they seek.

Somewhere in the long history of education the curriculum became
pictured as a vehicle for perpetuating the cultural heritage of the existing
society. Which means, I suppose, the passing from one generation to the next the
"eternal verities" of THE SABER-TOOTH CURRICULUM. Unfortunately we
are living in a period of such rapid scientific and technological innovation that it
is impossible for us to anticipate the conditions under which succeeding generations will live. The challenge of education today is to structure the curriculum so
as to develop in youth the ability to utilize cultural change for the advancement
of all mankind.

These Rights and Privileges

In my youth it was customary for commencement orators to thunder down at new wearers of these academic costumes, telling them in good round terms what they ought to do for themselves and their country now that they had earned their degree. In the last few years, particularly since September, 1939, and even more especially since August, 1945, many commencement speakers have adopted a decidedly new role. Instead of passing advice and admonition from on high down to the graduates, they assume a humble air, saying the world is in a terrible state, we older people having made a mess of everything, and now it is up to you to straighten things out. Where the earlier orators spoke down to the graduates, saying, "Listen to me and do as I say," the newer ones speak up to the graduates contritely, with hat in hand, saying, "You are better than we ever were, you better be or the world is sunk."

Both these attitudes are entirely proper and have much to recommend them. In my own case, tonight at least, I feel that I am temperamentally unfitted for displaying either of them. I do not want to talk down to you, Ladies and Gentlemen of the Graduating Class. I do not want to talk up to you. I just want to talk at you. I do not speak tonight, therefore, as an older man addressing younger people. Neither do I speak humbly or in any other fashion as an apologist for my generation. I am proud of my generation. I have eaten its bread gladly, and without too much trouble I have pulled in my belt when it had no bread to give. But I do not defend it here, I think it needs no defense.

Instead I want to talk at you as one teacher to another. I want to speak of certain rights and privileges of our academic profession — rights and privileges that go back a long way into history. For almost one thousand years we people of the Western European tradition have had higher educational institutions. For exactly four hundred years in the Western Hemisphere we have worn these academic gowns and granted these medieval degrees. The Royal Pontifical University of Mexico in New Spain and the University of San Marcos in Lima, the City of Kings in the Viceroyalty of Peru, were both founded in 1551. In what is now the United States of America, we people of English speech and background have had college education for more that three centuries. In all this time, but particularly in the last hundred years, the institution of higher education on Western European and American models has spread throughout the world. From

Convocation address at George Peabody College for Teachers, June 8, 1951.

the Valley of the Indus to that of the Nile, from the Alaskan Peninsula to the Cape of Good Hope, from the black Andes to the towering Hindu Kush, beside tropical forests and on the shores of Arctic seas, this pattern of the higher learning has been carried, modified, and put to work for all the purposes of thinking men everywhere in action for the changing of their ways.

Always at least once a year in these higher educational intitutions, we don our academic costumes, put on the caps and hoods of our scholastic grades, and confer degrees upon the recruits to our ranks. From the time of the first stadium generale at Paris, moreover, superficially the main features of these degrees have been the rights and privileges that they presumably carried with them. They were originally licenses to teach, to practice law, to heal the sick, or to expound theology, for example. They carried with them vocational rights comparable to those granted by the medieval guilds of craftsmen for whom the first concepts of modern higher education came. The first universitites, indeed, were simply guilds of scholars and teachers, and the license of a learned craft was the chief right they could bestow.

In the early universities, however, another class of rights was given with the degrees. The degree of doctor and master also carried with them the clerical privilege of being tried by canon law rather than in the civil court. They were thus worth good hard cash and sometimes exemption from the gallows. If one wished to steal or commit murder in certain European countries in the thirteenth or fourteenth centuries, it was a great advantage to be a master of arts or a doctor of laws.

The latter kind of academic privilege has happily fallen into disuse long ago. Today in this and in other democratic countries, wearers of these ancient costumes and regalia want no civil, economic, or social rights other than those which are freely granted to our least schooled fellow citizens. We do not believe in academic privilege in any medieval sense. In our very proper concern to give the highly educated man or woman no favors, we go even further. Except for a few phases of a few highly technical vocations, for example, there are still ways in which a person can enter many crafts or professions with little formal schooling. Even on the staffs of the great graduate schools in our finest universities there are always a few exceptional scholars who lack the usual scholastic degrees. In business, government, law, art, letters, invention, even in sciences, we Americans are particularly proud that we keep roads to the highest achievement open to men and women of talent who have developed their skills in non-academic situations.

With all this desire on our part to be democratic, we sometimes forget that a college degree still carries rights and privileges. It carries those rights and privileges with special force when some of these degrees today, as they all did in former times, carry membership in the teaching profession. To you new wearers of these costumes and holders of these diplomas, I wish now to list some of the prerogatives. They are privileges of the highly schooled man and most especially of him who holds a degree as a teacher. Without these privileges he is not educated, and his schooling is a sham though he be entitled to wear a dozen academic hoods.

The first of these is the privilege of extra work.

You say that the privilege to work is that of every citizen in a democracy, schooled or unschooled, and of course that is true. But the educated teacher's privilege is to work harder, more surely, and with greater effectiveness than is possible to his less well schooled fellows. His degree lies forever upon him as a burden. The shadow of his academic training is always across his path and in his heart. It tells him that he must put more weight behind his shoulder to the wheel of community progress than would have been possible without his education or he might as well turn in his diploma. It tells him that if his degree does not impel him to do more and better work by reason of his having earned it, he would do well to forget those letters behind his name. It tells him, in short, that he is a professional and that all the extra polish and precision of a proud craft must rest upon every product of his hands.

The second privilege of the educated teacher is that of serving the larger rather than the smaller community. I do not mean by this statement for one moment that the educated man should not properly work in a small village at a small job. Quite the contrary is of course true in many cases where a small job in a small place done by a truly educated teacher becomes a great job for a wide area of significance. I mean rather that while it may be proper, or at least understandable for a relatively uneducated person to work primarily for the happiness and welfare of himself, his immediate family, or his limited business or trade circles, it is the high responsibility and the distinguished honor of the educated man to work always for the larger group and the larger area in the truest sense. Because he is educated, he must be concerned not only for the welfare of his own children but also for that of all children. He cannot be content merely with the provincial and the narrowly partisan view; he must lift his eyes to the hills; he must perforce gaze down broad vistas; he must evaluate present events in the light of history; he must weigh immediate policies in their broadest social settings. His higher education will have taught him these things or it will have taught him nothing of any worth. It it has not taught him these skills, his scholastic honors are the cheap ornaments of a frivolous and useless show and his professional activities sink to the level of routinized pedagogical mechanics.

The teacher with a college degree has one more chief privilege. This is the highest, the most burdensome, and the most honorable of all the gifts that higher education can bestow. It is the privilege of constructive imagination in the service of one's people. The citizen who is forever a plodder, the man with his nose always on a grindstone, the cautious and timid soul who gets his views ready made, whether from the hireling pundits of press and radio, from the political boss in his ward or in the United States Senate, or from the dicta of the loud-voiced man who works at the next bench or desk, can be more readily forgiven or at least understood if he never plodded through an institution of higher education and above all if he never aspired to be a teacher. But for one who studied four or more years in higher schools such a course is impossible. For these colleges are not factories, they are not shops, and they are not market places. They are more than all these. These are associations of teachers who are devotees of disciplines. Those disciplines were all founded on constructive imagination. We call them disciplines, in effect, because they are made by controlled and directed dreams and yearnings and longings. The colleges which have best served teachers, scholars, and communities have marked their every advance by triumphs of new and daring ideas put into action. They live and grow by such ideas, and when they die, they die from the top down, the bottom up, or in both directions because freedom of inquiry has been denied them, either by outside pressure or their own inner sloth. For graduates of these colleges it is desertion in the face of the enemy to leave the hard, dangerous, and honorable path of self-directed, original, and constructive thought, speech, and action. The privilege of disciplined imagination must be proudly claimed by every educated man.

Long before this point it may be objected that what I am calling privileges are in fact duties. I recognize the justness of such an objection.

Why, then, do I say privilege instead of saying duty?

I say it because I believe the duty of an educated man and particularly of a teacher is a part of his privilege; it is in fact the only part of his privilege that counts. Certainly the privileges of degrees which are not duties are such insignificant or even uncomfortable things as an academic robe or the more than slightly ridiculous mortarboard cap. The privileges that count, it seems to me, are bound up in these three great tasks that educated men and women are vowed to perform.

It is unnecessary for me to emphasize the familiar fact that men and women without formal schooling of a college or even lower level often exercise these privileges much better than do people with college degrees. That fact simply illustrates the truth we have long recognized in this country. Perhaps we have recognized it here more readily than it has commonly been accepted elsewhere. This is the truth that all education is self-education and that he who does not learn to direct and operate his own education in a school will have to learn it out of school or remain sunk in practical illiteracy.

The degrees with their attendant privileges which you are receiving today are often regarded in the popular mind as gifts of some kind. The very language used for centuries in awarding degrees adds to this belief. It implies to the unthinking that these degrees are presents from a gracious giver to a grateful recipient, that we, the institution, the state, the organization, the people who have degrees to give, now bestow upon you who hitherto have lacked these honors, the reward of these degrees.

Most college men and women recognize the inadequacy of this view. They know that a degree is never a gift. They know that it has to be purchased at a price.

Nobody knows the full price except the man or woman who pays it. Some students can earn a degree with relatively little effort. They can get their academic privileges at cut rates. Others have to pay a very high price for their degrees in terms of hard labor, sacrifice or recreation, long hours of drudgery, and heroic support of families and fellow citizens. The man who pays must know all these elements of the price.

These academic goods of degrees and the education they symbolize are peculiar goods. Unlike material possessions, they have to be bought over and over again.

What is more pathetic than the sight of a man or woman who was never able to pay the original price for these goods and so lacks a college education?

It is the tragic sight of one who once upon a time bought his academic rights and privileges by hard work, by native edowment, by the support of his family, community, state, and country, and by good fortune to be born and reared in a particular locality — who received his degree with all the privileges thereunto appertaining, to use the ancient academic formula, and then, as the years went by, fell behind in his payments and could not keep up the installments on his education.

Now is the finest hour in these thousand years of higher education in the modern sense for a man or woman to accept the privileges of a college education. Now is the finest hour in these thousand years to be educated for teaching. At no previous time in the history of mankind has there been more work of a more difficult character for educated men and women to do. At no earlier time has there been so great a need for the skilled comprehension, the long view, and the broad understanding for which higher education supplies the tools and the techniques. At no other time has constructive, daring, inspired imagination had so many broad highways of endeavor open to its travel. I confess a lack of sympathy with those of my fellow commencement speakers who take a dimmer view of your opportunities, who see a road block of war around every corner and the ghastly hand of the A,H, or other alphabetical bomb reaching for every throat.

I remember that reason, warm hearts, and disciplined imagination have taken men, under God's good will, from the mud over these thousands years since our ancestors first shambled out on the plains of history; and I am persuaded that by God's continuing good will and men's continuing reliance on reason, warm hearts, and disciplined imagination they will go in the next few thousand years incalculable distances in the direction of the great ideals which they and their God have long held.

Will you exercise your pivileges as educated teachers to help move yourselves and your people along that road?

Will you pay the perpetual price for your academic distinctions every day you wear them?

If you will, I salute you, not because you will gain happiness thereby (although you are likely to gain a certain kind of happiness), not because such action will redound to your material credit (although it may possibly do so); but rather because you will be exercising your privileges on a high plane of our proud calling. Will you take up the privilege of rough, long work for your people, the privilege of developing meanings for yourself and your fellows where none existed before, and the privilege of cutting new paths and waging new battles through jungles of ignorance, prejudice, and ill will?

Will you take up these privileges or will you shrug them aside?

Will you fight or will you run?

Developing and Maintaining
The Morale of Teachers

It is relatively easy to recognize the presence or absence of morale in any group with whose activities we are reasonably familiar. It is often much harder to discover just what morale factors are present or lacking in a particular group situation, and it is usually very difficult to supply the missing factors even after a correct diagnosis has been made. These observations apply, I believe, to any human group, of whatever purpose.

The term *morale* was first developed in military situations. Since such situations are comparatively simple, let us start our examination of morale by looking at its manifestations in battle.

The enemy attacks our line in great strength, let us say. He hits a weak point in our front with tremendous artillery and air preparation. He throws armor and infantry in column against that point. He rolls our defending divisions to right and to left. He starts pouring his forces through the resultant gap.

But one of our divisions will not roll back. It will not budge. It fights from its slit trenches and fox holes with stubborn vindictiveness. Every man seems ready to die where he is, taking good care to inflict maximum damge upon the enemy as he passes. This division looks like the other divisions which have been rolled back. But it is not like those divisions. It is different. It is so fighting mad that it is cool and calculating in its determination to hit and hold the enemy.

The enemy commander sees that his time schedule is being upset. "Swing over to the left," he orders. "By-pass those fools who don't know when they are whipped."

But the fighting division will not be by-passed. When it sees its foes swinging away to go by on the other side, it arises from its fox holes and charges the enemy column. The enemy stops and strikes back. He sends two, three, as many divisions as he can dispatch against this insane outfit, which thereupon coolly digs in where it stands and starts its stubborn defense all over again.

Everybody, on both sides of this battle, who knows the facts of this action knows very well that this particular division has extremely high morale. Very often that is as far as one can go, however, in determining what made the division fight as it did. Were the officers better educated than those of the rest of the army? No. They seem to be just ordinary officers. Were the soldiers better selected or better trained than those of other divisions? Did they have superior

An address before a session of Schoolman's Week, March 19, 1947.

weapons, more artillery support, a larger supply of ammunition? No, apparently not. They just had higher morale; that seems to be all.

When we examine this division more searchingly, however, when we get down underneath surface matters like the education of officers, the selection of men, the training in mechanical skills of battle, and the like, we find that although such matters are undoubtedly important and necessary they are still not the crucial determinants of morale. These determinants of morale are so powerful that when they are present they can even go quite a distance toward overcoming the handicaps of having ignorant officers, poorly selected and partially trained men, and deficiencies in weapons and supplies.

The first of these determinants of morale is confidence in group ability. This is far different from mere confidence in the individuals who are in the group. It was not *members* of the division who came out of their fox holes and charged the enemy column. It was the *division* which crawled out of *its* fox holes and charged. This is the way the survivors think and speak of that charge.

This first determinant of morale applies to a teachers' group as precisely as to a military group. Morale is a group phenomenon. It never appears in just an individual setting. No individual ever experiences it except as part of a group in which he has enough confidence to say and think of it, "Our teachers' association can do this," or "Our principals' club will do that."

To develop and maintain morale among teachers it is, therefore, first of all imperative that the teachers should all belong to a common organization in which they have confidence.

Suppose we find a group of teachers in a community, all or most of whom belong to the local education association, but who have a relatively low morale. We find that as a group they lack the group counterpart of such qualities in an individual as self-confidence, resourcefulness, and courage.

They do not have confidence in their group or its leaders. They do not believe the group can do anything important. They do not want the group to do anything.

What is one of the first remedial measures to take in such a stiuation? Ordinarily it would be to seek ways of multiplying leadership. A group with high morale always has a wealth of leaders. The savage tribe falters in battle when its chief is killed. In a division like the one described earlier in this paper, the baton of leadership passes from hand to hand with easy assurance. "So the colonel, the captain, or the lieutenant in dead? There are sergeants, corporals, and privates in this outfit I can follow as well as I could follow a general officer from some lesser outfit." "My principal knows a lot about how to improve the curriculum, and there are plenty of teachers in this school who know how to work with the principal or to take his place."

Such statments as these suggest correctly that the second determinant of morale is closely tied to the first. That second factor is pride in group acievement. It is developed by confidence in the group's ability and at the same time it helps build up that group's morale.

If we find a group of teachers who are continually telling about what the teachers in other communities are doing and seldom refer to their own group except slightingly or apologetically, we do not have to search further to decide the general level of the group's morale.

We have heard a great deal about teachers' salaries lately. We need to have them raised, and we are going to have them raised. One of the chief reasons for having those salaries raised from their present generally low levels, in addition to supplying the actual physical needs of teachers and their salaries, is to support this factor of pride in the group which is so essential to morale. I want the salaries of my staff raised, first, because they actually need more money for food, rent, clothing, transportation, medical services, and many other necessities; and second, because their pride in their group is involved. I would no more willingly attempt to carry out a significant educational program with teachers who were not proud to be on the staff, than I would willingly go into action with soldiers who were ashamed of their platoon, battalion, or division.

Pride in the group can be encouraged by recognizing the achievements of the group. While recognition of an individual teacher's contribution is valuable, recognition of group achievement is much more valuable in building morale. This recognition should be definite and precise; it should not be mere vague praise. It should tell specifically what the teachers have done to improve the curriculum, the activity program, the adult education and recreation facilities, or any other feature of the community's school life.

The third chief determinant or morale is mentioned last, but it must be present from the first. Probably it is not more important than confidence in the group's ability and pride in the group's achievement, but it is certainly basic to that pride and that confidence. This third factor in morale is effective group action. In other words, the group must do something it can take pride in, something to justify its confidence in itself.

There are many teachers' groups which have all the abilities among their members necessary for very distinguished service, but which have low morale because they never work effectively as groups, and consequently have little pride or confidence.

School administrators must have confidence in the teachers' group, show pride in the group, and give the group something to do. These are the three requisites for the development and maintenance of teacher morale.

It may be said of any particular group, "I do not have confidence in them, because they are not intelligent or conscientious enough to merit my confidence." The first answer to this is that they will actually be more intelligent and conscientious if you display confidence in them.

Or it may be said of a group, "I cannot be proud of them, and they cannot be proud of themselves. Their record does not warrant pride." The answer to this is that there must be something about the group of which you can be proud and that in developing group morale one small toe-hold of pride in our own local outfit is worth a broad marble stair-case of pride for other and larger groups.

Finally, it may be said of a group, "They have done nothing in the past, do nothing now, and probably will do nothing in the future." The answer to this is that there is something for them to do right now as a group, and any effort to get them into action will be a first and crucial step in building their morale.

Riders to Set Upon Them

For my remarks on this occasion, I have chosen what I regard as a topic of great moment. That topic is embodied in the question: What education is of most worth to teachers?

The title by which I seek to symbolize this topic comes from an incident reported in the 18th chapter of the Second Book of Kings. Sennacherib, the mighty ruler of Assyria, was proposing a military alliance to King Hezekiah of Judah.

"And I will give thee two thousand horses," said the Assyrian monarch, "if thou on thy part canst find riders to set upon them."

Those two thousand Assyrian horses have been dust for almost three thousand years; so have Sennacherib and Hezekiah; so have the Assyrian empire and the Kingdom of Judah. They have all vanished into the overcast of history. Like drifting clouds, their forms, once seen for an instant of eternity, have floated over far away mountains and are forever gone.

So passed these rulers and their realms; so passed their vehicles and weapons; so pass all men and their materials of peace and their instruments of war. Omar Khayyam, as translated by Fitzgerald, put this fact in unforgettable words:

> They say the Lion and the Lizard keep
> The court where Jamshed gloried and drank deep:
> And Bahram, that great hunter - the Wild Ass
> Stamps o'er his head but cannot break his sleep.

What does this have to do with education of most worth for teachers? Am I merely commenting on a mystery?

I *am* commenting on a mystery; I am trying to give you as you cease to be students and become my fellow teachers, something of the mystery of our craft. It is a mystery which has everything to do with the problem of determining what education is of most worth to teachers.

The horses of Sennacherib are symbols of the material possessions and of our people, of any people, of every people who seek to work out their destiny in material terms. I have observed many of these peoples in history and a few of them in actuality in my own lifetime. The people I know best, are a people who with all their background of respect for non-material things, have a vast respect

Senior Convocation Address, Glassboro State College, Glassboro, New Jersey, June 2, 1963.

for material things. Some of them are, for example, about ready to give a young test pilot a governorship, a cabinet ministry, or even that highest of positions, a chairmanship of the joint chiefs of staff, because he rode some hardware around the earth twenty-two times.

Here I must point out that the riders Sennacherib wanted Hezekiah to set upon the proffered war horses are symbols of the ideas, principles, and forces of the spirits which have to guide and master the material belongings and institutions of a people. That education is of most worth for teachers which best nurtures and develops the forces of the spirit - the only forces that are able to control and direct the material powers of men. That education is of most worth for teachers because it is precisely the kind of education that all teachers have to use intelligently to make the total schooling which they give significant to their pupils.

Perhaps now we can begin to see in the heart of this mystery the dominant theme which must illumine it for our service and the service of our people. It is a theme of the pre-eminence of the spirit. It is a theme which most of our great world relations have taught us through the centuries. From the doctrines of Confucius and that Gautama who was called the Buddha to those of the founder of Islam, from the precepts of Judiasm to the teachings of Jesus who called himself the Son of Man and who was called by his followers the Christ, we have been told again and again in clear and unmistakeable language that the spirit is ever triumphant, that God gives final power to those who put their trust in the spirit, and that those who seek to operate their material enterprises in material terms alone will always fail.

This is a harsh truth. It cannot be grasped except by men and women who have received a high education of the spirit. It has been rejected century after century by people after people, and the highways of history are littered with the ruins of their societies to show the price they have paid for that rejection.

The essence of the optimum education for teachers is the learning of this harsh truth. I would ask you here to note that I say *education* and not *schooling*. Ordinary observers outside our professional field and to often, unfortunately, some members of our own profession, still confuse education with schooling. Schooling is a process that enables men and women to become educated, but it does not necessarily have that effect. Sometimes schooling, if improperly given and improperly assimilated, leads to deterioration. Otherwise, how can we account for the stark fact that the best-schooled people of Western Europe, within the last three decades, succeeded in taking graduates of the finest universities in Western Europe and turning them by a detriational *tour de force* into mosters who could casually watch a group of cowering, naked, huddled men, women, and children, the mothers and grandmothers kissing their babies goodby, whose only crime had been to have the wrong religious faith, nod to the sub-machinegun wielders, and say, "Commence firing!"

The essence of the education of the spirit for teachers and for the people whose spirits they are pledged to help educate is found in three elements of the riders whom they seek to set upon the material hardware of their society. Let us call these three elements the element of *manners,* the element of *style,* and the element of *drive.* We use all three of these terms in order of their importance. They all are necessary, and the first one is fundamental to the next two, the second one must be present for the third to be possible, and the third is the top element of the lot.

By *manners,* we mean *informed manners.* That is to say that no teacher can use his field for educational ends unless he has that foundation of scholarly information which we call erudition to give substance to the manners he seeks to pass on to his pupils. The element of manners is the one by which we teach our people better relations among men. This covers the whole field of human relations from the close companionship in families to the most tenuous areas included nowadays in the concept of international relations. Manners, here in this connection, are based on an understanding of the other person's wants, needs, and motivations. I think it was most dramatically illustrated to me not by a university professor or a professional teacher of any kind but by an elderly sergeant of cavalry who was teaching a group of us recruits what the army used to call elementary equitation. We were taking bareback drill, in other words, and we stood on this occasion dismounted, in a circle around our instructor. He was entitled to wear the Indian war ribbon because of his services against the Apaches some thirty years earlier. But he wore no ribbons that day. He stood on the near side of his single-mount, the only horse in the group who wore a saddle in the drill, and he stroked the animal's neck reflectively as he began his instruc-tion. "To learn a horse to lay down at the word of command," he said, "the first thing you gotta do is to remember that when the hostiles attack you wanta get that horse down where he is not so likely to get hit and you wanta get yourself down where you won't be so likely to get hit." At this point he tapped the big bay gelding on the chest and reached for the rifle in the scabbard on the saddle in the same motion. The horse and the man hit the ground simultaneously with the man's head nuzzled against the seat of the saddle and his cheek against the stock of the rifle with its muzzle across the animal's side menacing the hostiles. It was an elegant performance of a skilled horse-and-man team. As the sergeant and the horse got to their feet they seemed to be complimenting each other affectionately with congratulatory pats on the part of the man and playful nosings on the part of the horse. "The first thing you gotta do to learn a horse to lay down," continued the sergeant, "is to tap him on the chest like I did and never tap him there for any other reason because all our horses will lay down on that signal. My horse here will lay down for any of you men if you tap him there. Of course he probably won't lay down quite so fast for one of you recruits as he will for me. He will wait for just a second to see whether you get that Springfield out of the scabbard in time. No horse wants to lay down on a

Springfield rifle, and any army horse knows durn well it ain't good for the gun. To learn your own single-mount to lay down after the signal, you reach up over his withers like this, take hold of the off-cheek strap of his bridle, and then you can pull his head up toward you, and if you keep him from turning around too much you can, if necessary, throw him." Then the sergeant stopped and appeared to reconsider his words. "I made a mistake," he said. "That ain't the first thing you gotta do to learn a horse to lay down at the word of command. The first thing you gotta do to learn a horse anything is to like the horse."

This is, I think, in simple language exactly what constitutes the heart of the teacher's manners. The first thing a teacher has to do in dealing with his learners is to like the learners. The necessary informing process of course comes next and is always indispensable in manners.

The second element for these riders of the spirit is that of *style, imaginative style.* By that is meant not only the artistry of a teacher's organization of language, of teaching approaches, of research design, but also of the total pattern of his activities as a teacher and as a person in his society. The magnitude of our task in this connection is well exemplified by the long stretches of desert between style in terms of the contributors to *Vogue* and style as conceived by the professor of mathematics who strives to have his pupils do their elegant best in organizing their thinking in attacking their problems. Let us not be deceived by the simple notions of style current in most of our modern languages. This is an element that ranks next above the element of manners in the armory of the teacher's spirit. What is the style of a people whose states require the teaching of the evil effects of tobacco and whose mass media teach the youthful charm of tobacco? What is the style of a people that can send a simple test pilot around the world twenty-two times and cannot learn how to reduce the death toll on their highways?

The third and most authoritative element is that of *drive,* and its characterization in our mystery is that of a *daring drive.* No society ever became great or even attempted greatness in the grand manner whose teachers, whose leaders, whose mentors, consulted their fears more than their courage. I confess, if I may borrow the words of Sir Philip Sidney, "my own barbarousness" in that I look somewhat askance, somewhat contemptuously at these prophets of doom who say in awed tones that a lot of people on this earth are likely to be killed in the next war. That non-commissioned officer who came trotting along beside us at the *Bois de Belleau* on that delicate spring morning long ago and asked us, "Do you want to live forever?" made a more profound observation on this issue than I hear today from the heads of state, from leaders of the scientific community, and from other high ranking sources. The people of the world have always been facing death in horrible forms. Consider Europe at the time of the Black Death. Consider the millions who have died of hunger and whose souls have died within them as they watched their children starve to death. I would not go so far as to say that if we have World War III it might not be very important because it would not kill enough people. I merely repeat to myself the old question, "Do you want to live forever?"

But perhaps you will say that I am emphasizing to you a stupid form of courage to give substance to our drive. I hope it is not stupid because it seems to me that the chief lesson of history in that respect is that the greatest stupidities are usually committed in the service of timidity rather than in the service of an intelligent daring.

In deference to the circumstance that this is baccalaureate Sunday I wish to note that an education of informed manners, of imaginative style, and of daring drive cannot well be acquired in a narrow academic, nationalistic, or sectarian corner. The teacher must not have his mind fenced in. If the horses are going to be driven down a narrow lane with high walls on either side, they do not need to have riders set upon them; all they require is a whip across their backs and dogs at their heels. Even in a society like ours there are not wanting people in high positions who would like to furnish the whip of federal domination of the schools and the dogs of thought-police for this purpose.

A teacher must know the trails followed not only by the thinkers of his own approved group but also of men strange or even hostile to his people. There is no Christian teacher who will not gain educational stature by weighing the words of Mohammed: "If I had two loaves of bread, I would sell one and buy white hyacinths to feed my soul." There is no Buddhist scholar who cannot benefit by pondering the sublime statement of Micha: "He hath showed thee, O Man, what is good; and what doth the Lord require of thee, but to do justly, and love mercy, and walk humbly with thy God?" There are no Jewish or Christian teachers who will not be helped to an education of the spirit by studying Confucius' dictum that the good man is always more heedful of his obligations than of his rights. There are no teachers or learners of any faith who do not need to examine intently the warning of Jesus of Nazareth that they who take up the sword will perish by the sword.

The first fence that must be removed from the path of the educated rider is this barrier of any too narrow dogma.

The second fence that must come down before our riders is the time barrier. No man can understand the present who has not studied the past. Let us not forget that they must both be studied. It is as dangerous to neglect the one as to ignore the other. He who looks at what happened long ago without regard to what is happening now is a prisoner of the past. He who knows only his own era never understands it. The robe of time is seamless, and those who cut it arbitrarily are doomed forever to be tangled in its ravelings.

The third main barrier which must be cleared by one who would be a skilled rider of the horses of our modern world is that which fences in a particular region, area, or country. In many respects this is the most difficult obstacle of all to surmount. To overcome this barrier their teachers have to be acquainted with culture, languages, literature, government, and societies other than their own. They need to be as well acquainted with the ideas in history of people they hate as with those of people they love. All over the world we have erred grievously with respect to this purpose of our education. We talk about the power of education, but we do not trust it in matters of nationalism. We trust our secret police systems more. We must repair this error with all the informed warmth of manners, with all the imaginative style of design in our thinking and action, and with all the daring drive we can muster, or face again its familiar consequences in the provincialism, the jingoism, and the ultra-nationalism that offer the most fertile soil for wars.

Ladies and Gentlemen of the Class of 1963, you may say that I am outlining a tremendous amount of education beyond the small schooling you have received. You may modestly say that this is a task of impossible difficulty.

To this objection I must reply that to those who have learned how to forge even in a beginning way these weapons of the spirit, these elements of the manners, the style, and the drive, to carry as they ride the horses of material achievement, there is no educational impossibility.

Believe this with all your heart. Practice it with all your strength, form your squadrons, and ride.

We salute you now in the warm belief that on this quest your manners, your style, and your drive will put you over the barriers with honor and with significance. No educated man wants more.

Controversial Issues in American Life —
Their Effect on the School Curriculum

Are there any school systems anywhere in the world, in current or recent times, that have had no problems concerning the teaching of controversial issues in the schools?

Of course, there are many of them. In the last thirty years in particular they have flourished here and there throughout the world. They seem suddenly to blossom and sometimes just as suddenly to die, but they do not appear to die from peaceful causes. They seem rather to be vulnerable only to force.

Only dictators are ever strong enough to require, and only dictators and would-be dictators are ever stupid enough to propose, that education be conducted without giving the learners practice in making rational choices.

Even dictators know that education in certain fields is reduced to the level of inefficient training without this provision for practice in making intelligent choices. In natural sciences, mathematics, and engineering, for example, they are usually clever enough to realize that progress depends on giving the learner freedom to range far beyond memorized, approved facts and skills to search for new concepts and new techniques wherever his researches may lead him. But they find it hard, even in this area where freedom of learning is so obviously advantageous, to permit the process of learning through free choice among competing ideas.

It makes them nervous. You let these professors and students decide for themselves whether Lysenko's theory is right, and the next thing you know they may be thinking for themselves in some field where only the Big Boss in entitled to think. Thus we get a statement from some great "biologist" like "Professor" Stalin, setting all arguments at rest. No more controversy and no more research.

In the social sciences and even in the arts, the dictators have no doubts about what they want. They want completely dissensionless teaching. Under a dictatorship social scientists disappear. There is an account of the past to be memorized and repeated but there is not history. There is an appoved view of social groups to take but no sociology. There is a proper attitude to display government but not political science. Whether the dictator resides in the Casa Rosada, poses on a balcony in Madrid, or hides behind Kremlin walls, he always follows a simple pattern. "Let me do the thinking and the talking too on important matters, and any matter is important that attracts my attention. You

Statement to the joint meeting of the American Association of School Administrators, the National Council for the Social Studies, and the National Education Association's Department of Classroom Teachers, February 16, 1953, Atlantic City.

believe what I say, obey what I tell you to do, and work and fight at my command. Teach children to make choices among various ideas and courses of action? What seditious, atheistical, communistic, or bourgeois-capitalist nonsense as the case may be!"

A free society sets up barriers against this kind of outcome. In the United States our people invented their own peculiar system of public education in large measure for that purpose. They developed the independent lay board of control, close to the people, charged by the people with educational responsibilities only, and reporting to the people. No more effective device was ever developed to make it difficult for would-be dictators to control the schools. It can be done, of course, but it is very hard to do.

It is not surprising that groups wishing to reduce education in this country to a dissensionless training of their own choice often try to by-pass the school board, the state board of textbook examiners, the university board of regents or other legally constituted school authorities. The school boards are stubborn, they are responsible only to the people in most cases, they are independent, and they have tendencies to put the welfare of the children and young people above political considerations. So we have congressional and legislative committees undertaking examinations of textbooks and teachers, for example, for no reason of a proper legislative nature. They are not working on legislation; they are merely serving as sounding-boards and mouthpieces for the would-be dictators who find school boards much harder to handle than politicians.

The second great obstacle in the path of those who would have no controversial issues taught in our schools is the corps of professionally educated teachers and administrators. A free society has to have people in charge of its schools who are incomparably better equipped than those needed as trainers in a dictatorship. One who teaches a child to make intelligent choices among several possible courses of thought or action has to be of better quality in his own choices than a mere drill master who passes to his pupils what was passed to him and no more.

The third obstacle blocking the advance of those who want our education reduced to a dead level of training is that of the voluntary organization of school patrons. We invented the parent-teacher association in this country; we are just beginning to see its great potential. Here is the best channel of contact between school and people. The most effective means of mass communication still remains face-to-face conversations and shoulder-to-shoulder work among many people.

With a board that knows the school's task and its own responsibilities, a teaching corps that is professionally skilled, and school patrons who help determine and operate difficult curricular programs, the would-be dictators have tough sledding. That the would-be dictators do not always have tough sledding merely reminds us that these three great forces in American public education, like the free society to which they are devoted, have to be worked for every day and fought for at least every other day.

The Nature of Curricular Problems

Five separte times, in open warfare, Lone Buffalo had counted coup on the enemies of tribe, yet he was not given to overmuch boasting about his deeds. Only at ceremonial dances, when it was right and proper that such things should be done, did Lone Buffalo recount those coups. Even then, so thought many men of the Long Lances clan, he hurried too modestly when he told of his most daring exploit – how he once captured a Crow chief single-handed, disarmed him, stripped him of his warbonnet, and flogged him back in disgrace to the very outskirts of the enemy camp.

Not only was Lone Buffalo a brave warrior; he was also a skillful hunter and a kind man. He brought home buffaloes when other men could find only prairie dogs, and when he came in from a successful hunt he sent his wife with presents of good, fat meat to the lodges of widows and other poor people. It was easy for such a man to be rich in skins, food, weapons and horses without exciting the envy of his less fortunate fellows. His clansmen did not speak sneeringly of his success, but on the contrary they liked and trusted him so much that they made him chief of the Long Lances while he was still in the early middle winters of his life.

By any test applicable in Dacotah society, Lone Buffalo was an educated man. *He knew how to do those things that his social group wanted done.*

Lone Buffalo had a son. It was natural that he should want this son to become a brave fighter, a skillful hunter, and a good man. He knew well that to achieve this purpose the boy must be able to do certain definite things – to endure fatigue, hunger, and pain uncomplainingly, to shoot straight, to handle a lance with strength and dexterity, to follow a trail unerringly, to ride horses skillfully, to treat his fellow tribesmen well, and by means of prayer and sacrifice to behave properly toward those sacred beings who governed the lives of men.

Lone Buffalo realized that his boy could not learn all these things unless the conditions of the boy's life were favorable to the learning. The boy must *know* what to do, he must *desire* to do it, and he must have a chance to *practice* it. The father took care, therefore; that his son should hear the old men's stories of the brave and good deeds of other times, should attend dances where he could listen to war songs and the counting of coups, and should become familiar with what the Sacred Ones desired in a man. He showed the boy how to make and

From the November, 1934, issue of *Education* magazine.

handle weapons. He took him hunting and taught him the tricks of trailing and stalking. He explained to him the habits of animals, of men, and of spirits. He arranged all these conditions in the hope that when the boy came to a warrior's age he would bear himself in a manner worthy of his family, his clan, his tribe, and his nation. Lone Buffalo did not think this result could be attained without teaching, without conscious arrangement of the conditions for learning. He believed in education.

The elemental factors in this savage educational set-up may be summarized as follows:

1. There was a definite purpose behind the boy's education. The father and the whole community knew what kind of a person they wanted the boy to become. They wanted him to be a good member of the Long Lances clan of the Ogalala tribe of the Dacotah nation. They wanted him to be a socially valuable individual.

2. There was a clearly recognized set of experiences in which socially valuable individuals engaged. The members of the tribe had few if any doubts about their competence to decide just what these experiences were. The boy must do the things which men of the tribe had to do. If possible, he must do them as well as did leaders like Lone Buffalo.

3. There was an arrangement of conditions to facilitate the boy's participation in the socially approved experiences.

These three items in the Ogalala boy's education correspond to the three major problems of education for any culture in any period of history: the problem of *purpose*, the problem of *content*, and the problem of *method*. They may be summed up in three questions:

1. Why shall we teach?

2. What shall we teach?

3. How shall we teach?

The student of the curriculum is concerned primarily with the problem of content, but he cannot avoid consideration of the first and third problems also. The content which he sets up for the educational system must be directly related to the purpose of the educational system. The content must be arranged in such a way that it can be taught effectively with the facilities available. The content must originate in purpose and come to fruition in method.

The problem of content may be broken up into the following questions:

1. What general type of life are the pupils of the school going to live? For what kind of society whould they be prepared? In what sort of civilization will they work? Does the society toward which the curriculum is directed differ from the contemporary society? If so, in what way does it differ? Questions of this character are related to what may be called *the problem of the approved social order.*

2. What are the characteristics of a valuable member of the approved social order? What must he desire to do and what must he be able to do to fit into the approved social order? These questions exemplify what may be called *the problem of the socially approved individual.*

3. What particular experiences will lead the individual to acquire the skills and desires necessary for participation in the approved order? In what activities must he engage to develop socially approved characteristics? Such questions are directed toward what may be called *the problem of the socially approved content.*

Like many crucial issues in education, these three problems are easy to state but extremely difficult to solve. Let us examine some of the reasons for this difficulty.

First of all, curricular problems are difficult because any modern society has already answered them in part and answered them in conflicting ways. Indeed one of the characteristics of advanced civilization is a multiplication of answers to these questions. For example; what is the approved social order? Every social class, every economic group, every political organization, every religious sect, every patriotic society, every youth association, and many other special groups have a definite answer to this question, in some of its aspects at least. The approved social order is one in which property is sacred, in which every worker puts his extra cash into savings accounts, in which all citizens buy highly advertised articles from one another on the installment plan, in which all men worship God according to the doctrines of the Podunkite Church, in which the principles of the Buncombe Party prevail to the lasting aggrandizement of the party wheelhorses, in which members of the common herd are content with the stations to which it hath pleased God to call them, in which men die willingly for their country's diplomatic errors, in which the proletariat hold the reins of power, in which the motive of private profit is eliminated, or in which the pet ideas of this or that pressure group are triumphant. Where there are so many answers dictated by special interests, there is practically no answer at all. In a multitude of counselors there is sometimes only confusion.

Faced by this multiplicity of conflicting counsel, those who are professionally responsible for constructing the school curriculum may take the easy path of accepting the opinions of their own group. Ask school teachers and administrators to describe the characteristics of the approved social order or the socially approved individual, and the answer is likely to come pat in terms of the present curriculum. How many generations of educational authorities in the western European world have maintained stoutly that an educated man is one who knows the Latin classics! Why? Because for so many centuries the Latin classics have been designed to produce educated men. Intellectually, we have been reared within the confines of this argumentative circle. It is difficult for us to conceive the problem of secondary school content except in terms of the traditional secondary school curriculum.

The second chief difficulty confronting students of the curriculum is a technical one. It is the difficulty which arises from a lack of proper instruments and techniques for studying society, for determining the characteristics of the individual, and for deriving curricular content to serve a designated purpose. It is, however, a difficulty which can be overcome more readily than the difficulty first mentioned. The first is essentially an obstacle involving widespread and deep seated prejudices. The Second is an obstacle that can be attacked by directly formulating and testing techniques for the study and construction of the curriculum. The difference between the two obstacles is inherent in the fact that we have more love and hate for the subject matter of schools than we have for the processes by which the subject matter is derived.

Old Man Coyote and His Crystal Ball

I know certain characters who have served me faithfully in various books, and when I am stumped by a problem of exposition, I can always turn to one or two of them. For these remarks, therefore, I went to Old Man Coyote and his Loyal Opposition, Tom Gunn's Mule. I found these animals in Horse Heaven, Eastern Washington, just across the Columbia River from Umatilla, Oregon.

Old Man Coyote was seated on the crest of a hill staring down at the river, and Tom Gunn's Mule was cropping bunch grass beside him.

"Well, anyway they sure need it," said Old Man Coyote judicially, apropos of nothing.

The big mule stopped eating and stared at his companion. "I swear you're getting nuttier every day. Who you talking about? Who needs what?" he demanded suspiciously.

"The military," said Old Man Coyote. "I'm talking about their education, of course. That's their big need. If they have that, of the right amount and kind, their other needs will be met, will be added unto 'em, as the Good Book says."

"Good Book!" snorted Tom Gunn's Mule. "What do *you* know about the Good Book?"

"I have heard plenty of preachers," replied the elderly coyote with dignity. "You get within 500 yards of one of those summer tent meetings, and you have to hear 'em unless you're stone deaf."

"There you go again," said the mule wearily. "You not only don't know what you're talking about, but you keep changing the subject to show how many things you're ignorant of. You start on the education of the military and the next thing I know, you're makin' snide remarks about preachers. What has either one of those subjects got to do with the price of hay?"

"I'm not talking about hay; I don't eat the stuff," replied Old Man Coyote. "I'm talking about education for the defense of our country against all her enemies whomsoever, and I just happened to mention preachers as examples of people who believe you can be saved by the right kind of big idea. These two subjects go together much more closely than you might think."

"Yeah?" sneered the mule. "I've heard pretty near everything now, and too much of it from a coyote who never did a day of military service." The big animal tossed his nose back toward his near shoulder where the U.S. brand

An address given at the 4th Armed Forces Educational Conference, University of Maryland, December 7, 1962.

marked him as a reservist. "Big ideas, huh?" he continued. "It's drill on all the little things that count in the Army. In the old regiment where I've been curried and brushed by the numbers, *By detail, Off hip and off hind leg to hock, Commence grooming,* until my hide was thin as a cigarette paper, our stable sergeant took no guff from those dumb johns. He drilled 'em and and trained 'em until they could groom and pack and saddle and feed and water in their sleep."

"And sometimes did?" suggested the coyote politely.

"No, I didn't say any such thing," roared Tom Gunn's Mule. "I just said they *could* have. They didn't sleep around our stable sergeant or around the first sergeant either."

"How about your officers?" asked the coyote.

"Officers?" The mule seemed startled. "In my time," he said, "Our battery commander was Hole-in-the-Head Bellows. He had his non-coms handle most of the drill."

"Uh-huh," said the coyote. "You were in that jackass battery from 1916 to 1924, right?"

"Pack artillery!" snorted the mule. "How many times have I got to tell you damn' civilians our correct name. We packed howitzers, and every member of that regiment was a mule or a horse. The only burros I ever saw in those days were hangin' around some sheep camp, and the damn' coyotes were hangin' around the burros."

"Ah, yes," said Old Man Coyote tolerantly, "excuse me, but didn't you have some men in that outfit, too?"

"Well, of course," replied the mule. "I was just talking about the animals that did the work. All the men had to do was to put on and take off those barrels and trails and ammunitions boxes, put the guns together, load 'em, point 'em, and fire 'em. There was nothing to that. But you carry 200 pounds for thirty miles in one day over some of those Chihuahua roads when you're only three years old, and you'll feel like laying down and doggin' it. Anything to get that pack saddle off."

Apparently the veteran animal had some guilty memory dogging his conscience, for he alternated his ears in fore and aft stances as he spoke.

"1916," said the coyote admiringly. "You must be fifty years old?"

"Close to it," admitted the big mule. "But that's not very old. I'll bet I could still handle a real load if the Army only had a soldier who knew how to put a pack saddle on right!"

"Yes, yes," said the coyote soothingly. "Fifty years is not so long. You know what the Army drill was like fifty years ago, and I can tell you what the Army training is going to be like fifty years from now."

"You got a crystal ball, I suppose?" sneered the Loyal Opposition.

"I have the clear current of the past to look at," said Old Man Coyote, "and that is better." He stood up and walked to and fro staring at the river below the hill. Then he sat down on his haunches again and began his lecture with a magisterial wave of his right front paw.

"When I speak of the Army," he said, "I use the term broadly to include the whole defense establishment, since the Navy, the Coast Guard, the Air Force, and even the Marine Corps are all allies of the Army."

"Doggone it," interrupted Tom Gunn's Mule, "the correct term nowadays is the *Armed Forces!*"

"There will be time for comments and questions at the end of the lecture," said the coyote severely, "but I'll say armed forces if it will make you any happier. At the mid-point between 1915 and 2015, the Armed Forces, as usual, were about forty years behind the trend of events in their training concepts and programs."

"There you go again," snorted the Loyal Opposition, "always lookin' down on the military! Nothin' but a civilian yourself! Forty years behind the civilians, you claim..."

"I said nothing of the kind," rejoined Old Man Coyote. "I said merely that the Armed Forces were forty years behind the trend of events in their training concepts and curricula – the civilian educational programs are fifty to sixty years behind the times. Now suppose you stop snorting and stomping around and just listen to what I have to say. You might learn something."

"I doubt it," said the mule.

"Well, I agree with you in that doubt," said the coyote, "but we can try."

"You have seen fit to sneer at my civilian status," resumed the lecturer, "But you must remember that I have watched coyotes pretty carefully for a long time and I have seen them make the same three main mistakes these human beings make in their education. First, I will tell you what those three coyote-training mistakes are. Second, I will show you how those mistakes can be avoided. Third, I will look at the crystal flow of the river of events and tell you how the Armed Forces of the United States can whip those mistakes.

"We coyotes used to have a pretty easy life a long time ago. We had to find enough to eat and keep our enemies from killing us. The Indians didn't bother us to amount to anything. We just studied the tracking of jackrabbits, how to dig field mice out of their little burrows, and how to keep away from timber wolves,cougers, and bears.

"Then the white men came, drove out the Indians, killed all the buffalo, and built up their ranches. The ranchers' wives kept chickens, ducks, even geese and turkeys sometimes – mighty nice eating after a steady diet of jackrabbit and field mice. But the ranchers also packed firearms, pistols, shot-guns, carbines, sometimes even rifles. Every coyote, whether he hung around a henhouse look-ing for fresh eggs and nice tender chickens or not, had to study those guns. He had to know how close he could get to a man carrying a pistol, how much further he had to stay away when the man had a carbine, what to do when the man had a brand-new weapon with a telescopic sight on it.

"Here is where you can see all three of the coyote mistakes. The first was when an animal got to be so expert in the facts he learned about a subject — guns, for instance, — that he forgot his main job, what he was trying to do. I had an uncle who made that mistake. He was always telling us cubs about guns. Of course, he was often wrong. The longer the barrel, the longer the range, he used to say, for example, and then one of Jim West's boys got a little rifle that looked like a carbine, and that expert coyote knew his subject so well that he forgot that the main thing was to remember that he was trying to keep alive, and so he should be suspicious of all guns at all ranges. He let that boy get within 300 yards of him because he wanted to study that new gun. Just as the bullet hit him, he probably knew more about guns than any other living coyote. He died a victim of the mistake of shifting his major concern from his purpose to his subject. Let us call that the fallacy of the misplaced mission.

"Some other coyotes lost out because they had a favorite method or two which they became so skilled at that they neglected studying other methods. They were like the coyote who was digging a tunnel under Mrs. West's henhouse. Whenever somebody came out on the back porch of the ranch house, the coyote ran behind the horse stable, jumped over the rail fence at the corner of the corral and dashed into the sagebrush. He moved fast and precisely, always in exactly the same path, jumping over the same spot in the fence. When one of the West boys finally got him with a .30-30 just as he went over that fence, he was probably the most skillful living practitioner of that particular evasive technique. He died a victim of his strong point. Let us call that the fallacy of the favorite tactic.

"Of course all training, all education, is experience, and there is one thing about experience in general that many animals and men overlook, especially the most experienced ones. That is the tendency of all experience to slow up the animal's or the man's response when he meets a very new situation.

"We had a coyote one time in a pack I used to run with who never got within range of any guns — he was too experienced. He never stepped into a trap — he knew all about traps. He laughed at dogs and wolves and cougars — he was too smart for them. But when he went back to finish up eating a lamb killed the night before, there being no sign of traps, dogs, or guns, he ate heartily, and the meat was poisoned. Just before he died he certainly was the most experienced living coyote on guns, dogs, and traps, in all this part of the country. He died a victim of too much experience. Let us call that the fallacy of unexamined practice.

"How can these mistakes be avoided?"

"The first one, the fallacy of the misplaced mission, can be avoided only by studying the purposes from all angles. No matter what else the cub is studying, his main course of study should always be the mission.

"The second, the mistake of falling in love with a method, a technique, can be cured only by continual experimentation with new techniques.

"The third mistake, the fallacy of unexamined experience, is the hardest one of all to get rid of. It simply means that the more experienced you are in anything, the broader your views have to be. The older the coyote, the bigger the area he has to reconnoiter. This is where the big ideas I was talking about a while back come in. When a young, inexperienced coyote is afraid of big ideas, it is understandable. He will learn to accept them after he has had more schooling.

"But when an old, experienced coyote is contemptuous or afraid of new ideas, he is in a tough spot. He can learn new tricks only when they fit old ideas.

"Well, there you are," said the lecturer, as he stood up and started to walk away.

"Wait a minute," cried the Loyal Opposition. "You said you would tell how the Armed Forces could avoid mistakes like these."

Old Man Coyote patted a yawn delicetely with the back of a forepaw. "I have," he said. "I have laid down three general principles. Let the military people apply them. They can do that better than I." He turned and trotted away. Tom Gunn's Mule stared at the retreating figure and then resumed eating bunch grass.

As a disciple of Old Man Coyote and an admirer of the technical proficiency of the United States Armed Forces, I have only a few brief observations to make on the three fallacies of which the old fellow spoke.

First, I will say that the fallacy of developing the curriculum without sufficient regard to the mission is one of which United States military educators are not so guilty as are civilian educators. I stress the qualifying words, *United States,* because I suspect that there are many armies, navies, and air forces in the world today that have only the sketchiest notions of their real missions. They tend to think that all they need are atomic weapons to be really powerful military organizations.

I do not believe, furthermore, that the United States Armed Forces are very guilty nowadays of the fallacy of the dearly beloved tactic. You can more easily find that fallacy in civilian education and in other military establishments. As I read of the Chinese infantry advancing in the Himalayan front in mass formations behind mortar preparation, very much as they did when they came down from the Yalu in Korea a few years ago, I suspect that their commanders are becoming enamored with that technique. If so, I have no doubt that they are riding for a tremendous fall as soon as they run against commanders without any favorite tactic who will cook up new tactics especially designed for mass formations of burp-gun-wielding infantry behind mortar fire.

It is on Old Man Coyote's description of the third fallacy, that of un-examined practice, the restrictive effect of long experience, and the necessity of combatting it with what he called *Big Ideas* that I pause longest in reflective concern.

This is a fallacy that affects us all – in the schools and universities – in business, law, industry, government, art, scinece, literature, and all the affairs of mortal life.

We can teach our young people, civilians, soldiers, sailors, marines and airmen the scientific and mathematical facts and skills we think they need for the new era which seems to us, because of our long experience, to be a scientif-ically, mathematically dominated era. And how do we know that it will not be an era where learning to make behavioral analyses, learning to make moral decisions, even learning to make aesthetic choices will be much more important.

By 1980, to pick an arbitrary date which is fifteen years away, the guess-testing machines then available will make our present electronic computers look like children's toys. Those machines and the ones that will succeed them in 1985, 2000, and 2065 will of course require engineers to make them and set them up and mathematicians to program them, but even more the machines and their valets will be dependent upon visionaries, dreamers, hypothesis-makers to make the guesses which the machines will test against millions of possibilities.

Imagine, for the moment, a new Armed Forces Academy. I am not suggesting one, you understand, although the United States could well afford another one, in view of the size of the country and its military establishment. I am merely using this possibility as an expository device. Let us say that it is an academy which admits students to its entrance examinations who have com-pleted the two years of the junior college or its equivalent and who have already served a minimum of one year in one of the Armed Forces. We would have a three-year instead of a four-year program in this academy. We would have a variety of curricula because we would regard each student as an unique officer whom this academy would do its best to make a competent technician and a daring visionary. He would be given no general education of any kind, military, scientific, or civic. He would have learned that in his two years of college and one year of military training before he entered the academy.

Assuming further that these students would receive a baccalaureate two years after entrance and a master's degree on graduation, it is easy to see how competent engineering, chemical, ordinance, and intelligence technicians of various kinds could be trained in such an institution.

How would the great decision-makers and the great visionaries be educated? I am not Old Man Coyote, and so I will not trot away from that question. I will say that they will be educated in an atmosphere of extended freedom and extended responsibility from the first. The doctrine of the beloved subject, the technique of the approved tactic, and the creed of the uniform response should be hard to find in that academy. The problem of carrying out the country's missions would be studied, I assume, in every case from the scientific, historical, behavioral, and cultural standpoints. How they would be studied, with what emphasis and specializations, and with what future outcomes as goals — these would be questions particularly useful to military planners, decision-makers, and visionaries. The scholars of this institution, and the term *scholars* includes both the students and the professors, would be continually attacking such questions.

An educational program of this kind would of course be impossible in most countries. In the United States it is possible. In the United States I think the Armed Forces are closer to it now in many ways than most civilians realize, as the cooperative program between the Armed Forces and the University of Maryland will illustrate, but they still have a considerable distance to go. That they will close that gap and cover that distance, I have little doubt.

Both Old Man Coyote and I are optimists about the future of the United States Armed Forces and their education. If we are right, you will perhaps remember our prediction. If we are proved wrong, many of us, maybe most of us, will be in no position to fuss over memories.